*Marcia Hill, EdD*
*Mary Ballou, PhD*
*Editors*

# The Foundation and Future of Feminist Therapy

*The Foundation and Future of Feminist Therapy* has been co-published simultaneously as *Women & Therapy*, Volume 28, Numbers 3/4 2005.

*Pre-publication
REVIEWS,
COMMENTARIES,
EVALUATIONS . . .*

"THIS INSIDER'S CHRONICLE OFFERS AN INTIMATE POR-TRAIT OF FEMINIST THERAPY from the 1970s to today and the vibrant and courageous women who created it. The book celebrates the idealism, fierce determination, and innovative thinking of these therapists. It provides a map of the past, but more important, it gives us a moral compass for the future."

**Jeanne Marecek, PhD**
*Professor of Psychology
Swarthmore College*

"PROVIDES A HELPFUL LIST OF STRATEGIES for challenging erroneous assumptions in the service of enhancing cultural competence. . . . An excellent review of the history of the understanding of rape and social control. . . . Discusses contextual identity in terms of identities related to individuals, relationships, social identity, and human identity. . . . Points out how ignoring the interaction of class with other identifiers is problematic. . . . Recognizes the many contemporary feminists who have contributed to feminist theory. . . . Provides an interesting, engaging history of thought regarding contemporary issues, giving credit to still-living feminist mental health professionals, including psychologists."

**Lynn H. Collins, PhD**
*Associate Professor of Psychology*
*La Salle University*

"THIS BOOK IS ONE-OF-A-KIND AND PROMISES TO BE A CLASSIC IN THE FIELD of feminist therapy. It provides an excellent overview of feminist theory to date, and includes a call to action to insure that feminist principles are the cornerstone of psychotherapeutic training and practice in the future. It focuses on the work of feminist therapists who have made major contributions to psychotherapy theory, bringing together an understanding of how culture, ethnicity, race, class, gender, sexuality, language, age, health, trauma, and disempowerment affect women's lives."

**Nanette Gartrell, MD**
*Associate Clinical Professor*
*of Psychiatry*
*University of California*
*San Francisco*

The Haworth Press, Inc.

# The Foundation and Future of Feminist Therapy

*The Foundation and Future of Feminist Therapy* has been co-published simultaneously as *Women & Therapy*, Volume 28, Numbers 3/4 2005.

*The Foundation and Future of Feminist Therapy,* edited by Marcia Hill, EdD, and Mary Ballou, PhD (Vol. 28, No. 3/4, 2005). *"This insider's chronicle offers an intimate portrait of feminist therapy from the 1970s to today and the vibrant and courageous women who created it. The book celebrates the idealism, fierce determination, and innovative thinking of these therapists. It provides a map of the past, but more important, it gives us a moral compass for the future." (Jeanne Marecek, PhD, Professor of Psychology, Swarthmore College)*

*Therapeutic and Legal Issues for Therapists Who Have Survived a Client Suicide: Breaking the Silence,* edited by Kayla Miriyam Weiner, PhD (Vol. 28, No. 1, 2005). *"This book offers resources, understanding, and most importantly, company for therapists living with or worrying about the nightmare of client suicide." (Marcia Hill, EdD, psychologist in private practice; author of* Diary of a Country Therapist)

*From Menarche to Menopause: The Female Body in Feminist Therapy,* edited by Joan C. Chrisler, PhD (Vol. 27, No. 3/4, 2004). *"A definitive resource on women's reproductive health. . . . Brings this topic out of the closet. . . . The coverage is excellent, spanning the adolescent experience of menarche and moving from pregnancy issues to menopause and beyond. The chapter authors are clearly experts on their topics, and this edited book is admirable in its philosophical coherence. Feminist therapists working with young girls, women in their reproductive years, and older women will find clear information about how to understand and affirm their clients' experiences." (Maryka Biaggio, PhD, Professor and Director of Research on Feminist Issues, Department of Professional Psychiatry, Pacific University)*

*Biracial Women in Therapy: Between the Rock of Gender and the Hard Place of Race,* edited by Angela R. Gillem, PhD, and Cathy A. Thompson, PhD (Vol. 27, No. 1/2, 2004). *"A must-read. . . . Compelling and poignant. . . . Enhances our understanding of what it means to be biracial and female in society dominated by monoracial notions of identity and sexualized notions of biracial women. . . . Delves insightfully into a variety of biracial women's experiences." (Lisa Bowleg, PhD, Assistant Professor, Department of Psychology, University of Rhode Island)*

*Women with Visible and Invisible Disabilities: Multiple Intersections, Multiple Issues, Multiple Therapies,* edited by Martha E. Banks, PhD, and Ellyn Kaschak, PhD (Vol. 26, No. 1/2/3/4, 2003). *"Bravo . . . provides powerful and direct answers to the questions, concerns, and challenges all women with disability experience. The voices in this book are speaking loud and clear to a wide range of readers and audiences. . . . Centered on the core principle that quality of life revolves around one's mental health, a sense of strength, and resiliency." (Theresa M. Rankin, BA, NCE, National Community Educator, Brain Injury Services, Inc.; MidAtlantic Traumatic Brain Injury Consortium; Fairhaven Institute for Brain Injury/University of Wisconsin-Scott)*

*Violence in the Lives of Black Women: Battered, Black, and Blue,* edited by Carolyn M. West, PhD (Vol. 25, No. 3/4, 2002). *Helps break the silence surrounding Black women's experiences of violence.*

*Exercise and Sport in Feminist Therapy: Constructing Modalities and Assessing Outcomes,* edited by Ruth L. Hall, PhD, and Carole A. Oglesby, PhD (Vol. 25, No. 2, 2002). *Explores the healing use of exercise and sport as a helpful adjunct to feminist therapy.*

*The Invisible Alliance: Psyche and Spirit in Feminist Therapy,* edited by Ellyn Kaschak, PhD (Vol. 24, No. 3/4, 2001). *"The richness of this volume is reflected in the diversity of the collected viewpoints, perspectives, and practices. Each chapter challenges us to move out of the confines of our traditional training and reflect on the importance of spirituality. This book also brings us back to the original meaning of psychology–the study and knowledge of the soul." (Stephanie S. Covington, PhD, LCSW, Co-Director, Institute for Relational Development, La Jolla, California; Author,* A Woman's Way Through the Twelve Steps)

*A New View of Women's Sexual Problems,* edited by Ellyn Kaschak, PhD, and Leonore Tiefer, PhD (Vol. 24, No. 1/2, 2001). *"This useful, complex, and valid critique of simplistic notions of women's sexuality will be especially valuable for women's studies and public health courses. An important compilation representing many diverse individuals and groups of women."* (Judy Norsigian and Jane Pincus, Co-Founders, Boston Women's Health Collective; Co-Authors, Our Bodies, Ourselves for the New Century)

**Intimate Betrayal: Domestic Violence in Lesbian Relationships,** edited by Ellyn Kaschak, PhD (Vol. 23, No. 3, 2001). *"A groundbreaking examination of a taboo and complex subject. Both scholarly and down to earth, this superbly edited volume is an indispensable resource for clinicians, researchers, and lesbians caught up in the cycle of domestic violence."* (Dr. Marny Hall, Psychotherapist; Author of The Lesbian Love Companion, Co-Author of Queer Blues)

**The Next Generation: Third Wave Feminist Psychotherapy,** edited by Ellyn Kaschak, PhD (Vol. 23, No. 2, 2001). *Discusses the issues young feminists face, focusing on the implications for psychotherapists of the false sense that feminism is no longer necessary.*

**Minding the Body: Psychotherapy in Cases of Chronic and Life-Threatening Illness,** edited by Ellyn Kaschak, PhD (Vol. 23, No. 1, 2001). *Being diagnosed with cancer, lupus, or fibromyalgia is a traumatic event. All too often, women are told their disease is "all in their heads" and, therefore, both "unreal and insignificant" by a medical profession that dismisses emotions and scorns mental illness. Combining personal narratives and theoretical views of illness,* Minding the Body *offers an alternative approach to the mind-body connection. This book shows the reader how to deal with the painful and difficult emotions that exacerbate illness, while learning the emotional and spiritual lessons illness can teach.*

**For Love or Money: The Fee in Feminist Therapy,** edited by Marcia Hill, EdD, and Ellyn Kaschak, PhD (Vol. 22, No. 3, 1999). *"Recommended reading for both new and seasoned professionals.... An exciting and timely book about 'the last taboo.'..."* (Carolyn C. Larsen, PhD, Senior Counsellor Emeritus, University of Calgary; Partner, Alberta Psychological Resources Ltd., Calgary, and Co-Editor, Ethical Decision Making in Therapy: Feminist Perspectives)

**Beyond the Rule Book: Moral Issues and Dilemmas in the Practice of Psychotherapy,** edited by Ellyn Kaschak, PhD, and Marcia Hill, EdD (Vol. 22, No. 2, 1999). *"The authors in this important and timely book tackle the difficult task of working through ... conflicts, sharing their moral struggles and real life solutions in working with diverse populations and in a variety of clinical settings. ... Will provide psychotherapists with a thought-provoking source for the stimulating and essential discussion of our own and our profession's moral bases."* (Carolyn C. Larsen, PhD, Senior Counsellor Emeritus, University of Calgary, Partner in private practice, Alberta Psychological Resources Ltd., Calgary, and Co-Editor, Ethical Decision Making in Therapy: Feminist Perspectives)

**Assault on the Soul: Women in the Former Yugoslavia,** edited by Sara Sharratt, PhD, and Ellyn Kaschak, PhD (Vol. 22, No. 1, 1999). *Explores the applications and intersections of feminist therapy, activism and jurisprudence with women and children in the former Yugoslavia.*

**Learning from Our Mistakes: Difficulties and Failures in Feminist Therapy,** edited by Marcia Hill, EdD, and Esther D. Rothblum, PhD (Vol. 21, No. 3, 1998). *"A courageous and fundamental step in evolving a well-grounded body of theory and of investigating the assumptions that, unexamined, lead us to error."* (Teresa Bernardez, MD, Training and Supervising Analyst, The Michigan Psychoanalytic Council)

**Feminist Therapy as a Political Act,** edited by Marcia Hill, EdD (Vol. 21, No. 2, 1998). *"A real contribution to the field. ... A valuable tool for feminist therapists and those who want to learn about feminist therapy."* (Florence L. Denmark, PhD, Robert S. Pace, Distinguished Professor of Psychology and Chair, Psychology Department, Pace University, New York, New York)

**Breaking the Rules: Women in Prison and Feminist Therapy,** edited by Judy Harden, PhD, and Marcia Hill, EdD (Vol. 20, No. 4 & Vol. 21, No. 1, 1998). *"Fills a long-recognized gap in the psychology of women curricula, demonstrating that feminist theory can be made relevant to the practice of feminism, even in prison."* (Suzanne J. Kessler, PhD, Professor of Psychology and Women's Studies, State University of New York at Purchase)

**Children's Rights, Therapists' Responsibilities: Feminist Commentaries,** edited by Gail Anderson, MA, and Marcia Hill, EdD (Vol. 20, No. 2, 1997). *"Addresses specific practice dimensions that will help therapists organize and resolve conflicts about working with children, adolescents, and their families in therapy."* (Feminist Bookstore News)

**More than a Mirror: How Clients Influence Therapists' Lives,** edited by Marcia Hill, EdD (Vol. 20, No. 1, 1997). *"Courageous, insightful, and deeply moving. These pages reveal the scrupulous self-examination and self-reflection of conscientious therapists at their best. An important contribution to feminist therapy literature and a book worth reading by therapists and clients alike."* (Rachel Josefowitz Siegal, MSW, retired feminist therapy practitioner; Co-Editor, Women Changing Therapy; Jewish Women in Therapy; and Celebrating the Lives of Jewish Women: Patterns in a Feminist Sampler)

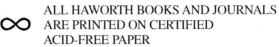

# The Foundation and Future of Feminist Therapy

Marcia Hill, EdD
Mary Ballou, PhD
Editors

*The Foundation and Future of Feminist Therapy* has been co-published simultaneously as *Women & Therapy*, Volume 28, Numbers 3/4 2005.

The Haworth Press, Inc.

New York • London • Victoria (AU)
www.HaworthPress.com

*The Foundation and Future of Feminist Therapy* has been co-published simultaneously as *Women & Therapy*™, Volume 28, Numbers 3/4 2005.

The Haworth Press, Inc., 10 Alice Street, Binghamton, NY 13904-1580 USA

Cover design by Lora Wiggins

**Library of Congress Cataloging-in-Publication Data**

The foundation and future of feminist therapy / Marcia Hill, Mary Ballou, editors.
     p. cm.
    "Co-published simultaneously as Women & therapy, volume 28, numbers 3/4 2005."
    Includes bibliographical references and index.
    ISBN-13: 978-0-7890-0201-3 (hc. : alk. paper)
    ISBN-10: 0-7890-0201-9 (hc. : alk. paper)
    ISBN-13: 978-0-7890-0217-4 (pbk. : alk. paper)
    ISBN-10: 0-7890-0217-5 (pbk. : alk. paper)
    1. Feminist therapy. I. Hill, Marcia. II. Ballou, Mary B., 1949-  III. Women & therapy.
RC489.F45F68 2005
616.89'14–dc22

                                                2004022800

# Indexing, Abstracting & Website/Internet Coverage

This section provides you with a list of major indexing & abstracting services and other tools for bibliographic access. That is to say, each service began covering this periodical during the year noted in the right column. Most Websites which are listed below have indicated that they will either post, disseminate, compile, archive, cite or alert their own Website users with research-based content from this work. (This list is as current as the copyright date of this publication.)

(continued)

(continued)

(continued)

(continued)

*Special Bibliographic Notes related to special journal issues*
*(separates) and indexing/abstracting:*

- indexing/abstracting services in this list will also cover material in any "separate" that is co-published simultaneously with Haworth's special thematic journal issue or DocuSerial. Indexing/abstracting usually covers material at the article/chapter level.
- monographic co-editions are intended for either non-subscribers or libraries which intend to purchase a second copy for their circulating collections.
- monographic co-editions are reported to all jobbers/wholesalers/approval plans. The source journal is listed as the "series" to assist the prevention of duplicate purchasing in the same manner utilized for books-in-series.
- to facilitate user/access services all indexing/abstracting services are encouraged to utilize the co-indexing entry note indicated at the bottom of the first page of each article/chapter/contribution.
- this is intended to assist a library user of any reference tool (whether print, electronic, online, or CD-ROM) to locate the monographic version if the library has purchased this version but not a subscription to the source journal.
- individual articles/chapters in any Haworth publication are also available through the Haworth Document Delivery Service (HDDS).

# ABOUT THE EDITORS

**Marcia Hill, EdD,** is a psychologist who has spent almost 30 years practicing psychotherapy. She is a former editor of the journal *Women & Therapy* and a member and past Chair of the Feminist Therapy Institute. In addition to therapy, Dr. Hill does occasional teaching, writing, and consulting in the areas of feminist therapy theory and practice. She is the author of *Diary of a Country Therapist* and has edited nine prior books about various aspects of feminist therapy, including *More Than a Mirror: How Clients Influence Therapists' Lives.* She is currently in private practice in Montpelier, Vermont.

**Mary Ballou, PhD,** is Professor of Counseling Psychology at Northeastern University, a practicing psychologist who holds a Diplomate from the American Board of Professional Psychology, Co-Chair of the Graduate Consortium of Women's Studies Programs in the Boston area, and Chair of the Feminist Therapy Institute. She has published five books in health counseling and feminist psychology and numerous chapters and research studies. Most recently she has been working with her students and multidisciplinary professionals on a project with Family Court to develop a tool to introduce psychosocial factors into judicial decision making in temporary child placement and restraining orders.

# The Foundation and Future of Feminist Therapy

## CONTENTS

Marcia Hill and Mary Ballou would like to thank Tina Jeong for her able editorial assistance.

# PART 1: FOUNDATIONS

# Feminist Therapy's Roots and Wings

## Marcia Hill

This is a critical time for feminism in general and for feminist therapy in particular. We have made many gains: feminist principles have been incorporated to some extent into ethics codes and into norms of generally accepted practice. Nonetheless, there has been a lengthy and increasingly powerful political swing to the right, especially in the U.S. This has not left the practice of psychotherapy unaffected. So although professional organizations now recommend sensitivity to a client's race, gender and sexual orientation, therapist autonomy is increasingly restricted to techniques and time lines that serve the insurance industry rather than clients. While awareness of violence against women is now commonplace among clinicians, human pain has become increasingly defined in medical, rather than psychological or sociopolitical, terms. Even the language of therapy has been co-opted by the insurance industry: Therapists are now "providers," clients are "consumers," and psychotherapy is "behavioral care" (as if all problems were behavioral). Words like "emotions" have been all but eliminated from the lexicon of

[Haworth co-indexing entry note]: "Feminist Therapy's Roots and Wings." Hill, Marcia. Co-published simultaneously in *Women & Therapy* (The Haworth Press, Inc.) Vol. 28, No. 3/4, 2005, pp. 1-5; and: *The Foundation and Future of Feminist Therapy* (ed: Marcia Hill, and Mary Ballou) The Haworth Press, Inc., 2005, pp. 1-5. Single or multiple copies of this article are available for a fee from The Haworth Document Delivery Service [1-800-HAWORTH, 9:00 a.m. - 5:00 p.m. (EST). E-mail address: docdelivery@ haworthpress.com].

http://www.haworthpress.com/web/WT
doi:10.1300/J015v28n03_01

*1*

psychotherapy. Language shapes reality, and the industry-driven language of therapy would have us see pain as biological and behavioral and help as drugs and the application of brief outcome-based "treatments." There is little place in this realm for looking at problems as responses to cultural injuries or for accompanying the client in a search for her own solutions and truths.

It is in this context that these authors contribute to this volume, which looks both backward to the roots of feminist therapy and forward to its possibilities. We offer also an analysis of the contemporary challenges to feminist therapy theory and practice.

We look at the foundations of feminist therapy from two organizing perspectives. One is its placement in time. The work of the earliest theorists (pre-1985) is examined by Susan Contratto and Jessica Rossier; Natalie Porter presents feminist therapy's primary theorists after that date. These authors have selected, in consultation with colleagues, those contributors to the foundations of feminist therapy whose work stands out either for originality or impact. The second frame is based more on content, pulling together four of feminist therapy's significant themes. Here, Susan Barrett reviews multicultural feminist therapy, focusing specifically on race and ethnicity. Laura Brown, Laurie Riepe and Rochelle Coffey look at the contributions of writers who have examined feminist therapy through the lenses of other differences, such as sexual orientation, ability and disability, aging, refugee and immigrant status, and social class. These perspectives come out of feminism's recognition that "woman" is not a unidimensional construct, and that to understand any woman, you must first understand her placement in her family; in her communities; and in the various social groupings of which she is a member, such as race or class (Barrett, 1998). Carolyn West describes the work of the relational-cultural theorists, whose influence has been significant in feminist therapy theory. Denise Webster and Erin Dunn review those authors whose work comes out of trauma theory, recognizing that in a culture of gendered and sexualized oppression, much of what women bring to therapy is a consequence of sexual abuse, battering and rape. All of these contributors end with a look at possible lessons that come out of the work they have reviewed, lessons that can and will be used as a foundation for feminist therapy's future.

These authors have done a remarkable job of sifting through almost three decades' worth of writing about feminist therapy to present its central themes and contributors. There is, naturally, a great deal of overlap, with some authors having substantial influence in more than one category. In addition, the choices of what work to include necessarily omitted many theorists whose work is both important and influential. Nonetheless, we believe that this compilation will give the reader a good overview of feminist therapy theory to date.

We look at this work keeping in mind that theorists whose writing is presented here all speak from their location not only in time but also in all of this culture's defining conditions. They speak as women of color or white women, as disabled or temporarily able-bodied. Their sexual orientation, age, class background and many other factors shape their understanding as much as does their gender. Too often these standpoints are mentioned only when they are "other," i.e., other than the perspective of the dominant culture. But growing up middle-class influences values as much as does growing up poor; being European-American determines one's vision as surely as does being Asian- American. In some of these reviews, notable those of Barrett and of Brown, Riepe and Coffey, these standpoints are at the center of the discussion; in others, they are unspecified (or only occasionally specified) and in the background. This reflects the reality of most writing and theorizing both historically and currently. The value of noting non-dominant status is that those outside the dominant culture are by definition bicultural and thus are in an especially powerful position to recognize and comment upon the "givens" that may otherwise be invisible. This is one of the gifts of feminism's analysis of gender, for example. The value of noting dominant status, however, is in reminding the reader that all perspectives are particular.

Where do we go from here? It is easy to feel defeated in today's climate. Sometimes it seems that the only and best future for feminist therapists is to hang on to what shreds of feminist perspective we can behind the closed door of the consulting room. Yet as the early feminist thinkers recognized, we cannot create a future that we cannot imagine; if we are to make real changes in both our cultural and clinical realities, we have to brave envisioning what those changes might look like. Thus, the second part of this collection imagines a future informed by feminist principles in the related arenas of psychotherapy, education for therapists, and community. These authors take up where the first section authors leave off, with visions that are informed by the lessons coming out of feminist therapy theory's history. Articulating dreams always runs the risk of sounding remote and unachievable, so these authors also include suggestions for actions both large and small that will help to make that future a reality.

If peering into the future is a risky enterprise, trying to create that future is like trying to build a home in the middle of a river: so little seems to take hold and make a difference. Further, the nature of the task is that the outcome is unobservable, often until well after one's lifetime. Yet what choice is there but to start? Malcolm Gladwell, in *The Tipping Point* (2000), describes the nature of change as being a matter of cumulative effort. That is, for complex problems there is rarely any one thing that makes a difference. Rather, each of many small changes adds to a kind of inevitability, with there being little evident effect until– apparently suddenly–the weight of the accumulated efforts creates a major shift in the picture. This is congruent with a feminist model of collaborative and grassroots change, as opposed to the traditional male mythology of autonomous heroic action as the fulcrum for change. Similarly, our attempts to change the cultures of community, education, or therapy are likely to appear either ineffective or minimally so. But these small efforts do accumulate. Do not think that nothing is changing simply because you cannot see it.

That said, as you read these visions of the future, consider for yourself where you might make a difference. What do you see as the most important place to begin? And, equally important, where is your own passion, what do you have the energy and commitment to do? One example of action has already come out of this volume, started by those who were involved with or heard about its creation. A number of women in the Boston area, including members of the Jean Baker Miller Training Institute, members of the Feminist Therapy Institute, urban health researchers, and others involved in service provision are meeting to consider how better to provide services based on feminist principles to local women. This group hopes to encourage support and collaboration among therapists and others who work with women, as a way to decrease isolation and provide solidarity in a shared feminist perspective.

Finally, we end this collection with a description and analysis of the challenges to feminist practice. We cannot hope to change that which we do not understand, and we wish you to be well equipped to grapple with and influence the forces that stand in the way of a feminist future. The work of remembering our roots, imagining and creating our future, and recognizing the threats to that future is as important now as it was when the second wave of feminism began. In fact, the Feminist Therapy Institute conference of 2002 was organized to do just that; the volume you hold is the outcome of that conference. We hope that in its pages you find both the groundwork and inspiration for action.

# REFERENCES

Barrett, S.E. (1998). Contextual identity: A model for therapy and social change. In M. Hill (Ed.) *Feminist therapy as a political act.* New York: Haworth.

Gladwell, M. (2000). *The tipping point: How little things can make a big difference.* New York: Little, Brown & Co.

# Early Trends
# in Feminist Therapy Theory and Practice

Susan Contratto
Jessica Rossier

**SUMMARY.** This article looks at some of the early writers in the feminist therapy movement, pre-1985. It highlights contributions of each as well as pointing out some of the internal debates between the women whose work is covered. It focuses on the diversity of contributions, the compelling political roots of the practice and unresolved questions. It concludes by raising points for consideration, which emerge from the consensual positions of these writers. *[Article copies available for a fee from The Haworth Document Delivery Service: 1-800-HAWORTH. E-mail address: <docdelivery@haworthpress.com> Website: <http://www.HaworthPress.com> © 2005 by The Haworth Press, Inc. All rights reserved.]*

**KEYWORDS.** Early feminist therapy writers, psychology of women, feminist therapy

Feminist therapy and feminist therapy theory emerged out of the ferment of the women's movement in the 1960s and 1970s. Women in

---

Susan Contratto is in private practice in Ann Arbor, MI. Jessica Rossier is in the graduate psychology program at Northeastern University, Boston, MA.
Address correspondence to: Susan Contratto, 1617 Cambridge Road, Ann Arbor, MI 48104.

[Haworth co-indexing entry note]: "Early Trends in Feminist Therapy Theory and Practice." Contratto, Susan, and Jessica Rossier. Co-published simultaneously in *Women & Therapy* (The Haworth Press, Inc.) Vol. 28, No. 3/4, 2005, pp. 7-26; and: *The Foundation and Future of Feminist Therapy* (ed: Marcia Hill, and Mary Ballou) The Haworth Press, Inc., 2005, pp. 7-26. Single or multiple copies of this article are available for a fee from The Haworth Document Delivery Service [1-800-HAWORTH, 9:00 a.m. - 5:00 p.m. (EST). E-mail address: docdelivery@haworthpress.com].

http://www.haworthpress.com/web/WT
© 2005 by The Haworth Press, Inc. All rights reserved.
doi:10.1300/J015v28n03_02

consciousness raising groups all over the country began to reveal previously unspoken and even unlabeled aspects of their lives. Affirmation, questioning, and self-revelation took place at a profoundly personal level. Women began to realize threads of similar experience with each other as women, as women in relationship with men, as women yearning for connections with other women, as daughters, as workers, and as lovers. As they discussed their experiences with therapists, or as therapists in these groups probed their discomfort with their training experiences, common themes emerged. Most problems were seen as internal to the individual. Most patients were blamed for their problems. Women's anger and frustration had no place in therapy. The pain and difficulties of everyday life–poverty, boredom, childrearing, isolation, and traumatic violence–were ignored. Early life events of a rather subtle nature such as "inadequate or insufficient mothering" were assumed to be the source of current problems. Women were labeled as neurotic, hysterical, depressed and were medicated or "helped to adjust."

It began to be clear that women's socialization in this culture created problems for them and that traditional psychology and therapy ignored this. "Real life" surrounding women's experience was ignored. Two vignettes from the clinical training of one of us (SC) give a flavor of the psychological climate around women.

The setting is a prestigious psychology clinic in a Northeastern city. The attending psychiatrist presented a case of a low-income family where the mother had committed suicide in particularly horrendous circumstances. The three children were under the care of the maternal grandmother who worked in the service industry. She had no car and depended on public transportation. The clinic had no evening hours. The staff psychiatrist supervising the case described her as "resistant" to seeking counseling for the children because she had difficulty getting to the appointments. This interpretation overlooked the circumstances and experiences of the grandmother by not recognizing her need to work in order to support three children who were suddenly placed under her care. At the same time the interpretation did not acknowledge the grandmother's grieving the loss of her daughter and struggling with the feelings accompanying the suicide.

Two teenage girls walking along a road in a public campground in early evening were picked up by a motorcycle gang and brutally gang raped. The first comment at the case presentation was, "You have to ask what they were doing walking along the road at night." In other words, they were asking for it. Statements like this are shocking for their cruel nature, as well as their existence in our seemingly more comprehensive approach to therapy these days. The ease with which women's experiences are trivialized and invalidated continues to be an issue for many feminist theorists.

The feminist therapy movement emerged from some of the major questions that women, practitioners and theorists struggled with. How much early experience is internalized and how is this done? How malleable is a woman's personality once stressors are understood or removed? Can a man be a feminist therapist? What techniques best suit feminist therapy? How should the feminist therapist equalize power in the therapeutic relationship? Is there a role for diagnosis or labeling or does that process always objectify the client? What is the place of political action in feminist therapy for the client and for the therapist? What is a feminist process in supervision?

The authors and books that we will be talking about are representative of and influential to the early growth of feminist therapy. They do not always agree with each other but represent a rich and exciting foundation in the field. In fact, a hallmark of the practice is its diversity. It is also a source of frustration for students; like any of the other vibrant therapeutic practices, we don't have a straightforward how-to book.

Two of the authors, Hannah Lerman and Nancy Chodorow, deal with how women became who they are. Susan Sturdivant, Edna Rawlings, Dianne Carter and Miriam Greenspan describe both philosophy of treatment and specific treatment techniques. Elizabeth Friar Williams and Iris Fodor concentrate their work in the practice of feminist therapy and the development of specific treatment tools. The work of Lynn Bravo Rosewater and Lenore Walker are some of the first forays of consequences and evaluation of violence against women. We will discuss the works in that order, noting at times debates within the literature.

## *HANNAH LERMAN*

Hannah Lerman (1986) clearly and accurately describes the final formulation of female psychological development, which Freud and his disciples leave as the heritage of post World War II psychoanalysis. These include: greater difficulty in development, a weaker superego, greater penis envy, narcissism, and problems with the expression of sexuality. These Freudians argue that normal women basically cannot traverse an Oedipal resolution and they endure the subsequent consequences for the rest of their lives. Why is this important? Lerman makes the case that in the 1960s and well into the 1970s psychoanalysis was the Cadillac of psychological treatment. Its concepts of early fixation, penis envy, repressed or contorted sexuality and cure within the transference model dominated psychological discussions of development and treatment. In fact, brief treatments at that time were treatments that allowed you to think psychoanalytically and make a measured decision as to whether the patient was able to understand a particular interpretation. The dominant alternative paradigms were the emerging humanist approaches including Rogers' counseling model (1977). These concentrated primarily in developing treatment options and had little to say about developmental issues, particularly gendered developmental issues. Clinicians, theory developers, and patients who were fortunate to be wealthy or have good insurance, chose psychoanalysis.

Psychoanalytic thinking heavily influenced the American reading public as well as public health practice in the '50s, '60s and '70s, primarily as it was transmitted through the work of Erik Erickson (1950). His books were readable, sensible and, because he focused on ego development, more meaningful to most readers than the jargon of journal papers. However, his theoretical assumptions were profoundly psychoanalytic— how to deal with the developmental challenges of life with the tools that the infant, toddler, child gained in managing libido and aggression in the pregenital period.

Lerman argues that there are a number of reasons for Erikson's pervasive influence in the United States. It was the first all encompassing theory to gain a hold. Its practitioners benefited from flexibility within the psychoanalytic institutes themselves so that varieties of psychoanalytic practice existed which departed in a variety of ways from Freud's original formulations. And, there was prestige and financial gain in being part of the elite psychoanalytic establishments. We would add that these ideas formed the basis of the increasingly popular child-rearing books of Dr. Benjamin Spock (1968) as well as well-baby pamphlets distributed in clinics by the Public Health Department.

Lerman also chronicles the earlier feminist assaults on psychoanalysis (1986, p.149-158). She describes writers including Chodorow, Jean Baker Miller, Eichenbaum and Orbach, who have undertaken feminist revisions of psychoanalytic theory and practice. She also reviews the work of other feminists working outside of the psychoanalytic framework.

After arguing that revisions, even feminist revisions, of psychoanalytic theory are flawed because the core is essentially rotten, Lerman proposes building our own theory. To that end she enumerates eight criteria for determining the feminist credentials of a theory of female development and applies them to current existing theories. These criteria are (1) clinical usefulness: "Coming as a clinician to the issue of personality development, I assert that any theory of personality development must be clinically useful, i.e., its concepts need to be readily translatable into what could and might take place with its use in a therapy session with a living woman" (p.173). She then asserts that (2) it must encompass the diversity and complexity of women and their lives. She comments, "We need to be especially careful to see that class, race, sexual preference, and ethnic identification as well as lifestyle (in all its dimensions) can be considered in any theories that we build" (p. 174). Lerman argues next (3) that the theory must view women positively and centrally. Further, (4) that the theory must arise from women's experience; "As a feminist therapist, I am aware that our best work comes out of our experience as women with women" (p. 174). And (5) that the theoretical concepts themselves should stay close to the data of experience. There needs to be (6) a recognition that the internal world is inextricably intertwined with the external world and that one experiences internal shifts as there are external shifts. (7) The theory should contain theoretical concepts that should not be confined by particularistic terminology or in terms of other theories. And, finally, (8) that personality theory should support feminist (or at minimum non-sexist) modes of psychotherapy.

These criteria are particularly interesting as they are the first feminist attempt to define a personality theory that works for women. The idea of criteria reappears in Brown's work (1994) and also in Worrell and Remer's (1992) book as well as others. In her footnotes, Lerman acknowledges the feedback and refinement process, which allowed her to come up with this list of criteria . . . a process, which is decidedly feminist . . . group collaboration without ownership.

## *NANCY CHODOROW*

Nancy Chodorow's book, *The reproduction of mothering* (1978), is by far the best known of the works in this chapter. Chodorow uses psychoanalytic theory, in particular object relations theory, to explain why women mother, that is why women themselves have a psychological investment in maintaining this traditional role and why men have an unconscious investment in that maintenance.

Chodorow is strongly critical of the traditional Freudian work on male and female development that portrays the infant as a narcissistic actor seeking drive gratification. She turns to British object relations theory, particularly as it was developed by Fairbairn, to argue a different development trajectory. This theory emphasizes the primacy of intersubjectivity: that the infant toddler is moving through the world in complicated relationship to other people (the objects of the theory). The internalization of relational experience that Chodorow describes in this book is mediated by conflict and fantasy.

Chodorow argues that the early relationship with a (usually) maternal caretaker is core to understanding later heterosexual tension, complicated issues within the mother/daughter relationship and women's drive to mother. Chodorow says that the outside experience is important: the degree of father absence and maternal presence are the social conditions that lead to the sexual differences that are part of our and other cultures. She argues that the greater the father absence, the more the generation of traditional sex roles and complicated mother daughter relationships. Socialization certainly reinforces psychological tendencies of girls and boys which have their etiology in early development; but socialization alone, Chodorow argues, could not explain the complicated passion and attachments that men and women have to each other and, differently, to their parenting and their children.

But Chodorow does not address the questions of what constitutes appropriate treatment. Lerman assumes, however, "Because she weaves psychoanalytic theory very heavily into her account . . . and has made it fashionable for feminists to reaccept psychoanalytic thinking, it would be easy to assume that she would find the techniques of psychoanalytic therapy acceptable although they do not generally accord with a feminist or even a nonsexist stance" (1986, p. 187). Lerman concludes her critique by saying, "If only she had left psychoanalytic theory out or had more adequately recognized the pitfalls that its acceptance has created for her own theories" (p. 188).

Chodorow asked a question that had previously been assumed to be so natural that it didn't need to be problematized: Why do women mother? It was akin to asking why people eat. And to answer that question she turned to a particular psychodynamic theory that was sensitive to social conditions. She tried to explain the inside's relationship to the outside. Her attempt to do this and the care with which she worked with the theories has been enormously influential on feminist psychoanalytic theorists to follow. Further, questioning the obvious and turning theory against theory has become a hallmark of much excellent feminist scholarship.

Her approach was to look at the human experience of passion and commitment that could not be explained by sex role socialization. She appealed to many feminist therapists and theorists precisely because they too saw the intensity of feeling, even irrationality that was generated in heterosexual relationships and in parenting. Many felt that while sex-role socialization explained much of women's experience, it did not fully account for the intensity and quality of these relationships.

## SUSAN STURDIVANT

Other authors' work is more explicit about techniques of practice than either Lerman or Chodorow. For example, Susan Sturdivant (1980) wrote *Notes on therapy with women,* which was both a critique of existing therapeutic treatments of women and a guide, and which tried to pull together the major feminist contributions to a philosophy of feminist treatment. Her historical background included an overview of the current (up to 1980) feminist movement, a critique of Freud in particular and psychotherapy in general and a description of the emerging field of Feminist Therapy.

Sturdivant raised the question of why a philosophy of treatment. She answered that it is the beliefs of the therapist about the inherent nature of men and women, his or her beliefs about the development of pathology, the therapist's thoughts and understandings about the nature of the social and cultural situation that the client finds him or herself in, and the therapist's world view of the way things should be which will determine the helpfulness of the treatment.

Sturdivant's basic argument is that the sex role socialization process for women is the reason why many women are dissatisfied and unhappy. She also notes that traditional therapy focuses on adaptation to the status quo, which for women means maintaining sex appropriate roles, avoiding conflict, denying anger, and engaging in self-sacrificing behavior. The role of feminist therapy is to increase awareness of the limits and pain of being a woman by exposing and illuminating the minority status of women, and ultimately, to provide a resocialization process for clients.

Certainly we are much more familiar with the damage of sex role socialization of women now than we were in the 1960s and 1970s. What Sturdivant makes clear, however, is that the principals governing the therapist, including preferred techniques, emerge specifically to heal women's gendered socialization experience. For example, she strongly argues that the therapist should share her struggles and her coping skills as a model setting participant rather than a technical expert. Further, she sees the all female group as the best modality for treatment since there can be validation, sharing, and mutual nurturing. She reminds us of a most important point: that most women are socialized to not only devalue themselves but also other women. The group becomes a means to recognize one's own strengths as well as the strengths of others. She notes that most feminist therapists see an egalitarian relationship as the hallmark of feminist therapy:

> To counteract the traditionally greater power of the therapist in psychotherapy, feminist therapists eschew the use of expert, coercive, and legitimate power in favor of reliance on reward and informational and referent power. This means that they do not use diagnostic labels or patronizing jargon and that they ask questions instead of making interpretations. (p.157)

## EDNA RAWLINGS AND DIANNE CARTER

Sturdivant relies heavily on work presented in *Psychotherapy for women: Treatment toward equality*, which is a volume of wide ranging essays edited by Edna Rawlings and Dianne Carter (1977). The excellent first two chapters of this book, written by the editors, describe a model of value change in psychotherapy. They argue that what the therapist believes about the patient will have a direct effect on how he or she does therapy as well as in the type of model he/she uses: whether a top down model, medical model, expert vs. patient, or one of reciprocal influences.

They write:

> The values, structure, and goals of sexist therapy are destructive to women. In the preceding chapters we have presented evidence that clients in therapy move closer to the values of their therapists. Sexist therapists accept the traditional/cultural definitions of women as essential to an adequate sexual identity, the sine qua non of mental health. However, we feel the traditional role of women in our culture is demeaning, powerless and negatively valued. Internalization of this role leads to low self-esteem and self-hatred. If sexist values are learned from a therapist, a woman client will be discouraged from expressing assertion, independence and power. (p. 49)

They go on to list the values of feminist therapy:

1. The inferior status of women is due to their having less political and economic power than men.
2. A feminist therapist does not value an upper- or middle-class client more than a working-class client.
3. The primary source of women's pathology is social not personal: external, not internal.
4. The focus on environmental stress as a major source of pathology is not used as an avenue of escape from individual responsibility.
5. Feminist therapy is opposed to personal adjustment to social conditions; the goal is social and political change. Other women are not the enemy.
6. Men are not the enemy either.
7. Women must be economically and psychologically autonomous.
8. Relationships of friendship, love, and marriage should be equal in personal power.
9. Major differences between "appropriate" sex-roles must disappear.

Rawlings and Carter outline the strategies of feminist psychotherapy (pp. 58-64) including their belief that diagnostic testing should not be used, that diagnostic labels should be avoided and, in accordance with Sturdivant, that feminist therapy is most effectively done in groups.

The book also includes two chapters by Patricia Ann Jakubowski, "Assertive behavior and clinical problems of women" (pp. 147-167) and "Self-assertion training for women" (pp. 168-180), that are a straightforward, readable guide to assertiveness training. Other issues covered in the book include career counseling, work issues, counseling with lesbians, feminism as therapy, consciousness raising groups, bibliotherapy, changes in women's studies courses, radical feminism, and social activism as therapy.

The two chapters by Hogie Wyckoff (1977) make clear the connection of feminist therapy to radical psychiatry. She states:

> We in radical psychiatry begin with a definite radical political perspective. We are not interested in being *hip shrinks* who service counter-culture people. We are community organizers; we want to teach people problem-solving skills and political awareness. We

want to provide protection to people while they make the changes
they want in their lives. We desire to put people in touch with their
power because we are interested in people reclaiming themselves
as full and potent human beings. (p. 370)

Wyckoff strongly advocates groups as well as political action for
both clients and their therapists.

## MIRIAM GREENSPAN

Miriam Greenspan is another author who developed innovative concepts in feminist theory. Her book (1983) *A new approach to women
and therapy* was noted for its vast contributions to the field of Women's
Psychology. According to Greenspan, in order to understand women's
problems one needs to analyze their personal history. However, to find
the real roots of the problem, one must look beyond the personal history, to the history of women in society, and to the history of traditional
psychotherapy itself.

Throughout her work, Greenspan develops concepts that capture, in a
very unique manner, the theories behind them. For example, the concept of "Man as expert Woman as Patient" highlights that the majority
of patients in all sectors of the psychiatric system are women, whereas it
is mostly men who take the role of psychiatrists, psychologists, and
medical doctors. She therefore concludes that male practitioners who
diagnose and treat female patients dominate the mental health system.
The problem with the concept of "Woman as Patient," explains
Greenspan, is that "once a woman comes to therapy with the identity of
a patient, she has already surrendered the part of herself she will most
need in order to help herself: her power as person" (p. 88). In other
words, women who adopt the patient's role sacrifice their own ability to
solve issues and expect "the expert" to take care of them.

Greenspan's second concept "Father knows best," describes, with
great objectivity, the major failures of Freud's psychoanalytic model.
She does, however, note the importance of psychoanalysis and its contributions to the world of psychology today.

Greenspan considers the problem to be that the Freudian approach
determined what then became "the ruling myths of psychiatric theory
and practice" (p. 16). She synthesizes those myths in three different areas. Myth 1: "It's all in your head." The basic premise of this principle is
that unconscious forces within the individual are the cause of emotional

pain, therefore ignoring the relationship between individual psychology and social structure. For Greenspan, the major problem with Myth 1 relates to the idea that the oppression and exploitation women undergo conveniently locates itself *within* the individual. Therefore, neither the workplace nor the social organization of the family requires transformation, but it is the individual woman who "needs to be fixed." In conclusion it allows for a pattern that focuses the blame on the victim.

Myth 2: "The medical model of psychopathology" considers that all emotional pain and illness can be treated the same way that one would treat medical problems. Based on these ideas, diagnostic and assessment tools such as the Diagnostic and Statistical Manual (DSM) were developed and utilized to reduce people's symptoms to a "pat formula" that requires specific treatment. This model works under the assumption that the problem lies within the person, and therefore treatment should concentrate on changing the individual.

Finally, the Myth of the doctor as "The Expert" leads to a therapeutic relationship based fundamentally on inequality of power between doctor and patient. Through this form of relationship patients learn to adapt to a sense of powerlessness therefore accepting it in other forms of social relationships. Specifically with women, the following may occur: "Woman as Patient learns, with the help of Man as Expert, to adapt to a situation of Father Knows Best" (p. 30). At this point in her book Greenspan rescues the deteriorated image of Dora, as she was portrayed by Freud when she fled therapy, as an example of how brutally cruel the punishment can be for women who dare to reject the expert's words.

> Dora tried to defy the myth of the expert: she told Father Freud that he didn't know best. For her effort, she was rewarded with the final weapon in the arsenal of the Expert-The expert's last hex. She was told she would never be cured until she accepted her pathology as Freud saw it. (p. 31)

Greenspan further explains that the use of this myth in traditional forms of therapy continues to reinforce women positively to accept and perpetuate social domination, therefore incapacitating women to experience a form of therapy that promotes more self-reliant or cooperative ways of solving problems.

In conclusion, Greenspan believes that the real problem lies within the male dominated society that depicts the normal feminine woman as a victim. "The Victim is the woman who has successfully adapted to a situation of social powerlessness. . . . The victim is the woman who sees herself through male eyes and thus learns to devalue, limit, and even hate herself" (p. 35).

To elaborate, Greenspan asserts that people who submit to domination bind themselves to self-destructive behaviors and develop "symptoms" that therapy must necessarily address and that often times hide an enormous amount of rage. These symptoms end up being a woman's adaptation of anger that allows her to continue to be feminine while at the same time rebelling against the psychosocial situation imposed on her. For her, a big part of therapy entails working with this anger and allowing it to come to the surface. But most importantly, it entails helping the woman realize how she "colludes with her own oppression" and adapts to the Victim role imposed by society therefore perpetuating her oppressed condition.

## ELIZABETH FRIAR WILLIAMS

Another author who considers it essential for women to learn the ways in which they help perpetuate their victimization is Elizabeth Friar Williams (1976) who in her book *Notes of a feminist therapist* describes her own practice of feminist therapy through case stories. She considers that "no woman's therapy is complete unless she is willing to give up whatever 'victim' behaviors are keeping her unrealized and frustrated" (p. 10). With this, Williams places this idea as part of the goals inherent to feminist therapy. Some other goals that she establishes for her patients coincide with Greenspan's ideas, for example, the shared objective to help women see the connection between their psychological situation and their condition as woman in a male-dominated society.

For Williams, women must understand that some traditionally female roles such as mother, homemaker, wife, etc., are not necessarily linked to the self-defeating feelings associated with them; and that women interested in expanding their roles in society do not need to give up more traditional ones, unless they choose to do so. Through this definition Williams makes acceptable the gratification these traditional roles can provide for the women who consciously choose them.

Williams also considers a basic function of feminist therapy to encourage women to find direction in terms of career or some form of productive work that keeps them from being dependent on someone else. Williams goes as far as to state that a "healthy woman is a woman who is able to support herself in work that is fun for her and gives her a sense of competence" (p. 9). This controversial idea provided fertile ground for strong criticism in the part of other feminist theorists and reviewers of her work.

Greenspan (1983) criticizes Williams' goal for women to have a job outside the home. First of all, she rescues the idea that the work women perform at home is not work at all because is not monetarily remunerated. Secondly, she emphasizes the fact that motherhood or child rearing is undervalued in our society, therefore provoking feelings of inadequacy or low self-esteem in women. Lastly, Greenspan suggests that in order for this situation to change, a lot more work is required than what one women can do in individual therapy, as Williams suggests in her book. Greenspan instead highlights the need of a "total restructuring of social life" in order to solve this problem, she considers that any other attempts will inevitably fall into the category of "Myth 1: It's all in your head" placing even more burden on women.

Further, Greenspan considers that Williams' ideas "end up putting women back in the same old bind: women are not mentally 'healthy' unless they feel and act more like men" (p. 138). For her, ideas like the one described above end up creating even more myths for women to live by. An example of this is the myth that women will be healthier if able to have a job outside the home, or in the opposite case, that they are not "Superwoman enough or liberated enough" (p. 143) if they fail to do so.

Other feminist therapists like Lerman (1976), considered that Williams, in her book, failed to address feminist issues "fully enough, sensitively enough, or meaningfully enough" (p. 748). She also, at points, perceived Williams as too critical of the women discussed in her book.

Finally, one of the strongest criticisms that Williams received from Greenspan for her work was that her book addressed issues that affected mainly white, middle class women in society, and some of her proposed solutions may even go against feminist ideals given that they include the oppression of other, less privileged women. For example, in her book, Williams includes the story of a patient who ends up hiring a live-in housekeeper to take care of her kids while she worked. The idea according to Greenspan would go against the ideals of "sisterhood" since "The 'liberated woman' who looks around and sees other women in chains is a contradiction in terms" (p. 142). Greenspan raises the question of the rights of the live-in maid and how this solution improves her situation? Or who takes care of the maid's own kids while she watches over someone else's?

However, Williams' work does share commonalities with the work of other feminist authors. She considers the role of socialization in women's lives fundamental to an accurate understanding of women's experiences. In her work she describes how society reinforces women's total dependency on men's approval and attention as a means to obtain self-esteem and value. She goes far back to society's upbringing of young girls:

> Young girls are still expected to live out the notion that future married love is the only focus around which to organize all their developing feelings and skills! Therefore women who have not achieved such a relationship come to therapy (and to other sources of consolation, personal change, or oblivion) believing that they *should* feel totally depressed, inadequate as human beings, worried about their "neuroses" or "inability to make contact," dissatisfied with their appearance, and hopeless about their chances for future happiness and personal security. (p. 28)

In her analysis of women's development, Williams defined what she calls "[her] own version of the Oedipus Complex." In it, she emphasizes the idea of power over sexual attraction as the primary force controlling young girls' behaviors. She considers that the important thing for both boys and girls is to obtain the approval of the powerful figure whom at first they believe to be their mother, but as they grow up realize to be their father. Boys get approval by being like their father, whereas girls need to obtain the father's approval of their sexuality and it is this approval that provides them with a feeling of power. This would then explain some women's need to get the constant approval of "father figures" in their lives.

Like other feminist theorists, Williams also analyzes depression in women. However, different from many feminists, she places more importance on hormonal levels than on sex roles. For her, the influence of sex hormones on the pituitary gland that produce hormones like norepinephrine tends to be at high levels in the body in depression. These influences are even more important during significant developmental periods such as menarche, menopause, and childbirth. According to Williams the tendency to "overemphasize women's feelings as the source of depression would end up blaming women for their depression" (p. 101). To a lesser degree, Williams considers that women's perceptions of themselves as having fewer options also contributes to the development of depression.

Finally, she discusses socialization as a contributing factor in maintaining depression: "[Women] have learned that it is appropriate for them to be sad and to feel helpless without a protector" (p. 105). But mostly she considers that depression has to do with the guilt women feel about being angry. Actually, she considers it therapeutic to help patients figure out the ways in which they act depressed instead of being openly angry.

## *IRIS FODOR*

Placing even more emphasis on the actual practice of feminist therapy, Iris Fodor in her work provides a different level of analysis. She proposes the use of behavioral therapy as a way to help women overcome some of the dilemmas imposed by sex role socialization. In most of her work, Fodor concentrates on what therapists should do to help women deal with sex role conflict and social change. She proposes that some of the techniques utilized in behavioral therapy such as desensitization, assertiveness training, role modeling, reinforcement, etc. could help women to better deal with the internal conflict women struggle with while trying to accommodate to the demands of gender roles.

> A behavioral approach could challenge the "morality" of conforming to sex role stereotypes and provide reinforcements so that prestige, competence or goodness can now be associated with new or expanded interests and role behavior. It could provide non-stereotypic female therapists for the patient to model as well as enable the patient to experience approval from male and female therapists for expanded role repertoires. (1974, p. 23)

Fodor concurs with Greenspan in that women have higher rates of mental illness. However, Fodor questions the explanation for such statistics, emphasizing that they could have various interpretations such as: greater readiness for women to seek help when needed, more mental illness, higher probabilities to be labeled sick, the possibility that labels imposed on women are a reflection of deviations from stereotypic behavior, or actual greater sex role conflict. Fodor also agrees with the idea that women's inability to express anger and the thought that it is unfeminine to do so are the main causes of depression. She proposes a behavioral treatment that includes techniques such as keeping records of the depressed moods, finding reinforcements of the depressed behaviors, and the use of assertive training.

Fodor places a great deal of importance on assertive training as a tool to improve women's lives. In a study performed by Fodor and Wolfe

(1977) three different methods were compared to measure their effectiveness in improving women's assertiveness skills. The first group included modeling and behavior rehearsal, the second group included the use of modeling, behavior rehearsal, and rational therapy, and the third one was a consciousness-raising group. Results of this study showed that the first two groups produced significant improvements in women's assertiveness skills, whereas the consciousness-raising group was considered to be ineffective. Therefore, this confirmed the author's idea that the use of behavioral techniques may bring great benefits to women's therapy.

According to Fodor, there are a series of irrational beliefs that women inherit from society beginning in early childhood that impede their assertive behavior. Examples include the idea that women need to be nurturing, docile, and submissive, and that failure to do so could lead people (especially men) to see them as "too masculine" or "aggressive." For Fodor assertiveness training programs must challenge these irrational belief systems and reinforce the use of new assertive behaviors and the elimination of old traditional ones (1975). Fodor's contributions are invaluable in that she studied trains of thought that would normally be considered as completely distinct and merged them in the practice of feminist therapy, complementing in that way the application and use of both approaches.

## LENORE WALKER AND LYNNE BRAVO ROSEWATER

In the field of violence against women, Lenore Walker and Lynne Bravo Rosewater began their separate and collaborate work in the early 1970s. Aspects of their work demonstrate feminist practice, theory, and politics. As a whole, their work provides many of our current understandings of domestic violence, family violence, pathology, treatment, and advocacy for victims of violence. They were active in the development of feminist therapy. They were both founding members of the Feminist Therapy Institute in 1982 and Walker was the first Chairperson. They published together in a particularly groundbreaking feminist way. Their co-edited book, the *Handbook of feminist therapy* (1985), gave all the women at the first Feminist Therapy Institute conference in Vail in 1982 an opportunity to present their ideas, regardless of writing skills or academic affiliation. To quote Rosewater:

> This commitment to disseminating ideas and finding others to help the women with their writing is to my mind truly feminist. This

book also set the precedence for the work of AFTI [Advanced Feminist Therapy Institute] to be chronicled in other edited books. (1995, p. 415)

Rosewater and Walker were political advocates in the public arena. Rosewater was a founding mother of "Women Together, Incorporated in 1976, the first shelter for battered women and their children in Ohio and the third shelter in the United States" (Rosewater, 1995, p. 408). Walker's public advocacy has included expert witness testimony on behalf of women who have killed an abusive spouse. By the mid 1990s she had appeared in approximately 350 such cases (Walker, 1995, p. 526). She was a pioneer in the theoretical development of the battered women's syndrome and was an integral part of its fight for acceptance as a legitimate courtroom defense throughout the country.

Both authors placed the woman in context. Rather than accepting the prevailing arguments about blame, they argued that women who were in violent situations developed predictable responses. It was not that sick women got in battering situations but that battering made women who might otherwise appear healthy to appear sick. Like Chodorow, they in theory and in practice turned conventional theory and practice in a feminist direction. For example, Walker (1979) proposed her theory of learned helplessness, which explained how the cycle of abuse led to an inability to self-protect, directly from the work of Martin Seligman with dogs. In a laboratory setting he found that dogs that were subjected to variable, aversive and random stimulation became unable to actively protect themselves and, strikingly, they did not leave their cages when the doors were open. Walker hypothesized that this experience mirrored that of battered women.

Rosewater also used a tried and true tool of psychology in her early work–psychological testing, specifically the MMPI (Rosewater, 1985). She argued that the testing profile of the battered woman (elevated scores on scales that measured anger, confusion and paranoia and lowered scores on scales measuring internal strength and coping skills) had been typically misinterpreted. Rather than indicating developmental, internal pathology such as psychosis or borderline personality disorder, she made the case that they are a predictable response to battering. This dramatic turn became the basis for PTSD and other situationally induced psychological syndromes.

Both Rosewater and Walker were active in struggles against misdiagnoses in psychology. They fought against the proposed diagnosis of Masochistic Personality Disorder, which was eventually changed to Self-Defeating Personality Disorder–for Rosewater an unacceptable compromise. She has been vocal in her criticism of personality disorders: "personality disorders, as they have been traditionally defined, posit that the behavior characteristics are irreversible; diagnoses like Post-Traumatic Stress Disorder, on the other hand, define behavior developed in response to trauma as being recoverable" (1995, p. 413). Needless to say their work has been invaluable to the field of Women's Psychology and to the creation of a new understanding of violence against women.

The authors discussed represent a major contribution to feminist thought and action. In writing this chapter we tried to emphasize the major differences between the author's ideas as well as the criticisms raised by each with the assumption that it is this ability to create, deconstruct, and re-create theories that has led to some of the current thinking in Women's Psychology.

As part of the early thinking in the field of feminist therapy and theory, each author established a path for future feminist authors to follow and build on, or in other instances, some of the errors committed in the development of theory and practice that have nonetheless led to new understandings. Either way, foundation for future feminist thought was created.

Besides some of the differences amongst them, we can also find common ground in identifying the major errors of traditional psychological paradigms, which helped perpetuate women's oppression and facilitated a misunderstanding of women's experiences. Authors discussed share an interest in finding new theories that presented women in a new and more positive light different from the male perspective. They were able to look beyond tradition and defy established societal and theoretical standards, leading to theories that validated and honored women's experiences and that gave voice to the repressed feelings and thoughts of women in earlier and present days. Therefore, they created a more comprehensive Psychology, one that is more inclusive of women's circumstances and lived experiences.

## LESSONS FOR THE FUTURE FROM THE PAST

It is instructive both for the present and the future to go back over foundational feminist therapy work. These remind us of certain key concepts as well as allow us to document the gains we have made. Among the noteworthy themes are the following.

1. Feminist therapy practice emerged at a time of intense political ferment. It had roots in the radical psychiatry movement as well as in the naming, sharing and actions of consciousness raising groups. As such it had a commitment to listening to women as experts in their own lives and to political action as part of a movement and as individuals, both clients and therapists. Have we stayed true to these roots?

2. Early writers focused on gender socialization as an important situational stressor in women's lives. Gender shaped the distribution of power in society as well as in relationships. It also defined the choices available to many women, both practical as well as emotional. Women who behaved in ways that were not traditionally feminine often ended up with psychiatric diagnoses. How does gender continue to play a role in our theory, practice and community actions?

3. In the 1970s and 1980s white males both as practitioners and as theoreticians dominated psychology. The field has changed with at least equal numbers of men and women and many more women in leadership positions and responsible for teaching and scholarship. How has this shift in number effected feminist practice?

4. And, finally, notably and understandably absent (with the exception of Williams) in the writers we have reviewed is a discussion of women's biology. This absence reflects the backlash against biology as destiny during this time period. There has been considerable movement in feminist biology and psychobiology since then. How is this reflected in feminist therapy practice and theory?

## REFERENCES

Brown, L.S. (1994). *Subversive dialogues: Theory in feminist therapy.* New York, NY: Basic Books.

Chodorow, N. (1978). *The reproduction of mothering: Psychoanalysis and the reproduction of gender.* Berkeley, CA.: University of California Press.

Erickson, E.H. (1950). *Childhood and society.* New York, NY. Norton.

Fodor, I.E. (1974). Sex role conflict and symptom formation in women: Can behavioral therapy help? *Psychotherapy: Theory, Research and Practice, 11* (1), 22-29.

Fodor, I.G. & Wolfe, J.L. (1977). Modifying assertive behavior in women: A comparison of three approaches. *Behavior Therapy, 8* (4), 567-574.

Fodor, I.G.& Wolfe, J.L. (1975). A cognitive/behavioral approach to modifying assertive behavior in women. *The Counseling Psychologist, 5* (4), 45-52.

Greenspan, M. (1983). A new approach to women and therapy. New York, NY: McGrawHill.

Jakubowski, P.A. (1977). Assertive behavior and clinical problems of women; Self-assertion training for women. In E.I. Rawlings & D.K. Carter, (Eds.), *Psychotherapy for women: Treatment toward equality* (pp. 147-167; pp. 168-180). Springfield Ill.: Charles C Thomas Publisher.

Lerman, H. (1976). One feminist therapist opens her notebook. [Review of the book *Notes of a Feminist Therapist*]. *Contemporary Psychology, 21* (10), 748.

Lerman, H. (1986). *A Mote in Freud's eye*. New York, NY: Springer Publishing.

Rawlings, E.I. & Carter, D.K. (Eds.) (1977). *Psychotherapy for women: Treatment toward equality*. Springfield Ill.: Charles C Thomas Publisher.

Rogers, C.R. (1977). *Carl Rogers on personal power*. New York, NY: Delacorte Press.

Rosewater, L.B. (1985). Schizophrenic, borderline or battered? In L.B. Rosewater & L.E.A. Walker (Eds.), *Handbook of feminist therapy: Women's issues in psychotherapy*. New York, NY: Springer Publishing.

Rosewater, L.B. (1995). Reminiscences, recollections and reflections: The making of a feminist foremother. *Women & Therapy, 17*, 407-418.

Rosewater, L.B. & Walker, L.E.A. (Eds.) (1985). *Handbook of feminist therapy: Women's issues in psychotherapy*. New York, NY: Springer Publishing.

Spock, B. (1968). *Baby and child care*. New York, NY: Meredith Press.

Sturdivant, S. (1980). *Notes on therapy with women: A feminist philosophy of treatment*. New York, NY: Springer Publishing.

Walker, L.E.A. (1979). *The battered woman*. New York, NY: Harper and Row.

Walker, L.E.A. (1995). The transmogrification of a feminist foremother. *Women & Therapy, 17*, 517-529.

Williams, E.F. (1976). *Notes of a feminist therapist*. New York, NY: Praeger Publishers.

Worell, J. & Remer, P. (1992). *Feminist perspectives in therapy: An empowerment model for women*. New York, NY: John Wiley & Sons.

Wyckoff, H. (1977). Radical psychiatry for women; Radical psychiatry techniques. In E.I.Rawlings & D.K. Carter, (Eds.), *Psychotherapy for women: Treatment toward equality* (pp. 370-391; pp. 392-403). Springfield Ill.: Charles C Thomas Publisher.

# Multicultural Feminist Therapy: Theory in Context

Susan E. Barrett
with
Jean Lau Chin
Lillian Comas-Diaz
Oliva Espin
Beverly Greene
Monica McGoldrick

**SUMMARY.** Psychological theory needs to be representative of the full range of human experience by being based in the experience of all groups of people. The women honored in this chapter, Jean Lau Chin, Lillian Comas-Diaz, Oliva Espin, Beverly Greene, and Monica McGoldrick, are all feminist therapists, researchers, scholars, clinicians and writers who have directed some substantial portion of their professional attention toward understanding the critical nature of minority and dominant group status on the development of psychological and feminist therapy theory. Together, their professional contributions and personal stories provide a powerful understanding of the nature of the intersection of race, culture,

Susan E. Barrett is a psychologist in independent practice in Atlanta, GA.

The author wishes to thank Beverly Jones for reading this manuscript and providing insightful comments.

Address correspondence to: Susan E. Barrett, 1904 Monroe Drive, Suite 200, Atlanta, GA 30324.

[Haworth co-indexing entry note]: "Multicultural Feminist Therapy: Theory in Context." Barrett, Susan E. Co-published simultaneously in *Women & Therapy* (The Haworth Press, Inc.) Vol. 28, No. 3/4, 2005, pp. 27-61; and: *The Foundation and Future of Feminist Therapy* (ed: Marcia Hill, and Mary Ballou) The Haworth Press, Inc., 2005, pp. 27-61. Single or multiple copies of this article are available for a fee from The Haworth Document Delivery Service [1-800-HAWORTH, 9:00 a.m. - 5:00 p.m. (EST). E-mail address: docdelivery@haworthpress.com].

**KEYWORDS.** Multicultural, feminist therapy, contextual identity

The legacy of the women honored in this chapter is vast and multidimensional, spanning the last two decades of psychological theory development. Their voices, as with the voices of other feminist therapists such as Jeanne Adleman and Gloria Enguidanos (1995), have grown stronger, more complex, and become more prolific over time, thereby contributing toward the development of a psychological theory that is truly based on all people. Those honored here, Jean Lau Chin, Lillian Comas-Diaz, Oliva Espin, Beverly Greene, and Monica McGoldrick, are all feminist therapists, researchers, scholars, clinicians and writers/editors who have directed some substantial portion of their professional attention toward understanding the critical nature of culture and race in the development of psychological and feminist therapy theory.

Individually and collectively the work of these women contributes to a very different paradigm for understanding human beings than that offered by mainstream North American psychological theories. Understanding the paradigm shift is essential to understanding the importance of their work. The old/current paradigm of psychology in the United States is rooted in the "European-American values of individualism, autonomy, control, and a belief in rights, liberty, the self, self-fulfillment, opposites, and progress" (Landrine, 1995, p. 16). These values are believed to be universal, not particular to this group, and are usually unacknowledged and invisible as the base of psychological theories. All people are then measured/assessed according to these theories, with people from other cultures with different values seen as not only different from this standard, but also deficient with regard to it (Chin, De La Cancela & Jenkins, 1993; Landrine, 1995).

In the new paradigm, *variability and diversity* of human experience, rather than *difference from one standard*, provide the conceptual frame. Human variability is the norm and each group's experience is part of the total description of human psychology (Espin, 1997a; Greene, 2003; Landrine, 1995). Frequently, behaviors have no label or meaning outside of the context within which they occur. "What researchers have understood to be ethnic or gender differences in the frequency or intensity of a decontextualized, superficial movement are not ethnic or gender differences at all; they are different acts in different contexts" (Landrine, p. 9). Understanding the context, including understanding European-American context, is essential for understanding the values, behaviors, and needs of a particular individual.

In more concrete terms, one way to think about the importance of diversity is through the lens of contextual identity (Barrett, 1998). In this framework, identity is a complex construct involving at least four levels, necessitating the integration of multiple views of one self. As an individual, we are each unique, exhibiting a variety of personality patterns and interests that allow us to differentiate ourselves from others. Second, we are embedded in a range of relational contexts including families, friends and small communities. Third, beyond these personal levels of identity, we have a sense of self based on larger social units, which include race, class, culture, sexual orientation, all of which are colored by power. Finally, we have an identity that is more universal, transcending differences, based on being human. Just what psychological characteristics we actually share with all others has been so heavily influenced by the thinking of those in dominant group positions that what is truly universal is far from clear.

For the work honored here, all of the women anchor themselves in group identity. All have some group identities that are dominant, e.g., educated. Without denying the privilege of the dominant aspects of her life, most of these woman firmly anchor themselves in minority group status as well, for example, racial, cultural, non-English speaking, lesbian, or recent immigrant. McGoldrick, on the other hand, examines the psychological impact of her white European-American dominant group identity. The power of group identity to frame life experience is illustrated in the personal story each author has contributed to this chapter. The stories show the author's lived experience of the intersection of race, culture, class, sex/gender, sexual orientation, physical ability, and immigration status. These group identities ground all of us, including those who are white, middle-class, heterosexual, etc., and the stories illustrate the power and necessity of understanding our own personal grounding in these areas.

The need for a coherent theory of feminist therapy to be rooted in the new paradigm has been eloquently discussed by Laura Brown (1995), Mary Ballou (Ballou, Matsumoto, & Wagner, 2002) and others. "Theories in psychotherapy are powerful tools for creating shared realities and directions for practice. The theory to which a therapist adheres prescribes not only the technique and approach used to make interventions, but also describes the nature of reality, normalcy, and psychopathology" (Brown, p. 143).

One useful way to think of theory is to see it as four interrelated parts (Bunch, 1987, pp. 244-5). First, theory describes what exists. Each of the women honored in this chapter describes the experience of people from a perspective of culture and race, clearly rooting the descriptions in the values of the culture they describe. Through the lens of a particular culture, they choose what to describe, giving it form and meaning.

Second, theory allows us to analyze what we describe. In this case, these women use a cultural/racial perspective to make sense of what they describe. Some of the writers also analyze the cultural behaviors in historical terms. Taken together, describing and analyzing people through the lens of culture and race provides a data base of information in which European-American experience is seen as particular, not universal, and the experience of people of varied cultural and racial roots is given equal weight.

Third, theory provides a framework for a vision. Based on this essential paradigm shift of recognizing, valuing and equalizing all group perspectives, what are our goals? How do we see the relationship of our clients to the European-American psychological values of the old paradigm? Beyond sharing a common therapeutic goal of valuing one's own culture and finding ways to live those values well, the women recognized in this chapter vary in how they address this question. For both a particular individual and for psychology in general, how much of the goal of feminist therapy is to accommodate to European-American values, change or expand them, or coexist with them?

Fourth, theory helps us with strategies. Our theoretical frame guides our therapy, helping us choose strategies that fit what we believe. All of the women herein give examples of how their understanding of feminist therapy theory is lived out through case studies.

One only has to read the works of these women to understand how deeply connected these theorists are with others. They draw heavily from the work of each other, other psychologists, literature of the particular groups they describe, philosophy, education, history, and social commentary and change. These women have spread their ideas through therapy, training/education of other therapists, lectures and conferences, and above all through writing. They have all written articles in journals, chapters in books, and sometimes articles for the public. In addition, each has written and/or edited more than one book, sometimes several. Through their work, they nourish other feminist therapists who participate in theory development on a smaller scale by encouraging them to write articles and contribute chapters in books they edit. Each of these women have received awards and honors from professional groups; for the women of color, this means they have been honored by predominately white professional organizations, no small feat. The impact of these women on feminist therapy is profound.

## *JEAN LAU CHIN*

Jean Lau Chin, EdD, ABPP, is Systemwide Dean of California School of Professional Psychology at Alliant International University. She is also the Praeger Series Editor for Race and Ethnicity in Psychology. For the past five years, she was President of CEO Services, a consulting firm providing clinical, educational and organizational services to health and mental health systems. She was also core faculty and Associate Professor at the Center for Multicultural Training in Psychology at the Boston University School of Medicine. She describes herself as "having a diverse career and unusual as a psychologist who has had her foot in clinical work, management, and scholarly pursuits" (Cantor, Chin, Gelman, Kaslow, 2002), spanning more than thirty years of work in mental health and health care.

Though her three professional foci are separate, Chin has woven them together, with each influencing the other. In addition to her decades of experience in management and consulting, and her clinical work with families, women and diverse populations, Chin has been a successful grant writer, managing over 100 government and foundation proposals; conducted numerous workshops and trainings, and written over 200 professional presentations and publications on cultural competence, psychotherapy, community health and mental health, women's issues and Asian American issues. She has published, with others, four books including, *Transference and Empathy in Asian American Psychotherapy; Diversity in Psychotherapy: The Politics of Race, Ethnicity, and Gender; Community Health Psychology: Empowerment for Diverse Communities;* and *Relationships Among Asian American Women.* Across all these forms of professional engagement, Chin focuses on cultural competence, community based services, integration of physical and mental health, and Asian American issues. Her work in the area of psychotherapy also overlaps with her other work on multiculturalism, diversity, cultural competence, racial/ethnic populations and underserved communities.

A major focus of Chin's work having relevance to feminist therapy theory is her analysis of the assumptive framework of European American psychology combined with a detailed vision of a psychological theory and practice that is truly culturally competent. She anchors herself firmly in her Asian American, bicultural roots, using that perspective to look deep below the surface of Western psychology to see the beliefs and assumptions supporting that perspective. She then offers an alternative perspective with a strategy for translating her perspective into practice for therapists.

With regard to therapy, Chin's goal is empowerment of individuals, including the development of bicultural identities based on race, migration experience and class as well as gender. To achieve this goal, therapists must view learning about a client's culture as a continuous process, and as a necessary but not sufficient step. To establish a good therapeutic alliance, the therapist must know her/his own assumptive framework, value differences, and integrate culture into the context for psychotherapy. Cultural differences are not good or bad, but must be used to facilitate good psychotherapeutic outcomes (Chin, De La Cancela & Jenkins, 1993).

Chin brings her outstanding ability to see beneath the surface to her description of some common assumptions that form the basis of Western psychology including: the quantitative measurement of certain traits, resulting in the deficiency of people who have too much or too little of it; the emphasis on sameness and commonality in describing human experience; having mainstreaming as a goal and acculturation as a desired process; viewing European practices viewed as modern and therefore better; a mythical ideal as to how therapy should be practiced; a belief in objectivity; overgeneralization when describing members of ethnic groups; and over utilizing the ideas of resistance and noncompliance when clients don't behave as expected (Chin, De La Cancela et al., 1993).

Chin then describes ten culturally competent concepts to challenge the above assumptions commonly used by Westerners. These include:

1. Look at qualitative, not quantitative differences when comparing groups, e.g., how they use language.
2. Use norms that are culturally specific, e.g., how the age of independence is viewed in different cultures.

3. Emphasize culturally specific services as the norm, not just as transitional services for newcomers.
4. Stress bicultural experience, rather than acculturation. Bicultural individuals may adjust their behavior patterns to fit the cultural context and develop dual self-identities to negotiate contrasting cultures. "In other words, dual selves are OK" (Chin, 2000).
5. Conceptualize therapy as empowering an individual, rather than using a traditional vs. modern paradigm.
6. Develop diverse forms of practice that match different clients, rather than working toward a mythical ideal of practice.
7. Shift from objectivity to valuing differences so manifestations of cultural differences are used as strengths.
8. Recognize the importance of process over content.
9. When making interventions, frame them to be consistent with the client's worldview; avoid the tendency to view client refusal as noncompliance.
10. Define different practices for different populations as therapists become culturally competent.

This insightful, thorough examination of the assumptions for change in psychotherapy forms the crucible for Chin's description of Asian Americans and Asian American women in therapy (Chin, 1994; Chin, 2000; Chin, De La Cancela et al., 1993; Chin, Liem, Ham & Hong, 1993). She both describes and analyzes the cultural, political and historical contexts and how significantly they are manifested in the lives and adjustment of individuals. For example, she describes help-seeking behaviors, psychotherapy, interpersonal relationships, emotions, communication styles, use of language, maturity, belongingness, identity, parent-child relationships, and time, and how they may differ because of culture (Chin, De La Cancela et al., 1993, pp. 82-89). In *Relationships Among Asian American Women* (Chin, 2000), she focuses on a feminist perspective and relates these concepts to issues of power and connectedness.

Chin's incredible thoroughness in conceptualizing of the problems inherent in Western psychology, her vision for what needs to be done, and her strategy for reaching that vision are all portrayed in language that is both broad in scope and intricately detailed, rendering her work imminently usable for the general population of therapists. She provides a conceptual basis for a true multicultural psychology. This is truly a gift to feminist therapists as we move from where we have been toward the future.

## Personal Story

Growing up, my parents were Chinese laundry owners as were prob-ably 80 per cent of the immigrant Chinese American families of my generation–it was an occupation of choice because there were no choices due to the Anti-Chinese legislation of the times. I was the youn-gest of four children, growing up in Brooklyn, New York. My parents immigrated from Toisan, China, a village of the GuangDong province. An emphasis on Chinese cultural values and practices was important during my early upbringing. My parents insisted that we speak Chinese in the home, and always reminded us to properly address and be courte-ous toward our elders and relatives. Responsibility to the family, hard work, and modesty, common values of the Chinese culture, were con-sistently emphasized in my parent's social conversations–their way to teach us and to make us proud. We lived modestly; only in later years did I realize how meager were our financial means.

Educationally, I did not have the mentors so common in today's envi-ronment. My peers were mostly the first in their families to attend col-lege. Typically, I was the only, or one of several, Asian students in the entire school throughout my schooling; this included my sister up through high school. The advisor for my high school honors program was a significant influence in my life; without her direction, I probably would not have attended college. She insisted that we stay after school to coach us on taking the SAT. She expected us to apply for college, and advised us all to apply to three colleges–a good private college, one of the city colleges (there was no tuition), and a safe school, i.e., a commu-nity college to which we would be assured of acceptance. I won a NY State Regents Scholarship, which helped to finance my college educa-tion.

Many contrasts characterized my life. Given my parents' village background, my mother finished sixth grade while my father finished ninth grade, a high school diploma was deemed an accomplishment. I went on to complete a doctorate to the surprise and pride of my parents. The differences between the Confucian and Socratic methods of learn-ing of Asian and Western education were subtle but striking in my edu-cation. While educated in Western, U.S. schools, my parents conveyed an observant and absorbent approach to learning typical of Chinese cul-ture. I was urged by my parents to be the recipient of knowledge; note that this is not viewed as "passive." Learning occurs through listening and taking in the wisdom and knowledge of one's elders and the mas-ters. In contrast, Socratic and Western forms of learning emphasize vocal classroom participation, challenging the status quo, and changing the obvious. I was often confused by these differences since there were no mentors to make the translation; I often found my motives and thoughts subject to being misunderstood and misjudged. While I always did well academically, I was often told that I was too quiet, that I should speak up; I was even questioned as to my ability to do public speaking, which I do quite frequently now.

Transformation and transcendence, both professionally and personally, characterize my career path. In one sense, I was always a "misfit." To all my professional roles, I brought my ability to look at things from the outside. In doing so, I felt I contributed an innovative and transformational approach to the services I provided. At the same time, others had a tendency to view me in rather stereotypic ways. My small size, distinct Asian culture, and different professional training evoked stereotypic expectations about passivity and powerlessness with which I was forced to grapple. Negatively, it made me question my managerial, clinical, and professional abilities. Positively, I remained anchored in the pride about who I was and committed to what I believed. Not only had I learned about my different ways of thinking, but also I had learned to advocate for that which I held dear, i.e., serving the underserved, promoting ethnic minority issues, social equity, valuing differences, and cultural competence.

My advocacy for community empowerment and community-based services was deeply influenced by the sixties. The expansion of social justice issues related to women's issues came later, not because gender was unimportant or because I was "delayed" in my development (as some have speculated), but because race and ethnicity were more prominent forces in my environment. Growing up in NYC, I was asked at least weekly about my racial/ethnic identity; "Are you Chinese or Japanese?" was usually the first question asked of me at social gatherings, by strangers, etc. The irony of living in cosmopolitan New York during the sixties amidst a race based environment did much to shape my views of these factors in training, research, and practice and the need to value and validated the diverse experiences of individuals.

My continuity with historical events helped shape me as well. World War II strongly influenced the lives of my parents, which in turn shaped my experience of the world. My mother escaped the Japanese invasion of Nanjing, China by three days; a day after she left by ship to immigrate to the U.S. in 1939, a second ship was bombed by the Japanese. The breakout of WWII, and subsequent conversion of China to communism, created a paranoid environment in the U.S. McCarthyism during the fifties led to fears of deportation and subjected our family to racist remarks and assaults. Any unfamiliar was eyed with suspicion, e.g., Chinese newspapers were surely communist. Messages of "you don't belong" or "you are inferior" were commonplace; this was evident in the overt and covert remarks of white customers when they brought their laundry into our store.

The challenge of integrating the cultures of the East and West is inherent in their contrasts. There is much that cannot be integrated. The vocabulary and language structure of English and Chinese are so very different as are the different emphases of social and cultural values. Urges to "speak up" from the West go against the mandate of "don't be so brazen" from the East; urges of confrontation from Western ideals go against those of promoting harmony from Eastern ideals. These contrasting differences require a consciousness and vigilance that is unnecessary if our society were not so race based. Social gatherings that bring non-Asians to an all-Asian gathering must be contemplated; will they feel comfortable? Differences in social customs, food, and values must be contemplated. For bicultural individuals like myself, it means creating two different realities that do not always mix. I have found my sources of support from the many colleagues with whom I have felt "of one mind" about the things for which we cared. I have found my sources of strength from my drive and passion to fix that which is broken and to heed the frequent reminders of my mother's teachings. I have learned that to resolve conflict sometimes means not to seek integration, but to seek divergence in the things we do and the thoughts we have.

## LILLIAN COMAS-DIAZ

Lillian Comas-Diaz, PhD, is currently the Executive Director, Transcultural Mental Health Institute in Washington, D.C., a Clinical Professor of Psychiatry and Behavioral Sciences and George Washington University School of Medicine and also maintains a private practice in clinical psychology. She has been incredibly prolific as a presenter, educator, writer, and editor giving over 200 presentations, participating in training videotapes, and being the Editor-in-Chief for *Cultural Diversity and Mental Health* and *Cultural Diversity and Ethnic Minority Psychology*, as well as participating in a multitude of editorial roles in many more journals. She has co-edited two books, with another in press, *Clinical Guidelines in Cross-Cultural Mental Health; Women of Color: Integrating Ethnic and Gender Identities in Psychotherapy* with Beverly

Greene; and *Ethnocultural Psychotherapy.* In addition, she has written over seventy articles and book chapters.

Her areas of interest include Puerto Rican women, Hispanic/Latino people, gender and ethnicity, women of color, global conflict and the psychology of women, psychopharmacology, professional women of color, family therapy, and with incredible depth and breadth, ethnocultural psychotherapy.

Comas-Diaz's contribution to feminist therapy theory is immense, covering all four areas of theory building, describing and analyzing the ethnopsychosocial situation of people of color, and developing a vision of the future with psychotherapeutic strategies for getting there. A central tenet of her work relevant for feminist therapy is the conceptualization of the status of people of color in the United States as that of being colonized, not just oppressed. Under colonization people of color in the United States are obliged to adapt to the norms of the dominant culture, with an inevitable sacrifice in the connection to one's culture of origin (Comas-Diaz, 1994, p. 288). Skin color, itself, becomes the sign of the colonized. Racism is a form of colonization, then, in addition to being a human rights violation. She brings race and skin color to the forefront in clear ways, saying "race is the greatest identifying characteristic in a racist environment, transcending gender, sexual orientation, and class identities (Almquist, 1989), and subordinating such identities to the condition of being colonized" (Comas-Diaz, 1994, p. 289). In her analysis of the nexus of racism, colonization, culture, gender and class, she ranges widely theoretically, including the work of social theorists with a liberation paradigm (e.g., Martin-Baro, Fanon, Memmi, Freire), social construction of self, and depth psychology.

Comas-Diaz describes the devastating psychological effects of living under colonization, both past and present. Complex Post-Colonization Stress Disorder is the frame she uses for making sense of the psychological result of the terror of colonization. She discusses identity problems, alienation, self-denial, assimilation, cognitive schema changes, somatic and psychological symptoms, depression, shame, rage, relational issues, becoming demoralized and losing hope. Her intricate and detailed analysis of this situation is profound (Comas-Diaz, 2000; Comas-Diaz & Greene, 1994b).

The vision Comas-Diaz puts forth ranges from the personal to the political. Her vision for the United States is rooted in the United States President's Initiative on Race (1998), which stated that the greatest challenge facing us is to accept and take pride in being a multiracial democracy, not a melting pot. This vision is repeatedly challenged as the

United States becomes less white and more peopled with individuals with dark skin. On the personal level, Comas-Diaz's vision for individuals and families is psychotherapeutic decolonization, a process involving the following:

1.  Recognizing the systemic and societal context of colonialism and oppression, thus, becoming aware of the colonized mentality.
2.  Correcting cognitive errors that reinforce the colonized mentality, for example, working through dichotomous thinking (superior-inferior, the colonized is good, the colonizer is bad, etc.) and acknowledging ambivalence (toward self and others).
3.  Self-asserting and reaffirming racial and gender identity, as well as developing a more integrated identity.
4.  Increasing self-mastery and achieving autonomous dignity.
5.  Working toward transformation of self and/or the colonized condition (e.g., improving the condition of women, men, and children of color) (Comas-Diaz, 1994, p. 291).

Comas-Diaz has developed an integrative approach to psychotherapy based on the ethnopolitical perspective she uses. The psychotherapeutic relationship provides a central component of treatment. Through this relationship, the therapist can bear witness to the story of the client, using dyadic variables of empathy, intuition, and attributions of "the Other." In Comas-Diaz (1994), she describes three issues to attend to in women of color that address a woman's sense of self: her conception of womanhood, cultural pluralism in identity development, and spirituality. The integrative approach uses diverse therapeutic orientations and modalities tailored to the needs of the particular women, based on the assessment that includes a cultural frame. These could include psychodynamic theories, cognitive-behavioral modalities, tools such as EMDR and other desensitization methods, with all working simultaneously on the affective, cognitive, behavioral and systemic levels.

The level of intricate detail of her thinking is illustrated in her work on ethnocultural allodynia (Comas-Diaz & Jacobsen, 2001), an abnormally increased sensitivity to ethnocultural dynamics associated with past exposure to emotionally painful social and ethnoracial stimuli. A vigilance to racism is critical for people of color, however, such vigilance can misfire, resulting in an individual believing too many of the problems are caused by racism. She describes in intricate detail a case study illustrating her approach to therapy from her framework. The therapy includes an assessment of ethnocultural trauma, cognitive-behavioral desensitization, EMDR, provision of information regarding racism and its effects, and exploration of internalized racism, all done through the context of the therapeutic relationship, including positive and negative transference.

Through her work on colonization and integrative psychotherapy, Comas-Diaz provides an essential foundation for a framework of feminist therapy from a multicultural standpoint. She also has a whole body of work on the particulars of psychology for Puerto Rican women and women from other Latino cultures. The sum of all her work is the gift of a broad base from which all feminist therapists can work.

### Personal Story

My life reflects the impact of context on identity. Searching for the American dream, my working class parents migrated from Puerto Rico to the continental United States. They carried empty stomachs and spoke broken English. Resistance, negotiation, and perseverance seasoned my identity. Born with a cleft palate, at age four I became the first patient ever to undergo a radically new surgical repair at the University of Illinois Medical School. Although the operation was successful, I stammered until high school. This experience taught me flexibility, adaptation, and compensation in the context of physical disability.

I tasted culture shock at an early age. Trading the frigid Windy City for the tropical Caribbean, I moved "back" to Puerto Rico. A stranger in my own land, I became the other. I realized the pervasive influence of culture on behavior while dreaming in Spanglish. Family and school provided supportive systems. Identity reformulation led to my interest in healing. Physical disability solidified my role as a wounded healer.

My parent's marriage taught me the complex relationship between power and gender. An assertive nurse at work, my mother was a submissive wife at home. Her contradictory modern/traditional behavior was typical of other women of her generation. Disappointed that his oldest child was not a son, my macho father exhibited Latino paradoxical gender behavior. Clearly preferring my brother due to his gender, my father simultaneously encouraged my ambition. My whole family taught me how culture and gender shape behavior. These were the first lessons in feminism with an accent. Although later on feminism found a fertile ground in my heart, these flowers emit a diverse aroma. Subscribing to an empowering clinical perspective, I aspire to promote liberation in a gender specific and culturally congruent manner.

I entered college in the late sixties and was immersed in independentismo (Puerto Rico's pro-independence movement). As a liberation approach, the independentista movement integrated socialist and emancipatory influences within a cultural context. These influences nurtured my interest in the relationship between healing, oppression and liberation, while issues of agency, mastery and self-determination found their way into my conceptualization of clinical work. Notwithstanding the university's progressive perspective, women's liberation and racial issues were relegated to the back of the bus. Puerto Rico's colonial status resulted in an identity crisis where internalized oppression–when inferiority feelings caused by oppression are accepted and projected toward peers–was rampant. One of its highest manifestations, racismo, branded me as a jabá (a pejorative racial term denoting a person with kinky hair and yellow skin). These experiences nurtured my identity as a mixed race woman of color. Later on I coined the term LatiNegra(o) to affirm the Latiness of Afro Latinos. Adding insult to injury, some peers questioned my not being Puerto Rican enough due to my continental birth. Developing a historical and sociopolitical understanding of these dynamics helped me cope. I immersed myself in literature of people of color, particularly women of color. I re-framed intra-racism as self-hate, helping me integrate the contradictions caused by oppression.

Frustrated by internalized colonization, I migrated to the continent, searching for the Golden Fleece in the form of a doctorate in psychology. Armed with a Master's degree in clinical psychology, I was unaware that I was entering battle. Coping with culture shock, lacking English proficiency, and deficient in racial socialization, I became an easy target for racism and sexism. Once more, my identity adapted to a new environment. Interested in the relationship between gender and race, I explored the confluence of the Civil Rights movement and feminism. Today I continue to be at home within feminism, albeit critically articulating its limitations with respect to women of color.

Within a community context I began to work with folk healers. Collaborating with them was a humbling experience that changed my assumptions about psychology. At that time I was a cocky clinician armed with scientific tools to "help" people. Although familiar with folk healing through cultural osmosis, I did not respect this model. Consequently, I thought that my professional role was "superior" to that of an espiritista's because of my formal schooling. This elitist insensitivity was promptly challenged when I began to work with folk healers as equals. These espiritistas and curanderas were Latinas who empowered themselves and others with indigenous knowledge. With its emphasis on female-centered spiritual development, folk healing affirms the historical role of women as healers. As I personally come from a long line of women healers, my folk colleagues helped me recover my ancestral memory. Listening to them, I learned that so much of what clients say is about spirituality–the meaning of life, pain, and death–areas in which I was not clinically trained.

Growing up in a culture full of magical realism that emphasized the permeable boundaries of reality familiarized me with ways of knowledge other than the intellectual. The folk healers provided me with a different paradigm, one that embraces holism in a culturally and gender specific manner. Since psychology of liberation teaches us to integrate indigenous perspectives into clinical, I developed a model of working within alternative healing and mainstream psychotherapy. My model's tenets include the importance of balance, the perspective that problems are opportunities for growth, and the belief that transformation and transcendence are developmental goals.

Working with communities of color in the continental United States gave me a new identity: cultural warrior. Viewing colonization as a special type of oppression that denies collective definitions, I envisioned liberation psychotherapy as promoting empowerment, reconciliation, and healing while advancing the integration of a fragmented colonized identity. This approach restored my hope in the psychologist's impact at the individual, family, group, and societal levels.

My professional efforts concentrate on scholarly, organizational, and social justice areas. Three themes organize my scholarship, namely, ethnic minority/cross cultural mental health, women's issues/feminism, and social justice/international psychology. Integrating these topics, I have found a nexus between psychology and political repression in the field of ethnopolitical psychology. Viewing colonization as a special type of oppression, I envisioned psychology as promoting empowerment, liberation, and healing. In addition to human rights investigations, I have been a member of mental health delegations to the former Soviet Union, Eastern Europe (1993), South Africa, India and Nepal. Moreover, I have contributed to the American Psychological Association/Canadian Psychological Association Initiative on ethnopolitical warfare in addition to being a member of the APA Task Force on Increasing Resilience in Response to Terrorism. At the international arena I continue to examine the relationship between race, gender and class. I gained new insights regarding feminist therapy with women of color and women's resistance to violence in underdeveloped countries.

## OLIVA ESPIN

Oliva Espin, PhD, is Professor Emerita, Department of Women's Studies, San Diego State University and California School of Professional Psychology-San Diego. In "Giving Voice to Silence: The Psychologist as Witness," her acceptance address for the 1991 APA Award for Distinguished Professional Contribution to Public Service, Espin describes a core part of her professional orientation. "As a young woman in my early 20s, I lived in four countries and three different continents in the course of three years. . . . My own experience of not being heard, seen, or understood created in me a passion to give voice to others' experience" (Espin, 1993, p. 408).

She has published numerous articles and book chapters as well as given many presentations ranging from the local to international level. Her four books are: *Refugee Women and Their Mental Health: Shattered Societies, Shattered Lives; Latina Healers: Lives of Power and Tradition; Latina Realities: Essays on Healing, Migration, and Sexuality;* and *Women Crossing Boundaries: A Psychology of Immigration and the Transformations of Sexuality.*

Primary areas of interest and focus for Espin include the effect of migration on women's lives; the intersection of ethnicity, race, class and gender; sexuality, including sexual orientation; language in therapy; the development of self and identity, including adolescent identity; healing and sainthood; and qualitative research methods. As a researcher and theoretician, she has used her knowledge and skills in qualitative analysis, narration, self-reflection and social construction to bear especially on the process of migration and all that it entails for women. She brings a broad perspective to the psychology of women, including theories of the psychology of oppression and resistance to oppression, language (bi and multilingualism), identity development, and spirituality/healers, all of which she uses to enrich the portrait she paints of women.

Espin's work puts experience into words, telling the stories of people often invisible. Through this process she describes the experience of women of color, Latinas, migrants, lesbians and other subgroups of women. She then analyzes these descriptions, with a focus on the impact of social forces on individual psychological development (Espin,

1997a). Espin's belief and trust in the power of story telling runs throughout her work. She says "a self needs a story in order to be" (Espin, 1997a, p. xi), and that "cultures provide specific plots for lives and how social prescriptions become individually appropriated as one constructs a life story and a sense of self" (Espin, 1997a, p. xii). She uses this frame to look at life passages, including migration, and the development of the story.

Espin's article on the "Psychological Impact of Migration on Latinas: Implications for Psychotherapeutic Practice" (1997b) contains many of her ideas on migration, ideas she develops in other writings. She discusses the psychological process of migration including the initial decision to relocate (women may not be consulted), whether or not the move was to escape dangers and/or a positive choice, culture shock, grieving the old, and adapting to the new. Through poetic language reflecting both English and Spanish, she tells the story of many people and their process of translocation.

Espin then focuses on Latinas in particular, understanding the process through their stories. She discusses the high incidence of somatic complaints, which must be taken seriously and examined for psychological meaning as well, and PTSD that may result from trauma before and during migration. She describes and explains gender role conflicts, often with large contradictions between the home and host cultures. In the United States, women may be more employable than men, further upsetting gender roles.

Race and class are important aspects of the stories. In many Latin home cultures, class is an issue, but race is not. In the U.S., race and class are both social issues with light skinned, younger and educated people receiving a more favorable reception; this may be a new and distressing experience for some people. In this article and others, Espin does an eloquent job of rendering visible the intricate process of migration, adolescent development, sexuality and language. Immigrant children acculturate faster than their parents, causing familial distress. In particular, sex and sexuality may be a major area of conflict for women and their families. To be "Americanized" is equated with being sexually promiscuous, causing a clash of cultures around a central aspect of women's development and identity. Espin describes how Spanish, as the first language, is the language of emotion, even if a woman is fluent in English. A woman client may switch back and forth between English and Spanish, depending on the subject, with English acting as a facilitator for the emergence of forbidden topics such as sexuality, while other concerns can only be expressed in Spanish.

From the position of a lesbian Latina immigrant, with powerful tools of intellect and language, Espin tells the stories of women. She uses psychological theories and also theories of oppression and transformation. She understands why and how migration is so difficult as well as the strengths needed within the women and their families. An implicit goal seems to be for immigrant women to know both cultures and to navigate their own personal path of adapting to the new. She gives numerous examples of women in therapy, providing a story line for other therapists to follow.

### Personal Story

I have lived most of my adult life removed from my country of birth. Undoubtedly, my own personal experience of migration has been a major influence in my professional life. It definitely informs my interest in the psychological impact of migration on women's lives. Migration for me, as for most immigrants/refugees has provided a dual and contradictory legacy. It has given me safety and success, yet it has also brought losses. In my professional work as a teacher, therapist, and researcher I have tried to understand for myself and for others what this experience entails.

The experience of migration is, in most cases, connected to the issue of language. The immigrant learns to "live in two languages" and two social worlds. Learning a new language is not only an instrumental process. It implies becoming immersed in the power relations of the specific culture that speaks the specific language. A new language challenges one's self-definitions and the forms of self-expression so familiar within one's first language. To this day, there are things I cannot share with my monolingual English-speaking friends no matter how close we are. I can translate, but translated feelings like translated poetry are just not the same. Even when feelings are supposedly not directly involved, the task of producing scholarly work or doing therapy in another language magnifies the difficulties of the experience. Conversely, the ability to "live in two languages" opens up worlds and comparative perspectives on "truth" that are usually not accessible to monolingual individuals. This, in turn, enriches scholarly work and therapeutic skills.

During my childhood, my father and my uncle were very significant figures. They always assumed that I could do whatever I wanted in life. My being a girl was never even mentioned. They made me feel that I had a right to achieve and thrive as a full person. One of the greatest shocks of my life was to discover in early adulthood that others expected me to keep quiet because I was a woman.

My years as a graduate student in the U.S. coincided with the beginning of the second wave of feminism. The ideals of the women's movement resonated within my own experience. Luckily, in a department where all professors were male, my dissertation advisor gave me, over thirty years ago, opportunities that some feminist doctoral students do not yet have.

The experience of living in Boston for more than a decade, at a time when feminist ideas were being developed, was a unique and powerful. I know how significant it was to be in Boston during the seventies and eighties. Even before the Stone Center and other Boston theorists became famous, there was a feminist effervescence in this city that, in fact, may have played an important role in making those theorists coalesce.

However, the beginning feminist perspective on psychological theory that provided me with an intellectual home, confronted me over and over with perspectives in which culture, class, race, and ethnicity did not seem to exist in the lives of women. I learned early that those of us who combine in our experience several categories of oppression are more often than not confined to the margin and need to construct our understanding from the perspective of that margin. My firsthand knowledge of the interlocking nature of oppression presented me with a challenge. Whatever research I have done has been an attempt to shed light on the interlocking of gender, ethnicity, class, and sexual orientation. My attempts to create theoretical understanding on the basis of the information provided by my experiences and that of my therapy clients, research participants, and students for over thirty years, hopefully contribute one vital thread to the tapestry of a renewed psychology.

I have not been alone in this process. Even though my experience is in one sense absolutely mine, individual and unique, it is in another sense generalizable to any person, particularly women, who has ever experienced the effects of similar events. Many women I have met and connected with at FTI, and other feminist psychology groups, have made an enormous difference in my life. They have nurtured, supported, and reminded me that I was neither alone, nor "crazy." In my search for supportive perspectives about social justice and psychology, I also found inspiration in the work of two men: Brazilian educator Paulo Freire and social psychologist and Jesuit priest, Ignacio Martin Baro. Both emphasized the importance of listening to the voices of all people, particularly those who are usually disenfranchised.

Being in a Department of Women's Studies since 1990, working with women from different disciplines and backgrounds in a wonderful atmosphere of collegiality, has taught me a lot, expanded my horizons beyond psychology, and enriched my thinking. Most of my work has come to fruition during my years in this, the oldest Women's Studies Department in the U.S. Paradoxically, a teaching institution has provided more support for my scholarship than the research institutions where I had worked previously. It has also allowed me to develop and teach courses that I could not have taught in a department of psychology. Preparation for these courses has played no small part in developing my own knowledge base and theoretical perspectives.

I am sure that these last few years, in the company of women, have also evoked my formative years studying in an all-girls school with nuns and lay female teachers, where I learned that women and men are equal in the eyes of God and where spoken and unspoken messages told us girls that we were at the center. I know that for some people this type of environment may have been negative. Perhaps I was fortunate to have some good nuns as my teachers. Perhaps I chose to hear only the positive parts of their messages. In any case, having been in the company of women in several different intellectual environments in my life, beginning with my formative years, has played an essential role in making me who I am.

Finally, I want say that what I did with my professional career was part of something bigger than just me, i.e., all the women in the feminist movement and all the psychologists who struggle to make the discipline sensitive to issues of social justice. In retrospect, I know I could not have done what I did for only professional reasons. I was compelled to do it because it was my own tool for survival and growth. Hopefully, in the process I have made a contribution to other women's lives.

## BEVERLY GREENE

Beverly Greene, PhD, ABPP, a tenured Professor of Psychology at St. John's University, Jamaica, New York, and a practicing clinical psychologist, has contributed an incredibly rich, voluminous, detailed amount of information about the lives of African-American women and other women of color, therapy with women, gay/lesbian/bisexual people, the intersection of multiple minority group status, family therapy, and children and adolescents.

As a researcher and writer, Greene has contributed volumes to our understanding, from the inside out and from a historical perspective, of the interplay of institutionalized racism, sexism and heterosexism. Her books include writing or co-editing four volumes of *Psychological Perspectives on Lesbian, Gay and Bisexual Issues*; four versions of *Abnormal Psychology in a Changing World; Women of Color: Integrating Ethnic and Gender Identities in Psychotherapy* with Lillian Comas-Diaz; and *Psychotherapy with African American Women: Innovations in Psychodynamic Perspectives and Practice* with Leslie Jackson. She has also published over sixty articles and book chapters with many more in progress. Her work is incredibly well researched, detailed and comprehensive, and well-documented, resulting in a firm grounding for her statements about the lives of the people about whom she writes. The result is a detailed weaving of societal context and the psychology of women and other underrepresented groups, rich with specifics providing the grounding for her examination of the psychological treatments needed.

In terms of the frameworks of variability of psychological patterns, contextual identity, and theory building, Greene describes and analyzes, in meticulous detail, patterns of individual and relational identity from a perspective informed by her African slave, Native American, lesbian and intellectual descendancy. She uses a historical analysis of African cultural roots and slavery in the United States, as well as analyses of the current social situation in the U. S. to make sense of what she describes and to understand the strengths and resilience of socially disadvantaged people in response to their social and personal distress.

The scope of any one of her articles or chapters can be broad, such as her chapter on "African American Women" in *Women of Color: Integrating Ethnic and Gender Identities in Psychotherapy* (1994b), co-edited with Lillian Comas-Diaz, PhD, a book for which they received a Distinguished Publications Award from AWP and an AWP Women of Color Psychologies Publication Award. On the other hand, her work can be very focused such as that in "Hair Texture, Length, and Styles as a Metaphor in the African American Mother-Daughter Relationship: Considerations in Psychodynamic Psychotherapy" (Greene, White, & Whitten, 2000), for which they received a Psychotherapy with Women Research Award from Division 35 of APA and "Women of Color with Professional Status" (Comas-Diaz and Greene, 1994a). A particular strength for Greene is her detailed research and writing about the intersection of multiple group identities, including race, gender, class and sexual orientation (Greene, 2000a, 2000b; Greene, 1997a; Greene and

Boyd-Franklin, 1996; Hall and Greene, 2002) and the role of social privilege and disadvantage hierarchies in constructing the meaning of ethnic, gender, sexual orientation and class differences (Greene, 2003).

"African American Lesbian and Bisexual Women in Feminist-Psychodynamic Psychotherapies: Surviving and Thriving Between a Rock and a Hard Place" (2000a) is an excellent example of Greene's attention to detail as she describes the intersection of race, gender, and sexual orientation, in particular. The "rock" is traditional "feminist and psychodynamic therapy theories as challenges to culturally competent and lesbian affirmative practice" (p. 94). Psychodynamic therapy's exclusive focus on intrapsychic processes traditionally ignored social realities. Feminist psychotherapy historically emphasized gender inequities, but did little to understand race, class, sexual orientation and the interactive affects of all three inequities and identities on gender realities.

The "hard place" is the homophobia/heterosexism among African Americans. Although African Americans are very diverse, some African Americans are vested in presenting a monolithic, idealized view of the group to counter the harsh distortions and negative images of Africans and African Americans. The idealized view holds heterosexuality as congruent with authentic Black identity and any non-traditional or lesbian sexual orientation as racial disloyalty, even as an aberration. Greene discusses in detail the forms homophobia/heterosexism take within the African American community. These include emphasis on reproductive sexuality to counter real or perceived genocide; believing race (and heterosexuality) are given and not chosen, but that lesbian or gay sexual orientation is a poor choice; believing lesbian identity should be concealed and not "flaunted"; following the conservative nature of the African American church on issues of sexuality; believing that lesbian and gay sexual orientation did not exist in Africa and is a White person's disease.

Greene also shows in detail the psychological impact for African American lesbians trying to navigate between the rock and the hard place–of developing a positive African American identity and a positive lesbian identity. The family and community are incredibly important survival tools for African Americans, providing a buffer and a place to learn about racism. Coming out as a lesbian may put that place of safety in jeopardy. Psychologically, this can be an untenable position to maintain. Greene describes how good feminist-psychodynamic therapy can help an individual African American lesbian maneuver through this passage.

Throughout her writing, Greene's portrayal of the interplay of group identity with relational identity and individual identity is rich and deep. The total portrait, detailed and clear, is of the psychological experience of a particular group of women. Greene provides a rich database of understanding, an essential component of a diverse theory (Brown, 1995), built on the lives of the women about whom she writes. The description is used as a base for conceptualizing the mental health concerns, both strengths and vulnerabilities, for the women as well as implications for needed treatment.

### Personal Story

The earliest seeds of my work were sown long before my I entered graduate school or assumed a professional identity. I was born in the middle of the twentieth century. Coming of age during the height of the civil rights movement with relatives still living in a south that I visited frequently during my childhood certainly shaped my sense of the world and its workings. My personal heritage included growing up in a multi-generational household, with both parents, 3 younger siblings and a large extended family that always included the presence of a grandmother, as well as paternal aunts and uncles. Both my parents and much of my extended family were survivors of America's holocaust in their experience of the vitriolic racism in the Deep South. They were important role models as people who survived many indignities without losing their own dignity, graciousness, humor, and tenacity.

Difference and its meaning would be an early part of the conversations both internal and overt during my early my life. My family identifies as African American however my maternal and paternal grandmothers were both the products of racial admixtures of white, Native American and African persons. Just as our family was characterized by its difference from a majority culture, we were also characterized by a combination of differences within. Early on in life I would become aware of the ways that I personally differed from the rest of them as well. Differences, embedded in similarities, with their meaning and their negotiation was a constant theme in my mental life.

Most of my family members had little formal education, working as domestics, factory and blue-collar workers. One paternal great aunt stands out as a schoolteacher in the south at a time when it was unusual for African Americans to do so. My father and his father were carpenters and made their living working with their hands. In his fifties my father resumed his studies and completed his GED, often while working a full and part time job. My mother completed high school and worked outside the home until I was 8, resuming that activity some 10 years later. Despite the absence of formal education, the adults in the family were surprisingly literate, read avidly and were serious about the importance of learning, as well as formal education for the next generation. My paternal aunt, a domestic worker by trade, avidly read the *New York Times* and was the family member who introduced me to that paper. When the families she worked for threw away books, she brought them home to us. Put simply, we were always surrounded by books.

Children in our family were given license to "speak," to be aware, to have questions and opinions and to express them; to be curious about the world we lived in and how it worked. The permission to speak was such a normative part of my early experience that I took for granted that everyone had such permission. It is most likely the reason that I never really struggled about whether or not I had the right to write down my thoughts and impressions and share them with people in the form of publications. The children in my family were also socialized to understand that we would not always be judged fairly because of our race and came to identify race as a potential barrier to our strivings. Perhaps more importantly, we were taught that racism would create problems for us but that the problem was not in us, it rests within those who are racist and in a pattern of social systems that denied us equal access to the opportunities accorded to others. We were also encouraged to have dreams, make plans and to try to find our place in the world with the sense that one's place was a function of skill and ability rather than inherent worth. I recall hearing my father often say that if you knock on a door and it doesn't open, it doesn't mean that the door is forever closed or that you should stop knocking.

Another part of this tutelage included learning to view the world with a "skeptical" intelligence. I recall many evenings at the dinner table telling the events of the day and having our father challenge what we learned or asking just how we knew whatever we professed to know. I believe that he was exercising his understanding of the world as one in which his children needed to be aware of what was going on in the world around them, to understand how to think critically, not just accept what they were told, and be able to assert their knowledge with conviction. This was instrumental in teaching us that we should not believe, without question, what we are told about ourselves or others simply because someone in a position of authority said so. Our mother made it clear that you sometimes had to obey people or agree with them because they were in a position to hurt you if you didn't, but this did not mean that they were right. Hence, she taught us that it was important to pick the time and place that you choose to challenge someone. I came to understand the importance of trying to make conscious decisions about when to challenge attempts to treat me as a second or third class person, rather than just react. It was in these early experiences that I came to understand how important it was not to accept uncritically, information about whom I, or "my people," were when that information was presented by those who have a stake in believing the worst about us.

The next most profound later influences in my development as a scholar were found in the person of Dr. Dorothy Gartner, then Chief Psychologist at Kings County Hospital where I spent almost the first decade of my work as a psychologist and where I thought I would be happy to remain. Perhaps more than anyone, Dorothy insisted I teach seminars in cultural diversity for the hospital training programs. Despite my reluctance she persisted and won out, encouraging me to write about this material for professional venues. My thinking at that time was strongly influenced by my work with a clinical supervisor during graduate school, Dr. William Johnson. Bill, among few Black psychoanalysts at that time, put forth a very different take on psychodynamic thinking and on cultural and racial transference and counter-transference. It was during this work with him that I was able to see how psychodynamic work could be important to African American clients, lesbian and gay clients, women of color and other disparaged people. Still, I wrote reluctantly and after the publication of 2 early papers thought that would be the end of it. Along came Adrienne Smith, Ellen Cole and Laura Brown. Having read the early papers each, apart from the other, got hold of me and squeezed yet a few more papers from my reluctant grasp. By this time it was getting to be fun and felt more like playing in the intellectual sandbox than the drudgery I expected. I began to write and publish more than clinical positions would allow and made the, I suppose, inevitable shift to academia. It now seems exactly where I should be, however without those early experiences and timely influences, I doubt that I would be. I am forever in their debt.

## MONICA McGOLDRICK

Monica McGoldrick, MA, MSW, PhD (Hon), is currently Director of the Multicultural Family Institute of New Jersey, Adjunct Professor of Clinical Psychiatry, UMDNJ-Robert Wood Johnson Medical School, and Visiting Professor at the School for Social Service at Fordham University. Her Honorary Doctorate, from Smith College for her contributions to the field, makes her only the third person in the school's history to be awarded such an honor.

McGoldrick has several decades of experience as a family therapist. In addition to her clinical work, McGoldrick has taught, done research and written about the theory and practice of family therapy. She has been honored several times for her work in family therapy, including the award from the American Family Therapy Academy for Distinguished Contribution to Family Therapy Theory and Practice. She is on the editorial boards of seven family therapy related journals, has published eleven books and written 33 articles and book chapters. Books directly related to ethnicity include *Revisioning Family Therapy: Race, Culture and Gender in Clinical Practice* and two editions of *Ethnicity and Family Therapy*.

One extremely important aspect of McGoldrick's work is that she is a white therapist, embedded in the primarily white professional context of family therapy, thinking and writing about the relevance of ethnicity, including the importance for white Americans of understanding the importance of their own ethnicity.

McGoldrick's primary focus is on ethnicity which she describes as referring "to a common ancestry through which individuals have evolved shared values and customs" and is "based on a combination of race, religion and cultural history" (McGoldrick, Giordano & Pearce, 1996, p. 1). Ethnicity pertains to everyone and must be integrated into therapy. It "interacts with economics, race, class, religion, politics, geography, the length of time since migration, a group's specific historical experience and the degree of discrimination it has experienced" (McGoldrick et al., 1996, p. 2).

McGoldrick's written work has provided an arena for a description of families from a wide range of ethnic backgrounds, including American Indian, African, Latino, Asian, and Middle Eastern (McGoldrick et al., 1996). However, one of the distinguishing characteristics of her work is the detailed description of a range of European ethnic influences on American families, including her own work on Irish women and Irish mothers (McGoldrick, 1990).

In "Culture: A challenge to concepts of normality," McGoldrick (2002) discusses her most recent ideas on the importance of placing oneself, including European Americans, culturally. In general, she values helping families adapt to the dominant American culture, while she recognizes the importance of ethnicity in conceptualizing human development and defining family. She values cultural competence in therapists, which means a deep appreciation of our own cultural values, respect for the limitations of our perspective, and an ability to be respectful with those whose values differ from our own (McGoldrick, p. 3). One of her therapy tools is a cultural genogram, which can "help us contextualize our kinship network in terms of culture, class, race, gender, religion, and migration history" (McGoldrick, p. 5).

McGoldrick, by virtue of her training groups, presentations and writing has taken the lead as a white, European American therapist in underscoring the fact that the dominant group position in the United States is specific, not universal. While envisioning non-dominant groups adapting to the dominant values, she recognizes the critical importance of understanding oneself culturally, and approaching others with both respect and tools for understanding their worldviews.

### Personal Story

I am a family therapist who is a fourth generation Irish American. I was born in Park Slope in Brooklyn, living there until I was six. After that, until I was 14, we lived on a beautiful farm in Bucks County, Pennsylvania, where I grew up with my mother and my caretaker and my two sisters, while my father lived and worked in New York and came home on weekends. My background was very privileged, but as I grew up I did not realize this. I thought I was just a "regular" American–not a woman, not an Irish woman, not a white woman, and certainly not a privileged white woman.

The mystification I grew up with on issues of race, class, gender and culture have profoundly affected my identity. My sisters and I were raised with the expectation that we would go to Ivy League colleges if we tried and that we should try. Then we should get PhDs in whatever subject interested us, and then we should marry Prince Charming and be his helpmate for life. On the surface, this was almost what my mother had done. She, like her sisters, had attended an Ivy League college and had a successful career in public relations before marrying my father, who was at the time comptroller of New York City in the La Guardia administration.

I did not realize the contradictions in my life until long after I finished all my formal education, which included two degrees from Ivy League schools where I felt distinctly marginal, uncomfortable, and that I did not belong. I then received a social work degree from Smith, to which my mother could barely bring herself to refer, because to her social work was a distinct downturn in status from my days in Russian Studies at Yale. During all those years I was completely ignorant of the fact that my Ivy League schools had been supported by the slave trade. Nor had I really noticed that these schools, like all the other schools I ever attended, were almost completely white.

I now realize that my family's story is a typical story of white upward mobility toward the power of the dominant group. At the core of my privileged childhood was Margaret Bush, an African American live-in maid, who worked for our family from the month I was born in 1943, when she was 41, until her death of a stroke 18 years later, nine months after I had left home for college. She was the person to whom I was closest all my life. But I did not understand the perverse social structure by which she, whose ancestors had been in this country so much longer than my own, forcibly brought here by the same cultural group that had dominated my own ancestors in Ireland, was the servant who made my family's lives visible. At the same time her history, her story and her relationships remained invisible, and she was given a back seat always in our lives. It was years before I realized how pernicious this was.

I did not question or even really notice the evil racial structure in which I was brought up, which gave me privilege on the back of Margaret's limitations. My education was fostered. She, on the other hand, felt she had to hide from my mother the fact that she couldn't read. When finally my mother found out and hired a teacher for her, when she was 50, her education took place behind closed doors in her private room, with us spying at the door to figure out what she was doing. I never realized that it was my people, white people, who made the inequitable rules of education and kept them in place, as we are still keeping such inequities in place, even in the supposedly integrated town where I have just finished raising my son.

I grew up also unaware of my Irish roots. As my mother said, "We're Americans now, Monica! Never mind where we came from." I did not know I was Irish until June of 1975, when at age 31, I went with my whole family on a trip to Ireland, during which I realized that I was still profoundly Irish, even though I had by that time married a Greek immigrant. This is, I now believe, the effect of white people in the U.S. trying to "pass" for the dominant group. They are made to feel that the way to success is to obliterate their own history and focus on the dominant group's history. What they lose in the process is their identity. Like my whole cultural group, I ended up mystified, lacking confidence, all the more so because we were so well able to fit in.

I also grew up not realizing I was a woman, in spite of the fact that I grew up in what was most of the time an all female family. Only very recently have I been realizing the many subtle ways in which I was made to feel in college and graduate school that I did not know the rules and that I was a fraud. I was struggling to fit in to such a male dominated world. The mystification that there were no women in the realms toward which I was striving was kept from my awareness by the way the system operated, and it has taken many years to begin to understand how that cultural structure contributed to me feeling inadequate.

Somehow, this background drew me, and my two sisters as well, toward an interest in multicultural issues. One of my sisters has spent years traveling in various cultures as an architectural photographer. My other sister teaches history to high school students and has developed international teacher exchanges and programs to promote cross-cultural and antiracist understanding. Somehow, in the fabric of our privileged background, we also received the messages that led us to challenge the mystification and the structures in which we are embedded.

Still, the question of what factors in my life's journey have contributed to my interest in multiculturalism is one for which I cannot offer any real answer. Why, I ask myself, did I marry an immigrant, which forced me to live in two cultures and to migrate with my husband and son back and forth to Greece, never fully belonging in one place? Did I just fall in love with someone who was in profound ways much like my beloved father, or was multiculturalism important? Or does my interest in culture derive from the fact, which I learned only after my mother died, that she had wanted to become a cultural anthropologist? Maybe I am living out what she was unable to do.

Do I feel I owe it to Margaret to try to make the world a different place to make up for what my ancestors and I did to keep her and her ancestors and descendants from having a fair share in our country? Surely I do. Do I feel I owe it to my friends of color, to make up for the fact that their mothers had to work to make white families visible and hadn't as much left over for their own children? Definitely. Do I worry that my son has it too easy as a privileged white male and that he might not take his responsibility to make the world a better place? Definitely. So I am a work in progress, trying to unpack my privilege, trying to notice the structures in which I have been embedded, and trying to look at the issues of psychotherapy with individuals and families from a multicultural pro-feminist position. And I am aware every day of how hard it is for me to stay conscious of my privilege, of the power of white supremacy, and of the insidious effects of patriarchy, racism, anti-Semitism, homophobia and classism on our world.

## FROM THE PAST INTO THE FUTURE

Centuries ago, the peoples of this country had varying shades of brown skin, living in tribes and groups while developing a range of cultures. When the white Europeans came, they imposed their cultural values, gradually expanding their influence across the entire land. In this twenty first century, the United States is in another transition, with skin color again at the center of the shift. More than one million legal and undocumented immigrants arrive annually, most from Asia, Latin and South America (McGoldrick, 2002). The United States President's Initiative on Race (1998) concluded that the greatest challenge facing North Americans is to accept and take pride in defining themselves as a multiracial democracy. "Given the United States' difficulties in assimilating its citizens of color, this is a formidable challenge" (Comas-Diaz, 2000, p. 1319).

Along with the racial changes come cultural changes. Europeans and now European Americans share some cultural values, values that influence how we think about human beings, psychological well-being, psychological growth and development, and the creation of webs of connection with others. As our population changes, it is clear that being white in American is a particular point of view, not a universal statement. Western psychology is poised on the edge of a major paradigm shift away from believing the European American values Landrine (1995) identified as the values everyone should have, away from one understanding of human beings, and away from a central dominant view against which all are measured. The work of the women honored here challenges the European American dominance and points the way to parts of the paradigm shift. Some changes are stated directly and some are merely hinted at, but all speak to the increase in complexity in psychology that is ahead of us. Some issues include:

1. An individual's group identity influences the relative importance of an individual self and the self-in-connection. The European American emphasis on the individual is very different from the emphasis of the self as a connected person inherent in

other cultures. How do these two aspects of identity work together?

2. Who/what constitutes a family? The European American ideal family still is seen as nuclear and heterosexual. For many other cultures, extended families are the norm with the possibility that non-relatives are family. Grandparents, siblings, other adults, and sometimes lesbian and gay adults may raise children. Much of Western theories on child development have been developed within an assumption of a two-parent nuclear, heterosexual family. Child development will be rethought.

3. Gender roles are different in different cultures. "Traditional gender roles" in the United States still refers to roles in white, middle-class families with the father working to support the family and the mother at home raising children. "Traditional gender roles" has quite another meaning in African-American families and other cultures of color. African-American women (and most lesbians) are presumed to have to both work and raise children if they have them.

4. White, western society has not assigned women strong roles. In fact, if many women do a particular thing, the value of that role is diminished. Some other cultures see women as strong–as wage earner, child raiser, and matriarch.

5. The west has a value on youth and youth culture, devaluing age and aging, especially for women. Since we also value "doing" more than "being," elders, who may be less able to be active, are seen negatively, as needing care. Many other cultures honor their elders, and value their accumulated wisdom. They are also seen as continuing to be valuable contributors to society such as through raising children.

6. Any language directly impacts how people who speak it understand the world. It affects what we do and don't think about, whether or not there are words for some experience. In particular, in the United States, English has colored all our thinking. This has been compounded by the fact that, until the last couple of decades, being bi-lingual was seen as being an immigrant and inferior, a statement about the lack of an individual being a "real" American. This is in contrast to other countries in which speaking more than one language is viewed as strength and a sign of being educated. As more languages work their way into the United States we can use them to widen our knowledge of the complexity of human beings.

7. Feminists in the United States have, in the past, viewed gender as the most salient variable when addressing group identity because most white people don't grasp the relevance and impact of their own race and culture. At this point in time, race and skin color may be the most important group identity needing to be addressed in the United States. The interplay of gender, race, culture, class, sexual orientation, etc., is more than the sum of all the parts–the nuances and shadings of meaning will influence how we understand ourselves.

All of the women honored here have, thankfully, been prolific, and very willingly shared their particular piece of understanding. Psychologically, they are all contributing to a powerful base of theory from which we can continue to build as we move forward in the 21st century. Their work helps point the way toward developing psychological theory based on differences, not deficiencies; understanding normal human growth and development; resilience through difficult times; psychological distress; and, perhaps, even the continued psychological development of humans as a species.

## REFERENCES

Adleman, J., & Enguidanos, G. (1995). *Racism in the lives of women: Testimony, theory, and guides to antiracist practice.* Binghamton, NY: Harrington Park Press.

Almquist, E. (1989). The experience of minority women in the United States. In J. Freeman (Ed.), *Women: A feminist perspective* (4th ed., pp. 414-445). Mountain View, CA: Mayfield.

Ballou, M., Matsumoto, A. & Wagner, M. (2002). Toward a feminist ecological theory of human nature: Theory building in response to real-world dynamics. In M. Ballou, & L. Brown (Eds.), *Rethinking mental health & disorder: Feminist perspectives* (pp. 99-141). New York, NY: Guilford Press.

Barrett, S. E. (1998). Contextual identity: A model for therapy and social change. In M. Hill (Ed.), *Feminist therapy as a political act* (pp. 51-64). New York, NY: Haworth Press.

Brown, L. (1995). Cultural diversity in feminist therapy: Theory and practice. In H. Landrine (Ed.), *Bringing cultural diversity to feminist psychology: Theory, research and practice* (pp. 143-161). Washington, DC: APA.

Bunch, C. (1987). *Passionate politics: Feminist theory in action* (pp. 244-245). New York, NY: St. Martin's Press.

Cantor, N. E., Chin, J. L., Gelman, R., Kaslow, F. W. (2002, August). In A. N. O'Connell (Chair), The 24th annual symposium on eminent women in psychology:

Historical and personal perspectives. Symposium conducted at the APA Convention, Chicago, IL.

Chin, J. L. (1994). Psychodynamic Approaches. In L. Comas-Diaz & B. Greene (Eds.), *Women of color: Integrating ethnic and gender identities in psychotherapy* (pp. 194-222). New York, NY: Guilford Press.

Chin, J. L. (Ed.) (2000). *Relationships among Asian American women.* Washington, DC: APA.

Chin, J. L., De La Cancela, V., & Jenkins, Y. (1993). *Diversity in psychotherapy: The politics of race, ethnicity and gender.* Westport, CT: Praeger Press.

Chin, J. L., Liem, J. H., Ham, M. D., & Hong, G. K. (1993). *Transference and empathy in Asian American psychotherapy: Cultural values and treatment needs.* Westport, CT: Praeger Press.

Cole, E., Espin, O. M., & Rothblum, E. (Eds.) (1993). *Refugee women and their mental health: Shattered societies, shattered lives.* New York, NY: Harrington Park Press.

Comas-Diaz, L. (1994). An integrative approach. In L. Comas-Diaz & B. Greene (Eds.), *Women of color: Integrating ethnic and gender identities in psychotherapy* (pp. 287-318), New York, NY: Guilford Press.

Comas-Diaz, L. (2000). An ethonopolitical approach to working with people of color (Award Address). *American Psychologist, 55,* 1319-1325.

Comas-Diaz, L., & Greene, B. (1994a). Women of color with professional status. In L. Comas-Diaz & B. Greene (Eds.), *Women of color: Integrating ethnic and gender identities in psychotherapy* (pp. 347-388). New York, NY: Guilford Press.

Comas-Diaz, L., & Greene, B. (Eds.) (1994b). *Women of color: Integrating ethnic and gender identities in psychotherapy.* New York, NY: Guilford Press.

Comas-Diaz, L., & Griffith, E. H. (Eds.) (1988). *Clinical guidelines in cross-cultural mental health.* New York, NY: John Wiley & Sons.

Comas-Diaz, L., & Jacobsen, F. M. (2001). Ethnocultural allodynia. *The Journal of Psychotherapy Practice and Research, 10* (4), 1-6.

Comas-Diaz, L., & Jacobsen, F. M. (in preparation). *Ethnocultural Psychotherapy.* New York, NY: HarperCollins.

De La Cancela, V., Chin, J. L., & Jenkins, Y. M. (1998). *Community Health Psychology: Empowerment for Diverse Communities.* N.Y: Routledge.

Espin, O. M. (1993). Giving voice to silence: The psychologist as witness. *American Psychologist, 48,* (4), 408-414.

Espin, O. M. (1996). *Latina Healers: Lives of power and tradition.* Encino, CA: Floricanto Press.

Espin, O. M. (1997a). *Latina Realities: Essays on healing, migration, and sexuality.* Boulder, CO: Westview Press.

Espin, O. M. (1997b). Psychological impact of migration on Latinas: Implications for psychotherapeutic practice. In O. M. Espin. *Latina realities: Essays on healing, migration and sexuality.* Boulder, CO: Westview Press.

Espin, O. M. (1999). *Women crossing boundaries: A psychology of immigration and the transformations of sexuality.* New York, NY: Routledge.

Greene, B. (1994). African American women. In L. Comas-Diaz & B. Greene (Eds.), *Women of color: Integrating ethnic and gender identities in psychotherapy* (pp. 10-29). New York, NY: Guilford Press.

Greene, B. (1997a) Lesbian women of color: Triple jeopardy. *Journal of Lesbian Studies [Special Issue]: Classics in lesbian studies. 1*, 49-60.

Greene, B. (Ed.) (1997b). *Psychological perspectives on lesbian and gay issues Vol.3: Ethnic and cultural diversity among lesbians and gay men.* Thousand Oaks, CA: Sage.

Greene, B. (2000a). African American lesbian and bisexual women in feminist-psychodynamic psychotherapy: Surviving and thriving between a rock and a hard place. In L. Jackson & B. Greene (Eds.), *Psychotherapy with African American women: Innovations in psychodynamic perspectives and practice* (pp. 82-125). New York, NY: Guilford Press.

Greene, B. (2000b). Beyond heterosexism and across the cultural divide: Developing an inclusive lesbian, gay and bisexual psychology. In B. Greene & G. L. Croom (Eds.), *Psychological perspectives on lesbian, gay and bisexual issues Vol. 5* (pp.1-45). Thousand Oaks, CA: Sage.

Greene, B. (2003). What difference does a difference make?: Societal privilege, disadvantage and discord in human relationships. In J. Robinson & L. James (Eds.), *Diversity in human interactions: The tapestry of America* (pp. 3-20). New York, NY: Oxford University Press.

Greene, B., & Boyd-Franklin, N. (1996). African American lesbians: Issues in couples therapy. In J. Laird & R. J. Green (Eds.), *Lesbians and gay men in couples and families: A handbook for therapists* (pp. 251-271). San Francisco, CA: Jossey Bass.

Greene, B., & Croom, G. L. (Eds.) (2000). *Psychological perspectives on lesbian, gay and bisexual issues Vol. 5: Education, practice and research in lesbian, gay, bisexual and transgendered psychology: A resource manual.* Thousand Oaks, CA: Sage.

Greene, B., & Herek, G. (Eds) (1994). *Psychological perspectives on lesbian and gay issues Vol. 1: Lesbian and gay psychology-Theory, research and clinical applications.* Thousand Oaks, CA: Sage.

Greene, B., White, J. C., & Whitten, L. (2000). Hair Texture, length and style: A metaphor in the African American mother-daughter relationship. In L. Jackson & B. Greene (Eds.), *Psychotherapy with African American women: Innovations in psychodynamic perspectives and practice* (pp. 166-193). New York, NY: Guilford Press.

Hall, R. L., & Greene, B. (2002). Not any one thing: The complex legacy of social class on African American lesbian's relationships. *Journal of Lesbian Studies, 6*, 65-74.

Herek, G., & Greene, B. (Eds.) (1995). *Psychological perspectives on lesbian and gay issues Vol. 2: AIDS, identity and community.* Thousand Oaks, CA: Sage.

Jackson, L. C., & Greene, B. A. (Eds.) (2000). *Psychotherapy with African American women: Innovations in psychodynamic perspectives and practice.* New York, NY: Guilford Press.

Landrine, H. (1995). Introduction: Cultural diversity, contextualism, and feminist psychology. In H. Landrine (Ed.), *Bringing cultural diversity to feminist psychology: Theory, research and practice* (pp. 1-20). Washington, DC: APA.

McGoldrick, M. (1990). Irish mothers. *Journal of Feminist Family Therapy, 2*(2), 3-8.

McGoldrick, M. (Ed.) (1998). *Revisioning family therapy: Race, culture and gender in clinical practice.* New York, NY: Guilford Press.

McGoldrick, M. (2002). Culture: A challenge to concepts of normality. In F. Walsh (Ed.), *Normal family processes, 3rd Ed.* New York, NY: Guilford Press.

McGoldrick, J., Giordano, J., & Pearce, M. (1996). *Ethnicity and family therapy, 2nd Edition.* New York, NY: Guilford Press.

Nevid, J. S., & Greene, B. (2000). *Essentials of abnormal psychology in a changing world.* Englewood Cliffs, NJ: Prentice Hall.

Nevid, J. S., Rathus, S. A., & Greene, B. (1994). *Abnormal psychology in a changing world (3rd ed.).*. Englewood Cliffs, NJ: Prentice Hall.

Nevid, J. S., Rathus, S. A., & Greene, B. (1999). *Abnormal psychology in a changing world (4th ed.).* Englewood Cliffs, NJ. Prentice Hall.

Nevid, J. S., Rathus, S. A., & Greene, B. (2002). *Abnormal psychology in a changing world (5th ed.)* Englewood Cliffs, NJ: Prentice Hall.

United States President's Initiative on Race. (1998). *One American in the 21st century: Forging a new future.* Washington, DC: Author.

# Beyond Color and Culture: Feminist Contributions to Paradigms of Human Difference

Laura S. Brown

Laurie E. Riepe

Rochelle L. Coffey

**SUMMARY.** This article reviews the work of important feminist theorists and contributors in several areas of human diversity. Work on the topics of women and disability, women's sexual orientations, women and social class, women's aging, and women's experiences as refugees and immigrants is reviewed and discussed. We propose future directions for feminist therapy theory and practice that integrates this expanded body of knowledge about women's lives. *[Article copies available for a fee from The Haworth Document Delivery Service: 1-800-HAWORTH. E-mail address: <docdelivery@haworthpress.com> Website: <http://www.HaworthPress.com> © 2005 by The Haworth Press, Inc. All rights reserved.]*

**KEYWORDS.** Women, aging, disability, social class, sexual orientation, refugee, immigration, bisexuality, lesbianism

Laura S. Brown is Professor of Psychology at Argosy University Seattle and maintains a private practice of feminist therapy. Laurie E. Riepe is a psychotherapist in private practice in Seattle. Rochelle L. Coffey is completing the PsyD program in Clinical Psychology at Argosy University Seattle.

Address correspondence to: Laura S. Brown, PhD, 4131 First Avenue NW, Seattle, WA 98107-4910 (E-mail: lsbrownphd@cs.com).

[Haworth co-indexing entry note]: "Beyond Color and Culture: Feminist Contributions to Paradigms of Human Difference." Brown, Laura S., Laurie E. Riepe, and Rochelle L. Coffey. Co-published simultaneously in *Women & Therapy* (The Haworth Press, Inc.) Vol. 28, No. 3/4, 2005, pp. 63-92; and: *The Foundation and Future of Feminist Therapy* (ed: Marcia Hill, and Mary Ballou) The Haworth Press, Inc., 2005, pp. 63-92. Single or multiple copies of this article are available for a fee from The Haworth Document Delivery Service [1-800-HAWORTH, 9:00 a.m. - 5:00 p.m. (EST). E-mail address: docdelivery@haworthpress.com].

As has been true for many facets of human diversity and difference, feminist therapists have been among the pioneers in the mental health disciplines in the development of paradigms for understanding and responding to difference. As feminist therapy theorists began to abandon a unidimensional model of women that ignored women's diversity and complexity, focusing instead on the intersections between gender and other components of identity and social location (Brown & Root, 1990), a number of feminist voices became central to the discourse on a range of variables. This chapter will attend to those aspects of human difference that are not always included under the rubric of "diversity," but which have been treated by feminist therapy theorists as co-equal with questions of ethnicity, color and culture. The topics that the authors have chosen to discuss in this chapter in no way constitute an exhaustive list of diversity variables. Rather, they represent areas of the discourse where feminist theorists have made important contributions. However, they also represent corners of the discourse that have yet to be moved from the margins to the mainstream of feminist therapy theory.

We begin with our standpoints as authors, because we believe that knowing those standpoints allows the reader to discern the manner in which our experiences have biased the lenses through which we view the work of others. Two of us are lesbians. Two of us are parents. One of us has always lived in the middle or upper-middle class. All of us have white skin; one of us is a Jew. All of us are partnered. One of us has an invisible disability; one of us parents a child with an invisible disability. All three authors were born and raised English-speaking in the U.S.; one of us is the granddaughter of immigrants. We identify these standpoints because the topics that we will address here–social class, disability, sexual orientation, aging, and immigration–are all factors in which at least one of us has participated as a member of a target group.

We also take a theoretical standpoint on these issues that arises from the social constructivist branch of feminist theory (Hare-Mustin & Marecek, 1990; Marecek, 2002). It is our stance that all of these variables of difference hold meanings that are socially constructed rather than inherent. While some factors (e.g., being able to see or hear, being of a certain age) are biological, the *values* ascribed to those factors and a person's position in the matrix of dominance and submission is dependent on meanings made within the social milieu. It is our belief that one of the major contributions made by feminist theorists of difference has been the deconstruction of standard, disempowering, stigmatizing meanings, and the reframing these experiences of difference as central rather than marginal to the understanding of humanity (Brown, 1989).

Although multiple authors have contributed to feminist theory of difference, our charge in this chapter is to identify those women who have been major contributors. We define such major contributors as those whose work has influenced the thinking of others. Following on Ballou's (1990) construction of authority in feminist therapy theory, we have identified thinkers whose work occurred in non-academic as well as academic settings, in the form of personal testimony as well as empirical research, and from the perspective of consumer as well as that of therapist. When a particular author has appeared to be focal for her topic area, particularly in those realms where there has been a paucity of feminist commentary, we have taken the opportunity to go deeply into her work. On other dimensions where there has been ample feminist representation we have chosen to summarize more succinctly in order to recognize the multiplicity of voices.

## FEMINIST CONTRIBUTIONS
## TO THE SEXUAL ORIENTATION DISCOURSE

Lesbians and bisexual women have always been among the most visible of feminist therapists and theorists. Adrienne Smith, whose idea gave birth to the Feminist Therapy Institute, was also one of the first open lesbians in psychology. Laura Brown, one of this chapter's authors, is a lesbian who has been a major contributor to feminist theory. Many heterosexual feminist therapists are assumed to be lesbian in many instances due to the popular conflation of lesbianism with feminism. Feminist therapists and writers have been the major contributors to theory and practice with lesbian and bisexual women. This dominance of the topic by feminists has made the identification of only a few major contributors challenging, since so many women might fall into that category. We have, consequently, looked to the literature and to citations of authors to assist us in making our selection, and commented more briefly on the contributions of each.

The Boston Lesbian Psychologies Collective (Bragg et al., 1987) was a group of feminist researchers and practitioners. They organized the first (and apparently only) conference on Lesbian Psychologies in the middle 1980s, from which their foundational work, *Lesbian Psychologies*, emerged. The collective took the step of identifying lesbian issues as distinct from those of women in general, and created an intellectual space in which feminist theory of lesbianism could develop.

Marny Hall, a therapist in private practice with an emphasis on sexuality (1991, 1993, 1995a, 1995b 1996) has been one of the most visible and vocal feminist contributors to theory and practice with lesbian women. Her focus has been lesbians' sexual functioning. Hall addresses the apparent persistence and intractability of problems of sexual desire in lesbian partnerships, and the failures of dominant paradigms of sex therapy to effectively assist lesbians in having satisfying sex lives in the context of long-term relationships. Her paradigm of "un-sex" therapy in which she offers a model of deconstructing dominant narratives out of the sexual activities of lesbians has been a source of empowerment both for perplexed therapists and for lesbians who find themselves struggling to keep passion alive once early limerence has fled. She has also challenged the notion that sexual activity between women ought to be confined to the context of emotional intimacy, and developed the model of "genital incidentalism" (Hall, 1993) in which she argues that sex can be a friendly, as well as a romantic, form of exchange between women.

Laura Brown, a clinical psychologist who practices and teaches, has made numerous theoretical contributions to feminist paradigms of lesbianism. Her article, "New voices, new visions: Toward a lesbian/gay paradigm for psychology" (Brown, 1989), is frequently cited by others and has been republished in a number of feminist psychology readers. Brown's argument in this article, extended in later work (Brown, 1992, 1995, 1996, 1999) was that the experience of lesbian (and by implication, bisexual) women needed to be viewed as core to understanding human behavior rather than as a separate, intellectually ghettoized discourse. This recentering of the discourse on women so that it emerged from lesbians' experiences reflects an overall feminist paradigm, first noted by Lerman (1987) of making the experience of the "other" central to theory building.

Beverly Greene, a clinical psychologist currently on the faculty of St. Johns University in Brooklyn (1986, 1993, 1994a, 1994b, 1995, 1997a, 1997b, 1998a, 1998b, 2000a, 2000b, in press a, in press b; Greene & Boyd-Franklin, 1994; Greene & Croom, 2000; Hall & Greene, 2002), has been a prolific contributor to feminist theory of lesbians of color, with a focus on the lives and strengths of African-American lesbians. Greene has addressed the issue of "triple jeopardy" in the lives of lesbians of color, and in so doing has generated images of resilience and competencies, not only of wounds and distress. Moving away from a pathologizing model while still presenting strategies for working as a feminist therapist with lesbians of color, Greene has been able to maintain the delicate balance between a discussion of clinical needs and issues while never creating a meta-message of dysfunction inherent to the group. Her work on symbolic issues in therapy with African-American lesbian clients (1986) was the first to formally challenge the non-conscious racism, sexism, and heterosexism of therapists working with African-American lesbians, and is considered by many to be one of the major transformative pieces of writing in the field of anti-racist feminist practice.

Beth Firestein, a feminist counseling psychologist practicing in Colorado, has written some of the most important and cogent work on the frequently-ignored topic of bisexuality (1996). Although Firestein is still early in her career, she has been a consistent presence in the discourse on women's sexuality, affirming bisexuality as a normative, non-pathological orientation and challenging biphobia in both lesbian and heterosexual feminists. While her body of work is not yet large, by being singular, her contribution is important and deserving of recognition.

## FEMINIST CONTRIBUTIONS
## TO THE DIS/ABILITY DISCOURSE

Feminist therapy theory initially spoke little if at all about women with disabilities. When women with disabilities were mentioned, it was in the context of their being consumers of psychotherapy services. Feminist therapy conferences were frequently held in settings that were inaccessible to feminist therapists with mobility impairments or chemical sensitivities (Barshay, 1993), nor was there significant outreach to feminist therapists who are Deaf. (Authors' note: The convention of Deaf culture, in which the word Deaf is capitalized, will be used in this chapter.) The discourse of disability rights is, additionally, sometimes at odds with that of feminism, as we will discuss below. Within disability rights communities, issues of sexism have been as prevalent as in other groups struggling for liberation. Additionally, as is true for feminism, there is no one cohesive disability rights politic other than that of access and inclusion (Olkin, 1999). Many temporarily able-bodied people have little non-clinical interaction with people with disabilities. Feminist practitioners who are still temporarily able-bodied have frequently been uncertain as to how to take a stance of alliance in relationship to disability rights issues.

Adrienne Asch, a feminist social psychologist currently serving as the Henry Luce Professor of Biology, Ethics and the Politics of Human

Reproduction at Wellesley College has been for more than two decades a powerful feminist voice on the topic of ability and disability in women's lives. Prior to her receiving her doctorate in 1992, she was a practicing clinical social worker. Her writings have been foundational in bringing a disability rights discourse to feminism and feminist theory and analysis of gender to the disability rights field (Asch, 1984a, 1984b, 1989, 1990, 1995, 1997; Asch & Fine, 1984, 1986, 1988; Asch & Geller, 1996; Asch & Rousso, 1985; Asch & Sacks, 1983; Asch & Schiff, 1992; Fine & Asch, 1981, 1982, 1984, 1988). She has also been a major contributor to debates on reproductive ethics, integrating both feminist and disability rights perspectives into questions about the new reproductive technologies and their implications for disabled and non-disabled women.

All of the factors described at the beginning of this section combine to make Asch's contributions particularly valuable to feminist practitioners. Her body of work encourages the feminist practitioner to think in a complex and nuanced manner about the intersections between gender and disability, and between feminist and disability rights politics.

Asch's work has been instrumental in developing several themes about the intersection of gender and disability. Written from the standpoints both of personal experience of disability and feminism, her work began by interrogating the diversity within the lives of disabled women, noting that it is a convention of ableist social construction to define all women with disabilities as members of the same group. She challenges this construction of identity, encouraging her readers to think in specifics about this particular person, this particular disability, and its particular meaning in the current relational field. Asch and Fine (1988) query, "Why should a limb-deficient girl, a teenager with mental retardation, or a blind girl have anything in common with each other, or with a woman with breast cancer or another woman who is recovering from a stroke?" (p. 6). Asch and her collaborators have noted that what creates this diverse collection as one target group is not any shared inherent similarities, but rather the similar ways in which they are targeted by ableist dominant cultures and individuals for discriminatory treatment. Asch has repeatedly taken the lead in describing the huge variabilities that exist within the lives and experiences of women with disabilities, analyzing how intersections with race, social class, and types of disability have differential outcomes for women with disabilities.

Asch also has drawn attention to the commonalities of experience, especially those for women with visible disabilities. She has cogently commented on the desexualizing of the bodies of women with visible disabilities, an issue which goes beyond the question of whether a particular woman with disabilities might find a partner to the more general manner in which disability is constructed as an infantilizing (thus desexualizing) phenomenon. She has explored the stereotype of women as nurturers, noting that the woman with a visible disability such as visual or mobility impairment is socially constructed as unfit for the work of parenting because of suppositions that she will be the one requiring nurturance, rather than offering it. This, Asch and her collaborators note, reflects an overarching construction of disability as incompetence, intersecting with the definition of competence for women being situated in the mother role.

One of the particularly difficult issues addressed in Asch's work is the point of contention between traditionally feminist reproductive rights arguments about the rights of pregnant women to terminate pregnancies when they are carrying a fetus with a disability, and the disability rights rebuttal to this stance. A common rationale given by women choosing to terminate a pregnancy is that the fetus has been discovered to have a disability such as Down's Syndrome. In the disability rights movement, however, this argument is seen as advancing a form of prenatal genocide aimed at people with developmental disabilities (McBryde Johnson, 2003). Asch has written sensitively and powerfully from a standpoint that includes both perspectives (Asch & Geller, 1996; Asch, 1995), noting how female gender may disempower or silence the woman with disabilities in particular ways around reproduction. The reproductive rights struggle for woman with disabilities, especially visible disabilities, is frequently not that of the temporarily able-bodied women. The main reproductive struggle for women who have a disability affecting motor skills or cognitive functioning is for the right to be pregnant, not to end a pregnancy.

Asch's work fulfills one of the primary functions of feminist writing about difference in that it expands the vision of feminist practitioners well beyond the illusory unidimensional "woman" and clarifies the interstices of the complexity of identity at the intersections. Her work raises consciousness about what it might mean to be a person with a disability, and about how feminist practitioners might approach their relationship with colleagues and clients with disabilities from a stance of respect and empowerment.

Several other authors who identify as feminists have made important contributions to the discourse on women and disability. Their work has had less effect on theory and policy, and more on practice and awareness. Rhoda Olkin, a feminist clinical psychologist who both practices and teaches, has written and presented in a number of settings about disability rights and disability awareness (Olkin, 1999, 2003). Because she is a feminist, her work is informed by feminist sensibilities, but until very recently has not been specific to the topic of either feminist analysis or women with disabilities. Her work is valuable in large part because of its specific, informative, and consciousness-raising focus on what therapists can do to become accessible in their skills and their work-settings alike. She takes accessibility beyond the essentials of wheelchair access in one's office and restrooms to the feminist ethical responsibility of acquisition of non-pathologizing knowledge of the disability experience. In one recent and one upcoming publication (Olkin, 2003, in press), she specifically blends the feminist and disability rights standpoints, analyzing how she had previously chosen to focus on the disability issue because of her strongly felt commitment to making that voice heard in a context where feminist voices were loud and many.

Nancy Mairs (1995, 1996, 1998), a feminist essayist who has both physical and psychological disabilities, has contributed consistent, powerful, and thoughtful testimonies of the experience of life "waist high in the world," to borrow the title of one of her recent volumes. Her elegant essays convey the quotidian and relational aspects of her multiple realities. Her readers come to know her as a woman with progressive multiple sclerosis and recurrent major depression who is also a recent convert to Catholicism, an immigrants' rights activist, an acclaimed writer and university professor, married, and a parent of now-adult offspring.

## FEMINIST CONTRIBUTIONS
## TO THE DISCOURSE ON AGING

Women live longer than men. Growing older is an experience that is gendered by this biological fact. Additionally, aging is a de-genderizing process for women; the interaction of ageism and sexism serves to underscore the manner in which women are valued in dominant Euro-American cultures primarily for their nubility and fertility. Several feminist theorists and therapists have made important contributions to the discourse on age and its meanings as seen through the lenses of gender.

Nancy Datan, who was a feminist developmental psychologist and theorist of women's aging, created an essential foundation for a feminist analysis of ageism and a feminist vision of women's positive aging experiences. Datan, who worked cross-culturally and studied the experiences of women's aging outside of dominant cultural contexts, and who, sadly, did not live to experience the aging process that she studied, dying of cancer in her forties, was the first aging researcher to bring the feminist stance of self-reflexivity to the process of understanding how aging is studied. Her work is marked by a brilliance of conceptualization, methodological rigor, and an utter commitment to the feminist stance of inclusion and desilencing of multiply marginalized people. She treated her research participants as her collaborators and her teachers long before feminist methodologies became accepted in academic contexts. Her work is frequently co-authored with colleagues, demonstrating her commitment to sharing the power and prestige of authorship with students and mentees.

Datan's strong feminist contributions to aging research began with her work redefining women's aging process as a form of competency, rather than as a loss of functioning (Giesen & Datan, 1980). She and her collaborators redefined the concept of competence to include adaptive reactions to periods of disequilibrium and empirically demonstrated how this paradigm could be observed in the lives of poor and working-class Appalachian women as they aged. Datan's work next moved from reframing women's experiences of aging to the development of theory about how aging and ageism were inextricably linked to sexism and the objectification of women.

In her ground-breaking essay, "Corpses, lepers, and menstruating women: Tradition, transition, and the sociology of knowledge" (Datan, 1986), Datan looked retrospectively at her early studies of aging women, conducted when she was herself in her twenties. She examined her own biases as a young researcher, and their impact on the development of hypotheses that shaped both the study itself (Datan, Antonovsky & Maoz, 1981) and the ways the authors interpreted their findings. The essential contribution that Datan makes here is her naming and describing of what she calls "the narcissism of the life cycle." She makes it clear that while she was aware of her fellow researchers' sexism and argued energetically for a broader feminist conceptualization of both the hypothesis and interpretation, that she was unaware until many years later of the temporal bias that was present in all three of the researchers. Datan identified their collective bias for youth and modernity that treated aging and traditional culture as "other." Datan realized in reflection is that this bias was subtly and strongly bound to the notion of woman as object and "other" even if sexism is accounted for in a narrower way. Her explicit connection of the otherness of age to the otherness of female gender was transformative for the entire field of aging studies.

At the end of her life, Datan continued to address the intersection between gender and aging. In her *American Psychologist* article, "The challenge of double jeopardy: Toward a mental health agenda for aging women," co-authored with her former student and life partner Dean Rodeheaver (Rodeheaver & Datan, 1988), Datan identified the problem for older women as being the intersections of sexism and ageism. She and Rodeheaver noted the effects of social realities on the well-being of older women and explicitly discussed how infrequently that was taken into account in traditional discourse on mental health needs of this group. This article challenged the dominant discourse that aging, and especially aging in women, was inherently psychopathological, and offered both theoretical and empirical support for the position that old women are competent and capable, albeit frequently battered by the mounting losses engendered by heightened levels of discrimination. The authors assert that hope for real change lies in addressing the discriminatory and neglectful attitudes and practices of society, and working to develop models of healthy aging that accentuate the resilient strategies of the aging woman. Datan recentered the discourse on aging by making women's experiences and competencies core to her analysis of what a good old age might look like.

Another important feminist contributor to paradigms of aging has been Rachel Josefowitz Siegel, a clinical social worker in private practice and an active and visible presence in feminist therapy settings since the late 1970s (Siegel, 1982, 1983, 1990a, b, c; Siegel & Sonderegger, 1990; Sonderegger & Siegel, 1990) Siegel's work has been an illustration of the concept that "the personal is political." Deriving theory and practice from her own experiences as a woman growing older, Siegel has been a potent narrator of the story of older women's lives, with a particular focus on how images of mother and mother-blaming affects bias towards old women. Siegel's candid telling of her own story (1983) highlights the urgency that characterizes the reevaluation which occurs as childrearing comes towards an end and mortality begins to be known as an eventuality. Siegel describes her personal and professional journey as a movement from experience that is characterized by loss and emptiness to one of richness and stimulation. Once again we see the theme of a feminist analysis acting to reframe a marginalized experience and situate it at the center as a form of strength and competence rather than pathology.

In her work on the image of the mother in ageism, Siegel secured her position as a feminist theorist redefining the roles and advocating the real needs of aging women (Siegel, 1990a). She challenges the need of both dominant culture and younger feminist women to use old women as stereotypical mother figures who provide us with a target to alternately blame and idealize. At the same time that Siegel pulls no punches when examining the oppression imbedded in our treatment of old women, she sensitively acknowledges the very real and complex psychological and social relationship between daughters and mothers. Additionally, she succeeds at not making the mistake of letting the responsibility for this issue rest at the psychological level, instead calling for an examination of the very real need for 'good enough nurturing' as a responsibility that rests on the broader shoulders of an entire society and its institutions rather than those of aging women. Perhaps most powerful is Siegel's claim to empowerment in the middle of the article where she, as an old woman of 65 years, refuses the social projection onto her and says to the reader "I am not your mother." By creating a genuine moment of authenticity between writer and reader in which the reader is able to experience grief at the 'in the moment death' of projections of mother as all-powerful and all-evil. The reader of Siegel's work experiences a sober recognition of the author as a real and sovereign individual, not a generic mother. This is the grief and sobriety that precedes intimacy, whereby the reader may now be available to see the writer for herself. Siegel's article is a definitive expression of feminist advocacy and empowerment for the oppressed group of aging women.

In other work, Siegel (in collaboration with Theo Sonderegger, 1990a & b) approach the issue of aging and women from the perspective of ethical practice. The notion that fighting ageism is a feminist ethic, while consistent with other more general explications of a feminist ethical stance (Brabeck, 1999) is uniquely focused here on work with aging women. Siegel has also written broadly about clinical experiences as an old woman therapist with both young and old women (1982, 1990b, 1990c). She examines the manner in which issues of the symbolic relationship in therapy are affected by the mother stereotypes that she explores in other work, and how her own identity development, both personal and professional, has been shaped by her process of mindful and empowered aging.

A final important feminist contributor to the discourse on aging who will be discussed here was the late Shevy Healey. Healey, who was a clinical psychologist who worked professionally with people with MS, left only a small formal written record (Healey, 1991, 1993, 1994).

Much of her work took the form of speeches at conferences (e.g., Healey, 1999) and most importantly, political organizing among old women and consciousness-raising among feminist therapists. As one of the founding members of Old Lesbians Organizing for Change (OLOC), and as an activist for aging women's and lesbians' issues in a wide range of settings, Healey created the political context in which theory and practice that were anti-ageist could flourish. Her life and work are featured in several videos about older women. Her legacy to feminist paradigms of older women is in the form of a powerful model of how to be old and proud effectively in the face of ageism, sexism, and heterosexism. Her passionate verbal contributions at feminist therapy conferences had an effect on all present and raised the consciousness of many.

## *REFUGEE AND IMMIGRANT WOMEN IN NORTH AMERICA: FEMINIST DISCOURSES*

Almost every woman who lives in North America today, aside from American Indian women, is descended from someone who came from elsewhere. Many of those ancestors arrived as refugees, in flight from oppression, war, or torture. The relationship of North American dominant cultures, especially those of the United States, to immigrant populations has been ambivalent at best, and is often, as is currently the case, hostile. To this disempowered group, feminist therapists and theorists have brought paradigms arising from their own immigrant and refugee experiences. Four feminist theorists have had the most notable impact in this field.

The first of these is Oliva Espin, a professor in psychology and women's studies, born in Cuba and currently working in San Diego. While she is also well-known for her work specifically on the lives of Latina lesbians and Latina spirituality, as well as some fascinating work on the lives of women saints in the Catholic church, she has also taken leadership in bringing the attention of feminist therapists to the immigrant and refugee experience (Espin, 1987, 1992, 1993, 1995, 1996). Her discussion of immigrant women's experiences of having "roots uprooted" (1992), and of the long-standing effects of geographical dislocation, whether voluntary or otherwise, on women's identities and lives, has created an entirely new area of focus for feminist therapists as we move into a more internationally-aware era of practice.

Espin's (1987) writing on this topic has its own roots in her exploration of the migration experience of Latinas, examining issues of acculturation and assimilation. She emphasizes a distinction essential to feminist theory: the necessity for treating the client within her unique socio-political, historical and economic contexts. Espin contributes to our understanding of issues of power, whether related to gender, race or class, and how these issues are especially complicated and rich for the immigrant Latina who must navigate between world-views. Espin presents these issues as important determinants for the psychological struggles faced by this population and makes a strong argument for understanding many of the conflicts faced by the Latina immigrant as natural consequences of the difficult process of immigration, rather than pathological.

Espin's writing on this topic has expanded to the experiences of other women immigrants and refugees. In her introductory article for the special issue of *Women & Therapy*, Espin (1992) articulates and demonstrates three aspects of feminist psychology that are contributive to our understanding of the mental health needs of refugee and immigrant individuals. The first is an emphasis on the social-historical context. Secondly, Espin speaks of the importance of the personal story in research and the development of treatment protocols. Thirdly, Espin discusses the importance of the psychologist's personal story, and the relevance of mutuality in the process of research. This example of feminist scholarship is masterfully accomplished because Espin not only succeeds at talking about these different aspects but she models the process by using her own story of emigrating from Cuba at the age of 20.

Espin's work has also gone beyond the boundaries of feminist publishing to have impact on the dominant culture of psychological practice. Her *American Psychologist* article (1993) is core to her contributions to this topic, and models for a mainstream audience feminist ways of knowing. Here she charts her personal and professional development and growing awareness that her role as a psychologist is one of witness and empowerment to those who are invisible and 'without voice,' including immigrants, women, lesbians and others who are negatively and under-represented in the cultural world view. She speaks of her own experiences as an immigrant and lesbian. It is her understanding of these experiences in the context of social constructivism that provides the form for all of Espin's work. Finally, she asserts that her career has been based on an intuition, later more firmly understood theoretically, that the 'illegitimate' and unseen experiences of minorities and target groups become legitimate and part of what is understood to be 'normal,' when they can be voiced and witnessed. This is an essential and primary aspect of feminist theory and practice. Espin's contribution both in her practice of psychotherapy and research, and her capacity to understand and express theoretically, is evidence of the importance of her work in the body of knowledge about immigrant experience and treatment.

Espin's other work in this area has included studies of identity development in adolescent immigrant girls (Goodenow & Espin, 1993), and the interaction of personal and sexual identity with the experience of immigration for women (Espin, 1995, 1996). This work has examined ways in which the process of dislocation and uprooting from one's culture and place of origin creates dynamic tensions in the assertion of gendered identity issues and ways of sexual relating. In this work Espin makes clear an important distinction regarding identity development that is possible and sometimes unavoidable for the immigrant woman. Women who immigrate from more traditional cultures to industrialized and more secular nations such as the U.S. very often find that they develop perspectives on who they are and what behaviors are available to them that go beyond the cultural "borders" of their birth culture. Additionally, the immigration process leads to seeing and understanding one's traditional culture from a less embedded standpoint.

Espin also describes the parallels between the process of acculturation and identity reforming for immigrants and the coming out process for lesbians. She talks of how developing an identity that is partly formed by affirming and including oneself in a group that is "stigmatized" or "negative" due to its status as a racial and/or ethnic minority, is akin to a lesbian coming out in a heterosexual culture. She analyzes the difficult tension that a young immigrant female faces when struggling to be the repository and embodiment of traditional values *and* become a part of a new society with differing morals and expectations. Espin defines this tension as particular for women and exceptionally difficult for the immigrant who is a lesbian. By focusing her feminist lens on female immigrants and lesbians, with attention to sexuality, Espin brings to relief the experiences of many individuals whose life experiences are mostly untold. She fulfills what appears to be an imperative for her as a feminist psychologist, to help us to see the realities of those who, from the perspectives of the cultural center and mainstream psychology, are routinely invisible.

Adrianne Aron is a feminist social psychologist and political organizer for the rights of Central American refugees who, with her collaborators, has studied a particular aspect of some refugee women's experiences, that of confronting terror and torture in their countries of origin. Bringing both a feminist and internationalist perspective to her work, she raises difficult questions for feminist therapists in the United

States whose government is usually complicit in these forms of oppression. How can feminist therapists in the U.S. respond in alliance to these women?

Aron and her collaborators offer models for understanding how state-sponsored terror in Latin America has taken gendered forms (Aron, Corne, Fursland, & Zelwer, 1991). They specifically examine the use of sexually abusive and exploitive torture and threats. Their analysis of the research, descriptions and case vignettes are convincing evidence that women are exceptionally vulnerable to the use of sexual violence as a means of torture and oppression. Aron and her co-authors use psychological research to legitimize these refugees' experiences and give credibility to methods of treatment specifically targeted to account for those experiences. It is clear that in their analysis of the problem and treatment suggestions, the authors are standing in a relationship of advocacy with the women they are studying. It is in these two aspects, consciousness raising and advocacy, that Aron's work with refugees contributes in an important way to the feminist literature.

Aron (1992) then moves to presenting a model for working from a feminist therapeutic stance with tortured refugee women. In her article exploring the use of *Testimonio* or Testimony as a sociotherapeutic tool, she describes the reclamation of power and the redevelopment of community that is possible through the difficult process of telling one's personal story of injustice and survival. Aron makes a strong case for the use of *Testimonio* both in the setting of decimated communities where injustice has occurred, and in the safe haven of adopted countries and therapeutic settings where refugees might find themselves after their escape. Aron makes the point that the use of *Testimonio* can be particularly empowering and effective with women as it allows for the members of society with the least access to traditional means of power to claim their personal experience as the basis of truth and knowledge. This point, that *Testimonio* can be a means not simply of doing individual treatment, but also towards equality in the refugee community, sets this article apart as an exceptional addition to the feminist literature regarding work with refugees. Aron names the qualities of *Testimonio* as historically feminist and advocates for its use with whole communities as a means not only towards healing the pain of past political and military oppression but transforming the oppression of sexism in refugee communities.

Gretchen Van Boemel and Pat Rozee's (1992) award-winning article on the experiences of Khmer refugee women, while singular, is deserving of notice here because of the impact of their work both within and outside of feminist therapy practice. In this article they describe their research, as a medical worker (Van Boemel) and community action research psychologist (Rozee) with Cambodian refugee women who suffer from non-organic blindness that the researchers hypothesized to be the result of the horrific trauma these women witnessed and experienced at the hands of the Khmer Rouge during the Pol Pot regime. Here Van Boemel and Rozee conduct a study to explore treatment options for this population that has been under-diagnosed, misdiagnosed, and mostly untreated by the American medical and mental health systems. Their research is remarkable primarily in that they use the attention of the study on this population and their findings to actively advocate for adequate diagnostic and treatment resources for these women.

The authors strongly demonstrate the powerful use of feminist theory-in-action by not only addressing an important issue for a target population, but by surpassing the scope of traditional research and actively taking the results of their work to institutions and successfully lobbying to change policies. They reframed their research participants' experience as a deep not-seeing of a world in which they had been forced to witness intra-ethnic horror. Until this work the normative experience for Khmer refugee women such as these was to be untreated and/or categorized by the medical system as unable to treat due to diagnoses such as "malingering." Van Boemel's and Rozee's identification of the legitimate needs and treatment options for post-traumatic blindness changed the outcome for women refugees who otherwise were left isolated and suffering. Additionally, their work is an exceptional example of how feminist theory in psychology can be used to effect change at the level of power systems such as government offices, medical practice policies and policy decision making for mental health.

## SOCIAL CLASS:
## FEMINIST VOICES IN THE INVISIBLE DISCUSSION

Feminist psychologists have made progress in the articulation of various intersections of diversity. However, class has rarely been part of that conversation, and editorializing was often subsumed under conversation about race:

The scholarship of feminist psychology as been . . . exclusionary; many of the research participants in the studies reported in feminist psychology journals are university students and more likely to come from middle-class rather than working-class or poor backgrounds. Frequently, the assumption is made that paying attention to issues of racial diversity will cover matters related to class as well, as though the two variables were isomorphic. Such an assumption perpetuates dominant cultural stereotypes equating middle-class status with white people and poverty with people of color in the invisible caste system of Western patriarchies. (Brown, 1994)

Perhaps feminist psychologists may be reflecting the broader society's hesitancy to discuss economic class as an organizing heuristic, believing that a person's economic class is simply a description of income level that can easily be changed with hard work. Or perhaps because there are instances of economic mobility, the phenomenon of class status does not seem easily defined. Whatever the reason, the lack of attention to class as a social construction worthy of research, theory building and practice standards reflects the elitism of the field of psychology generally and psychotherapy specifically.

Cognitive, institutional and interpersonal distancing from working-class and impoverished persons, when combined with stereotypes and prejudice, comprises the definition of classism according to Lott (2002). Bernice Lott, a feminist social psychologist now Emerita Professor of Psychology at the University of Rhode Island, has been a primary feminist psychology theorist on issues of class, working from a social psychological perspective. While her text is applicable to all of society, her target audience is psychologists; her message is a call to action: "Psychologists committed to social justice must carefully document and analyze the barriers erected by classist bias that maintain inequities and impede access to the resources necessary for optimal health and welfare." Classism results from the unequal and unearned privilege of those who have the power to discriminate. Cognitive distancing includes stereotyping and personalizing another's economic disadvantage. The balance of Lott's article reflects the common mistake that class diversity can be investigated by considering the lives of those in the poverty class to represent the working-class as well. Lott's other work on this topic includes analyses of the "disruption of classism" (Lott, 2003), examining how psychologists can move from positions of guilt into those of disrupting classist social structure. Working with Saxon (Lott & Saxon, 2002), Lott has found empirically that social class, more than ethnicity or gender, can lead to negative evaluations of women by both women and men. She has examined the experiences of poor and working-class parents dealing with their children's public schools, once again finding that social class leads to devaluation, this time by teacher and school administrators who make assumptions that working class and poverty class parents (primarily mothers in this work) do not care about their children's education or academic advancement (Lott, 2001).

Some of the earliest and still most influential work by feminist theorists on class has emerged from grassroots activists rather than psychologists or therapists. *Class and Feminism* (Bunch & Myron, 1974) consists of essays by members of the Furies, an early feminist collective. Some of these reflections documented the experience of several women who grew up working-class and collided with the middle class when they went to college and when they joined the women's liberation movement. Other essays attempted to articulate a feminist position on class. The authors made astute connections between sexism and classism, noting that the sexual objectification of working-class women was more blatant than for middle class women, evidenced in the assumption that the former were sexually promiscuous as soon as they began to develop sexually. The authors also made the connection between classism and race. As Myron noted, "I grew up poor but I had white skin privilege" (p. 39). In fact, the sense of racial superiority was particularly salient as it was the one identifier that supplied a sense of value.

Brown (1974) identified two erroneous beliefs about class operating within the women's movement. First was the belief that "a working-class woman with a college education escapes her class background" (p. 16) and second that downward mobility of middle and upper-class women effectively removes class differences. Bringing the feminist concept of personal as political to the discourse, Brown noted, "Class is much more than Marx's definition of relationship to the means of production. Class involves your behavior, your basic assumptions about life, your experiences (determined by your class) validate those assumptions, how you are taught to behave, what you expect from yourself and from others, your concept of a future, how you understand problems and solve them, how you think, feel, act" (p. 15). The upwardly mobile working-class woman within the woman's movement experienced the effects of her background even as she became economically self-sufficient.

Early feminist theorists recognized the importance of class markers distinguishing middle class activists from working-class activists. At a time when downward mobility was fashionable as a political and cultural statement among progressive activists, these women came to understand that even when material symbols of wealth (expensive clothing, cars, houses, jewelry) were discarded, the class differences remained. The concept of passing became an important heuristic for understanding the experience of a working-class woman who grew up trying to hide her lower status by imitating the prestige and status markers of the middle class. Similarly, Penelope noted the importance of recognizing seemingly mundane class indices when she introduced *Out of the class closet: Lesbians speak* in 1994 with the observation that the "events and objects that initiate our explorations of class and its effects in our lives need not be large or important. It may be something that others regard as insignificant: toothpaste, toilet paper, the kind of plates we eat on, whether our last meal of the day, if we have one, is called *dinner* or *supper*, if our family can afford to *'stock up'*" (p. 42). Those early experiences endure and continue to define a woman even when she moves out of poverty or working class through education and career advancement.

One early experiential attempt to articulate and conceptualize those early experiences was developed by Califia Community. Califia, established in 1976, was "committed to the development of a multicultural community of the spirit of women through feminist education" (Murphy, 1983, p. 139). Marilyn Murphy, a primary organizer of Califia, was a writer and activist, now retired. Issues of sexism, racism, heterosexism, ableism and classism were addressed didactically and experientially. The "Passing Game" developed by Mary Glavin (a working class woman who earned her PhD) was a centerpiece of the experience. Ahshe Green wrote the introductory lecture which was later revised by Marilyn Murphy and titled, *"Did your mother do volunteer work?"* The lecture included a critique of the function of class within American society: The function of the ruling class is to determine policy, the middle class to enforce the rules. Similarly, she critiqued the women's movement for a similar hierarchy and values and noted the difference in communication styles.

> Women raised in crowds know how to talk loud, to yell when necessary. We learn to follow more than one conversation at a time, interrupt in order to get our two cents in. We communicate with our hands and faces too. Our language tends to be colorful and descriptive. We express ourselves differently than women who grew up in large homes, where children have their own rooms, where conversations can take place in various rooms, where the families are small and nuclear, where individuals are not competing for at-

tention. These differences are interesting. They need not be oppressive in our groups or in our love and friendship relationships. (p. 6)

Murphy discussed various ways a working-class woman might act out feelings about money through compulsive spending, deprivation within a context of plenty, sharing and compulsive saving. Education vs. intelligence, articulation and grammar, relationships within and across class divides, emotional vs. material support, scarcity and abundance work habits, and privilege and oppression were topics addressed within the introduction.

Nancy Lynn Baker has been a consistent voice in the community of feminist therapists on the topic of class. Baker, who now is in independent practice as a forensic and clinical psychologist in the Bay Area, and who served as a psychologist for the Lost Angeles County Sheriff's Department for many years, came to graduate study in psychology from the factory floor and years as a union organizer. Baker asserts that unlike gender or race, which are unchangeable, class is at least partially defined by occupation.

> Becoming a psychologist or a psychotherapist does not prevent one from remaining a person of color or a woman. . . . But obtaining the privilege and the tools to participate in the intellectual discourse of theory construction and critique, especially in the U.S. which lacks a tradition of working-class intellectuals, almost simultaneously separates a person from membership in the working-class. One may be from the working-class, or even attempt to work in the interests of the working-class, but as a therapist or psychologist one's relations to the world and the world of work are fundamentally different. (p. 16)

Baker goes on to critique the lack of class definition in feminist theory. Even more importantly she notes that critical constructs, for instance "physical vs. mental labor" have not been identified to adequately reflect class experience beyond income. The lack of theory-building research is particularly problematic when ignorance about the real lives of working-class women may lead to inappropriate interventions with clients. Baker illustrates this point by noting that a middle-class therapist might encourage a woman to report sexual harassment, which in some occupations (law enforcement for instance) could put her in physical danger.

Rather, "therapy with women who have been harassed needs to include a reality-based analysis of all options" (p. 20).

Beyond specific experiences, Baker addresses the importance of the client's perception or meaning of the experience, which is "concretized in values and perspective" (p. 20). Baker notes the danger that a therapist may project her professional middle class values on the client. She may erroneously assume that empowering a client will mean that the client will want to move out of her working-class circumstances and adopt values of the middle class. By seeing class as a stratification construct, there is an inherent continuum of worth and an assumption that women should want to move "upward."

The fact that a therapist from a working-class background has made that "upward" move and presumably adopted a lifestyle that made it possible for her to accomplish that move, has implications for how she views her clients. Baker's answer is to resist the tendency to see class as a stratification category. Instead, she argues for the use of feminist cross-cultural therapy models that are grounded in awareness of our socially constructed values. By discovering the richness of our client's socially constructed meanings of their class locations we can add to theory-building that will reflect the diversity of women including their experiences of class.

Therapists must also consider the intersection between race and class as an area for further consideration. Karen Wyche, a professor of psychology at the University of Miami, has specifically addressed this intersection. She notes (1996) that in addition to the added economic discrimination, an African American woman is likely to continue identifying her class status as working-class even when she is affluent. This may be due in part to the sense of new wealth that may not include cash assets.

## VOICES OF WORKING-CLASS WOMEN

Many collections of narratives from working-class women have been published primarily in women's studies literature. While no one name stands out as distinctive among these authors, all of these contributions, because they are still rare, themselves stand out. These have included voices from working-class girls in a longitudinal psychoanalytic qualitative study (Walkerdine, Lucy & Melody, 2001), from working-class lesbians (Penelope, 1994), from women in academia (Dews & Law, 1995; Tokarczyk & Fay, 1993), from women in the workplace (Johnson, 2002) and from working-class women of color (hooks, 2000). As noted by Walkerdine et al. (2001), "class is at once profoundly social and profoundly emotional, lived in its specificity in particular cultural and geographic locations" (p. 53). It is not surprising that much of the literature on working-class women is largely descriptive rather than theoretical. Hill (1996) notes, "Class and classism is in the position that gender and sexism was in thirty years ago: denied, surrounded with myth, and silenced. Class is complicated and difficult, but the first problem with class is that we don't talk about it. We can't afford that kind of silence" (p. 5).

The difficulties we encountered in attempting to find definitive feminist voices on social class indicates that "that kind of silence" persists within feminist therapy theory, and perhaps in practice as well. Class, particularly working-class status, remains little attended-to.

## CONCLUSIONS AND FUTURE DIRECTIONS

One of the enormous challenges inherent in writing this article was that of limiting ourselves to the topics and authors that we discussed. Feminist therapists and theorists have made important contributions to the discourse on human difference, recentering marginalized experiences and calling into question dominant psychological models for understanding people on the margins. We have also re-discovered the depth and creativity of feminists' writing about these variables of diversity; feminist theorists have not simply started the discussions, but have expanded awareness for all therapists.

Yet there is work to be done by the bulk of feminist therapy theorists and practitioners. This work, while prodigious, is not in the mainstream of feminist therapy yet. The mere fact that it was deceptively easy to identify the one or two major contributors to each topic within the feminist discourse on difference beyond ethnicity and "race" communicates something important about future directions emerging from the work reviewed in this chapter.

Each of the authors we have discussed here has made a palpable impact on feminist theory. Yet with the exception of the work on sexual orientation, each of these authors remains almost singular. Other feminist therapists and theorists do not appear to have picked up the threads woven by these women and integrated them into the core of feminist practice. Many of these authors are rarely cited in the feminist practice literature; again, the striking exception to this trend can be found in work on sexual orientation.

This body of work argues for a rededication among feminist therapy theorists and practitioners to the concept that "woman" is a multi-faceted phenomenon. One important lesson emanating from the writings of these authors is that the complexity of women's identities, social locations, and biopsychosocial contexts must be affirmatively embraced. Age, social class, sexual orientation, disability, and immigration status are all experiences that intersect with and redefine the meanings of gender. The work of multicultural feminist author Pamela Hays (2001) offers an excellent paradigm for conceptualizing identities that reflects the focuses of this chapter. Her ADDRESSING model (*A*ge, *D*isabilities, *R*ace/*E*thnicity, *S*ocial Class, *S*exual Orientation, *I*ndigenous heritage, *N*ational origin, *G*ender) argues for seeing all people within a framework of intersecting experiences and target group memberships. The authors we review here offer strong feminist grounding for our understanding of those factors (e.g., everything except gender) that feminists have not routinely included in our theorizing.

The conflicts among and between women are also highlighted by the work we have reviewed. Asch's discussion of the tensions inherent in reproductive rights arguments that are founded on the devaluing of potential disabled lives, and Murphy's analysis of the hidden wounds of class in women's relationships are both examples of this sort of conflict. Perhaps as a corrective to millennia of internalized misogyny that disrupted women's relationships, much feminist work to date has focused on women's bonds and connections, even across difference. The authors we review here ask feminist practitioners to create space for uncomfortable difference, perhaps unresolvable differences, between one woman and another. We are challenged, as Siegel (1990d) suggested, to find our unity in the things that divide us, not simply in our common biology.

This work also creates the opportunity for feminist therapists and theorists to explore our definitions and epistemic strategies. What do we mean, after all, when we as feminists speak of social class? Since the economic realities that create class locations and class consciousness are in a continuous state of transformation in the U.S. and elsewhere, how can feminist thinkers generate concepts of class that reflect women's lived experiences? How can feminist theorists and therapists become more actively engaged in knowing about the lives of migrant and immigrant women? As a younger generation of non-heterosexual women are creating their own language and self-definitions, often in reaction to feminist theories of lesbianism, where if at all does feminist practice have a place?

This call to expand the range of feminist practice and to vision women's lives in a fuller and more complex manner is not a new one. The quality and depth found in the work of the authors who we have reviewed makes it imperative for feminist theorists and therapists to be either more inclusive in their future work, or more willing to delineate the restrictions on the generalizability of what they write or say or do. The future holds the promise of a truly multicultural feminist theory.

## REFERENCES

Aron, A. (1992). Testimonio, a bridge between psychotherapy and sociotherapy. *Women & Therapy, 13* (3), 173-189.

Aron, A., Corne, S., Fursland, A. & Zelwer, B. (1991). The gender-specific terror of El Salvador and Guatemala: Post-traumatic stress disorder in Central American refugee women. *Women's Studies International Forum, 14*, 37-47.

Asch, A. (1984a). Personal reflections. *American Psychologist, 39*, 551-552.

Asch, A. (1984b). The experience of disability: A challenge for psychology. *American Psychologist, 39*, 529-536.

Asch, A. (1989). Reproductive technology and disability. In S. Cohen & N. Taub (Eds.), *Reproductive laws for the 1990s* (pp. 69-124). Clifton, NJ: Humana Press.

Asch, A. (1990). Surrogacy and the family: Social and value considerations. In D. Bartels, R. Priester, D. Vawter, & A. Caplan (Eds.), *Beyond Baby M: Ethical issues in new reproductive techniques* (pp. 243-259). Clifton, NJ: Humana Press.

Asch, A. (1995). Some thoughts for practicing bioethics: Extending the feminist critique. In M. Grodin (Ed.), *Meta medical ethics: The philosophical foundations of bioethics* (pp. 149-155). Boston, MA: Kluwer Academic.

Asch, A. (1997). Women with disabilities: What do we know? What must we learn? *Journal of Disability Policy Studies, 8*, 239-242.

Asch, A. & Fine, M. (1984). Shared dreams: A left perspective on disability rights and reproductive rights. *Radical America, 18*, 51-58.

Asch, A. & Fine, M. (1986). Women and disability: Setting an agenda. *Disability Studies Ouarterly, 6*, 1-2.

Asch, A. & Fine, M. (1988). Introduction: Beyond pedestals. In M. Fine & A. Asch (Eds.), *Women with disabilities: Essays in psychology, culture and politics* (pp. 1-37). Philadelphia: Temple University Press.

Asch, A. & Geller, G. (1996). Feminism, bioethics and genetics. In S.M. Wolf (Ed.), *Feminism and bioethics: Beyond reproduction* (pp. 318-350). New York: Oxford University Press.

Asch, A. et al. (1984). *Building community: A manual exploring issues of women and disability.* New York: Educational Equity Concepts, Inc.

Asch, A. & Rousso, H. (1985). Therapists with disabilities: Theoretical and clinical issues. *Psychiatry, 48,* 1-12.

Asch, A. & Sacks, L. (1983). Lives without, lives within: Autobiographies of blind women and men. *Journal of Visual Impairment and Blindness, 77,* 242-247.

Baker, N. L. (1996). Class as a construct in a 'classless' society. In M. Hill & E.D. Rothblum (Eds.) *Classism and feminist therapy: Counting costs* (pp. 13-23). New York: Harrington Park Press.

Ballou, M. (1990). Approaching a feminist-principled paradigm in the construction of personality theory. In L.S. Brown & M. P. P. Root (Eds.) *Diversity and complexity in feminist therapy* (pp 23-40). New York: Haworth.

Barshay, J. (1993). Another strand of our diversity: Some thoughts from a feminist therapist with severe chronic illness. *Women & Therapy, 14,* 159-170.

Belle, D. (1990). Poverty and women's mental health. *American Psychologist. 45,* 385-389.

Belle, D., Doucet, J., Harris, J., Miller, J., & Tan., E. (2000). Who is rich? Who is happy? *American Psychologist. 55,* 1160-1161.

Brabeck, M. (Ed.) (1999). *Practicing feminist ethics in psychology.* Washington DC: American Psychological Association.

Bragg, M., Dalton, R.D., Dunker, B., Fisher, P., Garcia, N., Obler, L. K., Orwoll, L., Paiser, P., & Pearlman, S.F. (Boston lesbian psychologies collective) (Eds.) (1987). *Lesbian psychologies: Explorations and challenges.* Chicago IL: U. of Illinois Press.

Brown, L.S. (1989). New voices, new visions: Toward a lesbian/gay paradigm for psychology. *Psychology of Women Quarterly, 13,* 445-458.

Brown, L.S. (1992). Until the revolution comes: Towards a lesbian feminist psychotherapy. *Feminism and Psychology, 2,* 239-254.

Brown, L.S. (1994). *Subversive dialogues: Theory in feminist therapy.* New York: Basic.

Brown, L.S. (1995). Lesbian identities: Concepts and issues. In a. D'Augelli & C. Patterson (Eds.) *Lesbian, gay and bisexual identities over the lifespan.* (pp. 3-23) New York: Oxford University Press.

Brown, L.S. (1996). Preventing heterosexism and bias in psychotherapy. In E.D. Rothblum & L.A. Bond (Eds.) *Preventing heterosexism and homophobia.* (pp. 36-58). Thousand Oaks CA: Sage.

Brown, L.S. (1999). Dangerousness, impotence, silence and invisibility: Heterosexism in the construction of women's sexuality. In C. B. Travis & J. W. White (Eds.) *Sexuality, society, and feminism.* (pp. 273-298). Washington DC: American Psychological Association.

Brown, L.S. & Root, M. P. P. (Eds.) *Diversity and complexity in feminist therapy.* New York: Haworth.

Brown, R.M. (1974). The last straw. In C. Bunch & N. Myron (Eds.) *Class and Feminism* (pp. 13-23). Baltimore: Diana Press.

Bunch, C. & Myron, N. (Eds.) (1974). *Class and Feminism.* Baltimore MD: Diana Press.

Datan, N. (1986). Corpses, lepers, and menstruating women: Tradition, transition, and the sociology of knowledge. *Sex Roles, 14,* 693-703.

Datan, N., Antonovsky, A. & Maoz, B. (1981). *A time to reap: The middle age of women in five Israeli subcultures.* Baltimore: Johns Hopkins University Press.

Dews, C. L. & Law, C. L. (Eds.). (1995). *This fine place so far from home: Voices of academics from the working-class.* Philadelphia: Temple University

Espin, O.M. (1987). Psychological impact of migration on Latinas: Implications for psychotherapeutic practice. *Psychology of Women Quarterly, 11,* 489-503.

Espin, O.M. (1992). Roots uprooted: The psychological impact of historical/political dislocation. *Women & Therapy, 13,* 9-20.

Espin, O.M. (1993). Giving voice to silence: The psychologist as witness. *American Psychologist, 48,* 408-414.

Espin, O.M. (1995). "Race," racism, and sexuality in the life narratives of immigrant women. *Feminism and Psychology, 5,* 223-238.

Espin, O.M. (1996). Leaving the nation and joining the tribe: Lesbian immigrants crossing geographical and identity borders. *Women & Therapy, 19,* 99-107.

Fine, M., & Asch, A. (1981). Disabled women: Sexism without the pedestal. *Journal of Sociology and Social Welfare, 8,* 233-248.

Fine, M., & Asch, A. (1982). The question of disability: No easy answers for the women's movement. *Reproductive Rights National Newsletter, 4,* 19-20.

Fine, M., & Asch, A. (1984). Amniocentesis, treatment of newborns with disabilities and women's choices. *CARASA News, 8,* 2-6.

Fine, M. & Asch, A. (Eds.) (1988). Women with disabilities: Essays in psychology, culture, and politics. Philadelphia: Temple University Press.

Firestein, B.A. (1996). Bisexuality: The psychology and politics of an invisible minority. Thousand Oaks CA: Sage.

Giesen, C.B. & Datan, N. (1980). The competent older woman. In N. Datan & N. Lohmann, (Eds.), *Transitions of aging: Proceedings of the West Virginia University gerontology conference.* New York: Academic Press.

Goodenow, C. & Espin, O.M. (1993). Identity choices in immigrant adolescent females. *Adolescence, 28,* 12-31.

Greene, B. (1986). When the therapist is white and the patient is Black: Considerations for psychotherapy in the feminist heterosexual and lesbian communities. *Women & Therapy, 5,* 41-65.

Greene, B. *(1993). Human diversity in clinical psychology: Lesbian and gay sexual orientations.* The Clinical Psychologist: Publication of the Division of Clinical *Psychology of the American Psychological Association, 46,* 74-82.

Greene, B. (1994a). Ethnic minority lesbians and gay men: Mental health and treatment issues. *Journal of Consulting & Clinical Psychology, 62,* 243-251.

Greene, B. (1994b). Lesbian women of color. In L. Comas-Diaz & B. Greene (Eds.), *Women of color* (pp. 389-427). New York: Guilford.

Greene, B. (1995). Addressing racism, sexism and heterosexism in psychodynamic psychotherapy. In J. Glassgold & S. Iasenza (Eds.), *Lesbians and psychoanalysis: Revolutions in theory and practice* (pp. 145-159). New York: Free Press.

Greene, B. (1997a). Lesbian women of color: Triple jeopardy. *Journal of Lesbian Studies-Special issue: Classics in Lesbian Studies, 1*, 49-60

Greene, B. (Ed.). (1997b). *Psychological perspectives on lesbian and gay issues Vol. 3: Ethnic and cultural diversity among lesbians and gay men.* Thousand Oaks, CA: Sage.

Greene, B. (1998a). Ethnic identity and family dynamics: African American lesbians and gay men. In C. Patterson & A. D'Augelli (Eds.), *Lesbian, gay and bisexual identity: Psychological research and social policy (*pp. 40-52). New York: Oxford University Press.

Greene, B. (1998b). Stereotypes and erroneous presumptions: Barriers to effective practice with lesbian and gay patients of color. *(Special Issue) Medical Encounter: A Publication of the American Academy on Physician and Patient, 14*, 15-17.

Greene, B. (2000a). African American lesbian and bisexual women. *Journal of Social Issues, 56*, 239-249.

Greene, B. (2002). Older lesbians' concerns in psychotherapy: Beyond a footnote to the footnote. In F. Trotman & C. Brody (Eds.), *Women therapists working with older women: Cross cultural family and end of life issues* (pp.161-174). New York: Springer.

Greene, B. (2000b). African American Lesbian and Bisexual Women in feminist-psychodynamic psychotherapy: Surviving and thriving between a rock and a hard place. In L. Jackson & B. Greene (Eds.), *Psychotherapy with African American women: Innovations in Psychodynamic perspectives and practice* (pp. 82-125). New York: Guilford Publications.

Greene, B. (In press- a). Heterosexism and internalized racism among African Americans: The connections and considerations for African American lesbians and bisexual women. A clinical psychological perspective. *Rutgers University Law Review,54,4 LatCrit Symposium VI.*

Greene, B. (In press -b). African American lesbians and other culturally diverse people in psychodynamic psychotherapies: Useful paradigm or oxymoron? *Journal of Lesbian Studies-An Update on Psychoanalysis and Lesbians.*

Greene, B., & Boyd-Franklin, N. (1996). African American lesbian couples: Ethnocultural considerations in psychotherapy. *Women & Therapy, 19*, 53-64.

Greene, B. & Croom, G. L. (Eds.). (2000). *Psychological perspectives on lesbian, gay and bisexual issues Vol. 5: Education, Practice and Research in Lesbian, Gay, Bisexual and Transgendered Psychology: A Resource Manual.* Thousand Oaks, CA: Sage.

Hall, M. (1991). Ex-therapy to sex therapy: Notes from the margins. In C. Silverstein, (Ed.) *Gays, lesbians and their therapists.* (pp. 84-97). New York: W.W. Norton.

Hall, M. (1993). Why limit me to ecstasy? Toward a positive model of genital incidentalism among friends and other lovers. In E. Rothblum and K. Brehony, (Eds.) *Boston marriages: Romantic but asexual relationships among contemporary lesbians* (pp. 41-61). Amherst MA: U. of Massachusetts Press.

Hall, M. (1995a). Clit notes. In K. Jay (Ed.) *Dyke life: From growing up to growing old, a celebration of the lesbian experience* (pp. 195-215). New York: Basic Books.

Hall, M. (1995b). Not tonight dear, I'm deconstructing a headache: Confessions of a lesbian sex therapist. In K. Jay (Ed.) *Lesbian erotics.* (pp. 15-27). New York: NYU Press.

Hall, M. (1996). Unsexing the couple. *Women & Therapy, 19,* 12-25.

Hall, R. L. & Greene, B. (2002). Not any one thing: The complex legacy of social class on African American Lesbians' Relationships. *Journal of Lesbian Studies, 6,* 65-74.

Hare-Mustin, R. & Marecek, J. (1990). *Making a difference: Psychology and the construction of gender.* New Haven: Yale University Press.

Hays, P. (2001). *Addressing cultural multicultural complexities in practice: A framework for clinicians and counselors.* Washington DC: American Psychological Association.

Healey, S. (1991) Growing to be an old woman: Aging and ageism. In J. Alexander, D. Berrow, L. Domitrovich, M. Donnelly & C. McLean (Eds.) *Women and aging: An anthology by women.* Corvallis OR: Calyx Books.

Healy, S. (1993). The common agenda between old women, women with disabilities, and all women. *Women & Therapy, 14,* 65-77.

Healey, S. (1994) Diversity with a difference: On being old and lesbian. *Journal of Gay and Lesbian Social Service, 1,* 109-117.

Healey, S. (1999). *Untitled Keynote Speech.* Old Lesbians Organizing for Change conference, San Diego CA.

Hill, M. & Rothblum, E. D. (Eds.) (1996). *Classism and feminist therapy: Counting costs.* New York: Harrington Park Press.

hooks, b. (2000). *Where we stand: Class Matters.* New York: Routledge.

Johnson, J. (2002). *Getting by on the minimum: The lives of working-class women.* New York: Routledge.

Lerman, H. (1987). *A mote in Freud's eye.* New York: Springer.

Lott, B. (2001). Low income parents and the public schools. *Journal of social issues, 57,* 247-259.

Lott, B. (2002). Cognitive and behavioral distancing from the poor. *American Psychologist, 57,* 100-110.

Lott, B. (2003). Psychologists and the disruption of classism. *American Psychologist, 58,* p. 145.

Lott, B. & Saxon, S. (2002). The influence of ethnicity, social class and context on judgments about U.S. women. *Journal of Social Psychology, 142,* 481-499.

Mairs, N. (1995). *Remembering the bone house: An erotics of space and place.* Boston: Beacon.

Mairs, N. (1996). *Carnal acts.* Boston: Beacon

Mairs, N. (1998). *Waist high in the world: A life among the nondisabled.* Boston: Beacon.

Marecek, J. (2002). Post-modern feminism in personality psychology. In M. Ballou & L.S. Brown (Eds.). *Rethinking mental health and disorder: Feminist perspectives* (pp. 3-28). New York: Guilford.

McBryde Johnson, H. (2003). Unspeakable conversations. *New York Times Sunday Magazine,* February 16, 2003.

Murphy, M. (1983). Califia community. In C. Bunch & S. Pollack (Eds.) *Learning our way: Essays in feminist education* (pp. 138-153). New York: Crossing Press.

Murphy, M. (n.d.) *Did your mother do volunteer work?* Unpublished manuscript.

Myron, N. (1974). Class beginnings. In C. Bunch & N. Myron, (Eds.) *Class and Feminism* (pp. 36-41). Baltimore: Diana Press.

Olkin, R. (1999). *What psychotherapists should know about disability.* New York: Guilford.

Olkin, R. (2003). Women with physical disabilities who want to leave their partners: A feminist and disability-affirmative perspective. *Women & Therapy, 23,* 237-246.

Olkin, R. (In press). Women with disabilities. In J. C. Chrisler, C. Golden, & P. D. Rozee (Eds.), *Lectures on the psychology of women (3$^{rd}$ ed.).* New York: McGraw-Hill.

Penelope, J. (1994). Class and consciousness. In J. Penelope (Ed.) *Out of the class closet: Lesbians speak* (pp. 2-15). Freedom, CA: Crossing Press.

Rodeheaver, D. & Datan, N. (1988). The challenge of double jeopardy: Toward a mental health agenda for aging women. *American Psychologist, 43,* 648-654.

Sennett, R. & Cobb, J. (1973). *The hidden injuries of class.* New York: Vintage.

Siegel, R.J. (1982). A midlife journey from housewife to psychotherapist. *Voices: The Art and Science of Psychotherapy, 18,* 29-33.

Siegel, R.J. (1983). Change and creativity at midlife. In Robbins, J.H. & Siegel, R.J. (Eds.), *Women changing therapy: New assessments, values, and strategies in feminist therapy.* New York: Haworth.

Siegel, R.J. (1990a). Old women as mother figures: Ageism and mother blaming. In E. Cole and J. Knowles (Eds.), *Woman defined motherhood* (pp. 89-97). New York: Haworth.

Siegel, R.J. (1990b). Love and work after 60: An integration of personal and professional growth within a long-term marriage. In E. Rosenthal (Ed.) *Women, aging and ageism* (pp. 69-79). New York: Haworth.

Siegel, R.J. (1990c). We are not your mothers: Report on two groups for women over sixty. In E. Rosenthal (Ed.) *Women, aging and ageism* (pp. 81-89). New York: Haworth.

Siegel, R. J. (1990d). Turning the things that divide us into the strengths that unite us. In L. S. Brown & M. P. P. Root (Eds.) *Diversity and complexity in feminist therapy* (pp. 327-336). New York: Haworth.

Siegel, R.J. (1993). Between midlife and old age: Never too old to learn. In N.D. Davis, E. Cole & E.D. Rothblum (Eds.), *Faces of women and aging.* (pp. 173-181). New York: Haworth.

Siegel, R.J. & Sonderegger, T. B. (1990). Ethical considerations in feminist psychotherapy with women over sixty. In H. Lerman & N. Porter (Eds.), *Feminist ethics in psychotherapy* (pp. 176-184). New York: Springer.

Sonderegger, T. B. & Siegel, R.J. (1995). Conflicts in care: Later years of the lifespan. In E. J. Rave & C. C. Larsen (Eds.), *Ethical decision making in therapy: Feminist perspectives* (pp. 223-246). New York: Guilford.

Tokarczyk, M. M. & Fay, E. A. (Eds.). (1993). *Working-class women in the academy: Laborers in the knowledge factory.* Amherst, MA: University of Massachusetts.

Van Boemel, G.B. & Rozee, P.D. (1992). Treatment for psychosomatic blindness among Cambodian refugee women. *Women & Therapy, 13,* 239-266.

Walkerdine, V., Lucey, H., & Melody, J. (2001). *Growing up girl: Psychosocial explorations of gender and class.* New York: New York University Press.

Wyche, K.F. (1996). Conceptualizations of social class in African American women: Congruence of client and therapist definitions. In Hill, M. & Rothblum, E.D. (Eds.) *Classism and feminist therapy: Counting costs* (pp. 35-43). New York: Harrington Park Press.

# The Map of Relational-Cultural Theory

Carolyn K. West

**SUMMARY.** Psychological theory-building has long been dominated by White, European-male perspectives, perspectives that fail to account for the multifaceted experiences of diverse and marginalized populations. Feminist theory seeks to explore, encompass, and understand the wide range of human experience, a territory that is viewed as broad and complex and dynamic. Relational-Cultural Theory as it addresses the critical importance of relational exchange related to development and health provides an elaboration of some of the most basic feminist principles. Perhaps not surprisingly, this evolving theoretical model has emerged out of the relational work of five women and continues now within an ever-expanding and diverse network of women. This paper will present several elements of this work, its relevance to the larger work of feminist theory, and some of the major contributions of the founding "Monday Night Group." *[Article copies available for a fee from The Haworth Document Delivery Service: 1-800-HAWORTH. E-mail address: <docdelivery@haworthpress.com> Website: <http://www.HaworthPress.com> © 2005 by The Haworth Press, Inc. All rights reserved.]*

Carolyn K. West is a senior lecturer in the School of Arts and Sciences at Western New England College and has a private practice in South Hadley, MA.

Address correspondence to: Carolyn K. West, 29 College Street, South Hadley, MA 01075.

[Haworth co-indexing entry note]: "The Map of Relational-Cultural Theory." West, Carolyn K. Co-published simultaneously in *Women & Therapy* (The Haworth Press, Inc.) Vol. 28, No. 3/4, 2005, pp. 93-110; and: *The Foundation and Future of Feminist Therapy* (ed: Marcia Hill, and Mary Ballou) The Haworth Press, Inc., 2005, pp. 93-110. Single or multiple copies of this article are available for a fee from The Haworth Document Delivery Service [1-800-HAWORTH, 9:00 a.m. - 5:00 p.m. (EST). E-mail address: docdelivery@haworthpress.com].

http://www.haworthpress.com/web/WT
© 2005 by The Haworth Press, Inc. All rights reserved.
doi:10.1300/J015v28n03_05

**KEYWORDS.** Relational-Cultural Theory, psychological language, power, 5 good things, relational empathy, women's experience, connection, disconnection, being-in-relationship, mutuality

From the very beginning of psychological inquiry and practice there has been an attempt to capture and understand experience by building theory–theory that would explain development and delineate developmental stages and that, elaborated, could provide a framework for understanding development gone awry. This is certainly a worthy objective, and its attainment would potentially yield complimentary treatises regarding support and assistance and even prevention. What seemed to be either assumed or overlooked, however, was the question of whose experience, exactly, and whose development and under what conditions?

Early theories addressed the individual, observed from a clinical distance, excised from context, specimen-like in study, pathology-driven in practice, male-dominated in interpretation–a sort of "this is your experience and I will tell you about it" approach. Gradually, some developmental theorists such as Klein (1975), Winnicott (1958), and Fairbairn (1963) recognized interactional factors and a kind of universal species of relationship advanced into consideration. As the name suggests, Object *Relation* theory examined the influence of an other, albeit one who was stripped of context and seemed as two dimensional as the print that described her.

In this article, I wish to address more recent theory that not only incorporates the notion of relationship, but is built on it–relationship viewed as a vibrant, central, and multi-dimensioned feature of development. And, in particular, I intend to examine ways in which Relational-Cultural theorists have contributed to feminist theory building. Specifically, I will examine Relational-Cultural Theory as it addresses the foundational feminist principles related to experience and the experiences of all women, to issues of language and its importance in theory-building, to power as it interfaces with relationship, and to the imperative of feminist practice to address social change. The ideas represented here will be discussed largely within the context of the founding group of Relational-Cultural theorists including Jean Baker Miller, Alexandra Kaplan, Judith Jordan, Irene Stiver, and Janet Surrey. However, as I intend to describe, the nature of the theory holds implicit that there are many contributing voices–some informing and affirming of early thinking, others contributing directly and more recently to Relational-Cultural Theory, and, given the nature of the work, many contributions yet to be heard.

While the aforementioned theories of development emerging out of patriarchal vision and thinking seemed to establish and delimit "truth," making it neater in some ways, more sterile, more structured and lock-step, such constraints denied or failed to consider what did not fit, and alternatively, ignored or pathologized it. Indeed, these former theoretical models mirrored a style of thinking that Stephanie Riger (1992) describes as marked by "distance, power, and control." She cites Evelyn Fox Keller in suggesting an alternative methodology based "not on controlling but on 'conversing' with nature." Immediately one senses reciprocity, an exchange, an interaction . . . a relationship.

What I find particularly remarkable and appealing about feminist theory is that it is expansive rather than constrictive, a territory of inquiry much more vast than any single theory, a landscape holding many ideas and many truths. Its questions allow ambiguity, entertain difference, invite reflection, and encourage investigation into new perspectives without being reductionist, without needing to dismiss, edge out, or shout down. This allowing, it seems to me, this ability to stay open in the face of ambiguity, provides the space for a transformative process that is akin to the very nature of development itself. After all, what is being investigated is a process, and would seem best represented by a model that is, itself, flexible and receptive to change.

Indeed, perhaps because it arises out of an historical experience of being labeled and categorized and, to use Carol Tavris's (1992) term, "mismeasured," the process of building feminist theory rests on listening and considering-honestly, intelligently, and respectfully. This is not to suggest an atmosphere of polite agreement, as debate within the community is, has been, and hopefully will continue to be lively, pointed, fresh, and stimulating. But it is to suggest that carefully attended to, the contribution of many voices has the potential to invoke counterpoint rather than cacophony. In their writing, a working group involved in delineating the defining principles of feminist theory and practice, uses phrases such as "the joy of the process"; "the energy of the women"; and "the pleasure of honest, open thinking about ideas that define who we are" to describe this active, productive engagement (Brabeck et al., 1997).

The working image that comes to mind for me in thinking about feminist theory is one of a large map. This map represents an infinitely intriguing and rich territory too long rendered invisible, ignored or misrepresented. While there are certain elemental guideposts which are critical to its exploration, its boundaries are quite flexible and fluid and many perspectives are required to comprehend and appreciate its terrain. These multiple perspectives–the developing theories–can be envisioned as a series of transparent overlays. Each overlay, each perspective, is uniquely important in its own right; and at the same time each contributes a fuller topography to the map–one atop another, atop another–none singularly whole, separate, static, or competing, but each illuminating, overlapping, providing nuance and texture and expansion, and all together shifting the entire theoretical landscape toward a richer, more thorough understanding of women's–of human–experience.

Some of the ways in which Relational-Cultural Theory contributes to and enhances this map are evident by noting several of its foundational elements and how these in theory and practice embody and carry forward feminist therapy principles. So if the territorial map is feminist theory and the transparent overlay is Relational-Cultural Theory, one point of contact and overlap, a point where Relational Cultural theory helps to clarify and inform, is that of the valuing of experience. Indeed, the kernels from which this theory emerged were sown from the practice of women listening to women, empathically and over time.

My own theoretical acquaintance with this principle came from Carol Gilligan's *In a Different Voice* (1982) as well as from the work of Belenky, Clinchy, Goldberger and Tarule (1986). Some of these early works evoked not only resonance, but energized criticism and debate. At the same time they served to highlight the very basic notion that the individual, rather than a distanced "objective" other, is the best authority on her own experience. Working in the reverse and substituting a theoretical stage model as the authority not only denied the experience of individual women, a practice that Hannah Lerman (1996) calls the "pigeonholing of women's miseries," but truncated any potential for actually learning more.

It is also important to note that those women initially responsible for developing Relational-Cultural Theory respectfully acknowledge the contribution and influence of, among others, Gilligan and her colleagues and Belenky et al. "For a long time now Carol Gilligan's work has played a special part in our endeavors" (Miller & Stiver, 1997, p. x).

> Gilligan's analysis of the centrality of connection in women's sense of self shows how profoundly this basic experience of connection affects women's ways of approaching relational conflicts and crises. . . . The studies with girls as well as with women which Gilligan and women working with her have undertaken and the

continuing attention of this group to voice and language as integral to the understanding of psychological processes make their work centrally important to our understanding of women's development and to the development of a relational psychology. (Jordan, Kaplan, Miller, Stiver & Surrey, 1992, p. 3)

In acknowledging the influence of Belenky et al. (1986), these authors write "[they have] enhanced our understanding of women's special and different ways of knowing, in particular 'connected knowing'" (p. 3).

## *JORDAN, KAPLAN, MILLER, STIVER, AND SURREY*

It seems illustrative that Relational-Cultural Theory emerged out of the relationship of five women–all skilled practitioners, all seeking a better understanding of their work and experience through their relationships with one another. This core group including Judith Jordan, Alexandra Kaplan, Jean Baker Miller, Irene Stiver, and Janet Surrey began meeting in what they called the "Monday Night Group" in 1977. Inspired by the ideas of feminist writers, these women did not initially have theory-making as the group's purpose or goal. Yet, it was within these ongoing exchanges that the centrality of relationships in development, in health, and in psychological distress emerged.

So from feminist practitioners paying attention to experience-to the experiences of women as told in therapy, to the experiences and ideas of one another, and to those of other feminist writers–a new model began to take shape. This was theory built from the ground up. Rather than categorizing based on extant theory, the stories of women's lives being told and listened to in therapy provided a grammar of sorts, a way in which details related to the whole, and this grammar continues to echo across the many ways in which women define themselves.

It seems interesting, too, that Relational-Cultural Theory appears both to reflect and to be reflected by the process that created it. It was relationship, among five women in the beginning, and now among many women of diverse backgrounds and identities, that has provided the space for hearing and being heard, for thinking and learning, for connection and disconnection, and for growth and development.

What is also intrinsic to feminist theory, another of its guideposts, is that it should be sufficiently complex to hold not just the experience of the dominant group, but the experience of *all* women. Who we are and the context in which we function affects not only what we know, but how we come to know it. "A feminist theory of practice recognizes that any theory that does not acknowledge the diversity of experiences is greatly limited in its validity and usefulness" (Brabeck et al., 1997, p. 25).

These ideas, relatively new in the history of psychology, challenge the mythology of the value-free, objective scientist and the omniscient theorist. One of the criticisms of Relational-Cultural Theory as it evolved alongside the larger map of feminist theory, was that its early writings potentially shifted the dominant paradigm to another dominant paradigm. The need to understand oppression beyond the locus of gender is expressed unambiguously by Brabeck et al. (1997):

> One of the most problematic aspects of feminist practice in the past two decades has been the centrality of White women's voices in defining the categories and meanings of feminist analyses. Internalized domination has led many women to exclude the experiences of those for whom ethnicity, class, culture, sexual orientation, age, spiritual practice, and ability are the most salient aspects of their experience of oppression and liberation. (p. 25)

To have experienced and felt the damaging effects of exclusion and fail to be inclusive could be to merely substitute one paradigmatic caricature for another.

Yet as their work expanded and developed, "the theory group" as the initiators of Relational-Cultural Theory came to be known to their colleagues, continued to explore their own experience, in the process encountering the limitations of their own knowing as privileged white women. As is central to a feminist method, these women have worked and work to be clear about what elements of experience they are able to speak to with authority and they take care not to extrapolate their findings to all people or even to all women. They have engaged in ongoing inquiry into their own values and assumptions in order that they could be maximally open to the experiences of others.

In the introduction to a 1992 volume of writings from the Stone Center (Jordan et al.) the authors address the issue of voice and inclusion:

> It is especially important, in carving out a perspective on relational empowerment, to incorporate the patterns of relationship that exist with those who are marginalized by the dominant culture. Without this, there is no way that we can speak for all women. We do not want to repeat the error of other theoreticians: speaking as if there is one voice, one reality for humans, for women, when in fact we

recognize the exquisite contextuality of human life. We regret the limits of our model-building at this time and we have taken steps to include more minority women and lesbian women in the development of these ideas. We are trying to expand our understandings through more frequent dialogue with those who can teach us about other "realities" and points of view. (p. 7)

The evolution and expansion of the theory is mirrored by the evolution and expansion of its name from Self-in-Relation to Relational Theory to Relational-Cultural Theory. It has taken form gradually, and has been refined and elaborated, and voices of diversity have been welcomed and heard. Responsively, the theory has been reshaped, broadened, and deepened to include these voices. In the introduction to *The Healing Connection* (Miller & Stiver, 1997) some forty individuals are identified as those with whom the authors had recently engaged and from whom they had recently learned. Substantive writing from the Stone Center of Wellesley College includes works from Elizabeth Sparks on how relational cultural practice can be maintained and fostered in "cultures of disconnection" (2001) and Maureen Walker on the dominant paradigm of power–over and on cultural disconnections in the therapy relationship (2002). Both women are on the faculty of the Jean Baker Miller Training Institute and, among others, give voice to non-dominant perspectives.

What is also apparent in the writings from the Stone Center is that this engagement among women from diverse backgrounds and with diverse experience is often intense and the learning is as messy and difficult as it is rewarding and illuminating. This seems important to mention lest I communicate a sense that this is just women doing relationship. Doing what women do. Doing what they've always done–that which in some essentialist way, comes "naturally." That "relationship" is easy and that all one needs to do is listen and smile and perhaps, nod now and then. In *Building Connection Through Diversity* (1997), Cynthia Garcia Coll writes of her experience over six months of investigating diversity within what she refers to as a "microcosm of evolving relationships" among three women coming from very different backgrounds.

Throughout our regular meetings, we have experienced miscommunications and passionate arguments; we have also experienced sadness and exhaustion from sharing personal, painful experiences. We have become aware of our own misconceptions and prejudices about each other's experiences and have found some commonalities in areas that were quite unexpected. It has been hard work. Going from the personal to the political, the process has also evidenced very clearly to me that the notion that when women acknowledge their differences, the solidarity among them will be lost is a misconception. Actually, I am more convinced now that this process is necessary if a true new world order is to be established and feminism is to become the voice for many voices that feel excluded. (p. 176)

It seems clear from their writing that in order to have effected transformation in their work, the members of the core group have themselves engaged in the very process they describe-that of being-in-relationship. And through this being, with each other, and with others whose history and status and experiences have been different, their understanding and the scope and relevance of Relational-Cultural Theory has been and continues to be enlarged and enriched. This is not work that is over: "We've looked, we've seen, we know." Rather it is being incorporated into all levels of thinking in regard to theory and transforms that thinking and the resulting theory. Indeed, it seems as if this engagement with diversity is another way of being-in-relationship.

Laying the transparency of this theory atop the map of feminist therapy brings attention, also, to the issue of language-language and theory, language and therapy. Feminist thinking has long identified language as a critical variable in modifying reality and in creating experience (Riger, 1992). Words convey experience and when there are no words or when the words are inadequate, the experience is left unarticulated, is misunderstood or denied. That this awareness is held central to Relational-Cultural theory-building is expressed unequivocally by one of its founders, Jean Baker Miller.

> For a long time now, our group has had a strong commitment to demystifying psychological and psychotherapeutic language. We believe that the language commonly used in the field is not only mystifying but pejorative, denigrating, and distancing. Much of the subject matter it refers to is complex, but we believe that these topics can be discussed in more ordinary language. (This is a continuing struggle for us, and we ourselves may still fall into bad habits of language.) (Miller & Stiver, 1997, p. 5)

The use of more accessible, less blaming, perhaps more familiar language, is, of course, a double-edged sword. On the one hand, the experience being described becomes less clinical in the traditional sense and more graspable–the distance between the one who has known the experience and the one who is framing it, the theorist, is reduced. At the same time, the use of familiar language in complex ways creates the possibility of a different kind of danger–one with the potential of trivializing, or of being taken out of the nuanced context in which it is intended. Because the language of Relational-Cultural Theory is also widely familiar, even commonplace, e.g., *relationship, power, empathy, connection, disconnection*–like other ideas and tenets of feminist therapy, it may more readily be co-opted, misused, and its originators unacknowledged; or alternatively, it may be dangerously and grossly simplified, rendering it a mere description of "women's nature." This seems a necessary and courageous tightrope to walk, and this process is clearly ongoing.

Difficulty arises not only when familiar language is used to describe a theory of growing complexity and shadings. Relational-Cultural theorists simultaneously struggle with finding ways to express an experience that heretofore has not had any language for its expression. Judith Jordan (1997b) addresses this issue when she speaks of psychological theory's traditional tendency to objectify, to "it-ify," or render into "thingdom." This is a conceptual trap well supported by the language that holds it–that records and describes experience as discrete, separate, able to be objectively viewed and analyzed–a still photo devoid of context or consideration of the moment after or before.

Relational-Cultural Theory is really speaking to a different paradigm entirely, one that appreciates and investigates a relatedness, an interconnectedness-one, as described by Alexandra Kaplan (Miller & Stiver, 1997), that sees the "basic human motive" as that of participating "in connection with others, rather than the need to be gratified by others." What happens within this participating is what is of primary interest: the flow, the process of growth, both verb and noun, both being and becoming. How can this experience be represented without making it static or solid, without, in Judith Jordan's language, rendering it a "thing?" How can one speak to process using a linguistic code that has been developed to mirror the western style thinking of the separate, quantifiable, objective, and known? To use language that is accessible and emptied of psychological jargon, yet which represents accurately this dynamic flow has been, and is, challenging.

It is evident within the substantial writings of this group that the seeming ordinariness of individual terms combine in new ways in an attempt to describe concepts that have been experienced, but not previously named. The result is phrasing and language that:

> sounds strange–we have to use a long phrase like "movement in relationship" rather than one word–and (again) we believe that this is because our culture has not honored certain experiences and so does not provide us with ready words to describe them. (Miller & Stiver, 1997, p. 53)

This meticulous, considered attention to language is another place where the overlay of Relational-Cultural Theory has explored the landscape and enriches the map of feminist theory. Having been made acutely and painfully aware of what has not been said, the experiences that have remained unnamed, and the faulty and harmful assumptions rendered by the language of early theorists, Relational-Cultural Theory is creating a language of relationship, word by word and phrase by phrase. The care with which this is undertaken is highlighted by Judith Jordan's reminder that "In psychology we must be cautious with our language, for in naming, we give form" (1997, p. 21).

The critical and extensive terrain marked "power" is another place where the transparency of Relational-Cultural Theory contributes to feminist theory building. Principles of feminist theory and practice are rooted in such notions as egalitarian relationship, the reconfiguration of power inequities, and the dual intentions to hold issues of power at the forefront of all exchanges and to consciously model more collaborative ways of being in therapy and in the world (Hill & Ballou, 1998; Worell & Remer, 1992). Indeed, concepts regarding domination and subordination have been central to feminist critique:

> As feminist practitioners, we attend to hierarchies of power and dominance among and between people in all practice settings. We notice the ways in which we are both oppressed and oppressor, dominant and marginal, as well as the interactive relationships that emerge from these different positions of power. (Brabeck et al., 1997, p. 25)

The Relational-Cultural model which sees mutual empathy and mutual empowerment as the bases for development provides a refreshing alternative to previous developmental theories which rest on separation, independence, and the bounded autonomous self as a primary and necessary goal. Implicit in the successful negotiation of the stages delineated by these former developmental paradigms and the dominant values represented by them, is a power framed aptly by Maureen Walker (2002b). This is a developmental progression:

> associated with hyper-competitiveness, conquest, and might. [where] power mutates into "power-over," and is then viewed as the entitlement of the "winners"–those individuals who have attained the social ranking and the material accoutrements that signify value. (p. 1)

This is not only "power" as it is experienced within a particular dyadic relationship. But in keeping with feminist principles, it is power viewed on a much grander scale, power as it is manifested in the organization of socio-cultural strata, power as it is held by the dominant culture, power as it affects the relationships of those who have more to those who have less. The personal is indeed political.

Certainly, any discussion about relationship assumes the notion of power as integrally relevant since the distribution of power, power inequities, and shared power affect all that occurs within and because of the relationship. Relational-Cultural Theory sees authentic, mutually empathic (Jordan, 1997a), and mutually empowering relationships, a true "being-in-relation," at the heart of growth and development; and the absence of these characteristics, their distortion, breaches in the relational process, disconnection or violation of relationship–an "anti-mutuality"–to be a source of distress, the development of psychological problems and the very root of violence (Miller & Stiver, 1997).

Power as defined by Jean Baker Miller (Miller & Stiver, 1997, p. 198) is "the capacity to produce a change." It is not the denial of power differences, but the recognition of them, the mindful attempt to minimize differentials, and to, within the context of relationship, be *em*powered and to *em*power another that creates the change inherent in growth and development.

Of course, the most prominent area highlighted with the metaphorical overlay of Relational-Cultural Theory on the map of feminist therapy is that of relationship itself: that which is at the very foundation of this theory. Here the map becomes particularly rich in its coloration, intriguing in its pathways, and familiar, yet at the same time stimulating and complex in its terrain.

Yet, the familiarity of this territory and the language used to describe it may belie its depth and subtlety. Ellen Goodman, who coauthored *I Know Just What You Mean* (2002), writes concerning the connection fostered by women's authentic interaction, and cites Lois Braverman who refers to a "living current of conversation"–a phrase that seems to echo the fluidity of process and exchange that Relational-Cultural Theory seeks to describe. Goodman writes:

> We like that idea of the "living current." We've seen it and felt it in our own lives, and we know other women have, too. In the flow of conversation, back and forth, women hear each other out, take each other seriously, care and feel cared for. . . . When something happens at work or home that you can't quite, exactly, figure out, you take all that raw undigested feeling to a safe place–a friend–and come away clearer. . . . In these ongoing dialogues, women reveal themselves. Gradually, trust is tested and won; an intimate comfort zone is created. (p. 35)

Through their own extensive experience as practitioners, their own weekly conversations, and deep listening, the builders of Relational-Cultural Theory have identified a kind of DNA of psychological development. And they subsequently discerned and described the "five good things" (Miller & Stiver, 1997)–zest, action, knowledge, a sense of worth, and the desire for more connection–that emerge from the mutual empathy and mutual empowerment of authentic connection. These, according to Relational-Cultural Theory, are the elements that foster growth and development.

These five good things were most evident to me during an event in September of 2002. The following is a description of quite ordinary and at the same time extraordinary scope that is offered as an example of the Relational-Cultural Theory as it is experienced. I participated in a small gathering, the purpose of which was to provide a supportive send-off to a woman from Massachusetts who had been selected to participate in a world wide women's peace conference to be held in Geneva. I went to this circle knowing only the person who invited me and encountered there about twenty other women of varying ethnicities, ages, and socio-economic means. The circle, itself, was one of speaking and listening, a process that held within it a difficult to define and impossible empirically to measure, but very real, felt creative energy. About twenty women in dialogue, speaking, and finding their own truth as they spoke. Twenty women listening, exchanging, being changed and creating change.

Using language descriptive of Relational-Cultural Theory, women spoke of settings and circumstances that made it difficult for their voices to emerge, and of their feelings of being *en*couraged–of finding within the circle the courage to speak–and of their sense of connection and resonance as the circle progressed. I had arrived not knowing what to expect, how the evening would unfold, where my place in it would be; and I left having experienced the 5 good things: *zest,* an amazing energy, a sense of vitality–in the face of great and grave concerns, a feeling of truly being alive. There was an experience of *action* within the authentic exchanges that had taken place–we didn't merely speak our hearts and minds, rather the interaction moved us further within the dialogue itself, and in its interweaving, in the living current of conversation, a further current of action was empowered.

This circle was the genesis and the holding place of *knowledge*. It was education in its most true form, from "educare" or to call forth. Within the holding of the circle, within the non-judgmental listening, was the opportunity to truly know what one knew. This contrasts with the idea of knowledge as something that can be quantified, that exists separate from the knower, and is quite alien to traditional epistemologies. Sara Ruddick (1995) in speaking particularly of mothers, notes that speaking changes a speaker. "When developing voices are listened to," she says, " they will transform the thought they are beginning to articulate and the knowledge they are determined to share" (p. 40).

The palpable attention and acknowledgement within the circle also gave rise to an experience of *worthiness*–that one's thoughts and feelings mattered and were legitimate. And most profoundly, from this vitality and connection flowed *a desire for more connection,* something dynamic, a living current leading to mutual growth and empowerment, a seeking to remain within or to re-experience that flow of being-in-relation.

As is characteristic of the model, the language that names these 5 good things appears simple, without pretense or obfuscation. It is possible to understand what is being described largely because we have felt it, we can name people and circumstances that offer this connected relationship; and we have felt the reverse, as well. In some way this model offers the possibility of a personal mini-lab where as a relational encounter occurs, there is an immediacy of sensory and emotional and cognitive experience. It is not necessarily that in the presence of a mutually empathic exchange, one feels good in the sense of being happy, that the emotions experienced are pleasant ones; rather it is that one has been heard and understood. This is the centerpiece of Relational-Cultural Theory.

Finally, there is an additional section of this metaphorical overlay that may represent one of the most critical features of feminist practice and Relational-Cultural Theory at this time in history. Feminist practice has long been called to redress issues of power and to take its work out into the world. In writing of feminist methodology, Stephanie Riger (1992) frames it this way: "A feminist method should produce a study not just OF women, but also FOR women, helping to change the world as well as to describe it" (p. 736). Included in the principles that guide feminist therapy is an overarching commitment to social change. The western mantra of independence, achievement, dominance and power-over, what might collectively be seen as "anti-mutuality" in Relational-Cultural terms, has rendered the entire world a more threatening, violent, and disconnected place. I recall the first time I sat in the audience at a presentation made by Jean Baker Miller and Irene Stiver. During the discussion period, a participant framed a question about how relational theory interfaces with world conflict. My memory is that Jean paused only briefly before responding that those in a power-over position rarely cede their position willingly. Yet there are efforts to take this theory out into the world through many groups and workshops and trainings and through active collaboration with women throughout the world.

Relational-Cultural Theory has developed by listening to women's experiences and by bringing the understanding of growth fostering relationships into therapeutic settings. This spiral of listening and discussing and learning and re-informing therapy relationships has resulted in an evolving theory of both lovely simplicity and stimulating intricacy. But it has expanded well beyond the confines of therapy. For example, several Stone Center researchers have investigated how growth-fostering relationships affect the workplace (Fletcher, 1996) and how relational practice can be the basis for transformation in nonrelational work environments (Hartling & Sparks, 2002). Miller and Stiver (1997) also describe the example of the Harvard Union of Clerical and Technical Workers that, following "hard struggles," "won a contract that contains many unusual relational and growth-fostering provisions" (p. 194). These are beginning ways in which a theory of psychological development is moving beyond an individual model of intervention.

It is also important to note that the feminist notion of resistance is incorporated into Relational-Cultural inquiry and practice. Maureen Walker (2002b) provides powerful accountings of ways in which those who are politically disempowered have, in the context of a power-over situation, employed relational competencies while demonstrating both resistance and resilience. In referring to her mother, she relates a way of being in relationship which sought to "subvert the power paradigm." "She refused to believe the lies of the power-over paradigm; lies that defined her as less than human, unworthy of respect" (p. 6). This inclusion of marginalized voices in discovering the ways in which individuals have stayed connected to their own knowing and resistant to the dominant mythology is relational and critical and continuing.

In the forward to the second edition of *A New Psychology of Women* (1986), Jean Baker Miller talks about the huge undertaking involved in bringing full personhood into being. "Such an attempt," she writes, "encompasses all realms of life, from global, economic, social, and political levels to the most intimate personal relationships" (p. xi). Lest we feel the hopelessness of the oppression that at root is relational oppression, Jean Baker Miller and Irene Stiver suggest that:

> the study of how people participate in growth-fostering relationships opens up a vision of human possibilities that has been obscured. If this complex and valuable activity continues to be seen as a minor, personal one and the province of women only, however, then it will always be something that women do for others within a context of subservience rather than mutuality. Women will continue to be oppressed and men to be heavily pressured to proceed along a path centering on individual power and gratification. The violence to which the latter stance often leads will continue, and the structure and institutions of society will not change. We believe that studying women's lives offers us a crucial key to thinking about societal transformation–and that this transformation is essential. (1997, p. 62)

It is sadly too clear that we live in a world and at a time that is desperate in its need of being-in-relation. May we all collaborate in that being.

## FUTURE DIRECTIONS

While the entire map of feminist theory is gaining clarity and detail, a thorough understanding of its territory remains incomplete. Signposts evolving from Relational-Cultural Theory suggest that the following areas may prove fruitful in this ongoing exploration.

1. Using the Relational-Cultural overlay, disorder becomes less about the individual and more about what happens in the rela-

tionship. Disorder emanates from a breach between rather than within, and symptoms are seen as strategies of disconnection. How might these ideas translate to preventative measures? What medium can be useful in education and how might skills of relationship be incorporated into school curricula and workplace training?

2. The dominant power-over paradigm has established science and empiricism as the single broker of truth, a situation that restricts what questions are asked and what answers are considered credible. What paths of resistance can bring multiple truths to a broader audience? How does research using a model such as Relational-Cultural Theory get funding within a context demanding and reifying short-term cognitive and medicalized treatment modes?

3. The scientific methodologies of empiricism have largely devalued, negated, and even derided any consideration of spirituality as integral to human development and functioning. Yet there is within the Relational-Cultural model the intimation that something immeasurable and intangible is occurring between therapist and client. This model speaks to a therapeutic presence that not only includes cognition, but asks for a quality of "being-with," fully and in the present moment. This includes being aware of one's own sensory and somatic experience as information about what is happening in the interchange. There is clearly a suggestion of integrating body and mind and the sense that we can begin to know another's experience by being with them on a moment to moment basis, feeling with them as well as thinking about them. Perhaps this is a place where the language of western psychological thought offers little in the way of defining this presence and exchange. It seems as though this theory is at the edge of something other and that future conceptualizations and explorations may include a spiritual component, perhaps using the language of spirit in a new way.

4. The Relational-Cultural model in its current evolutionary state primarily considers adult relationships, although some attention has been paid to the college-age and adolescent population. How does this theory expand to work with children? What does therapy using this model look like with the most powerless in our society?

5. Neurobiological data that consider the impact of Post-Traumatic Stress Disorder, for example, provides clear evidence of

physiological changes wrought by situations of abuse. This is certainly helpful in understanding experience and has potential for assisting interventions, as well. It is important, however, that history does not repeat itself in the efforts of science to proclaim difference and so justify the status quo. To move too quickly to see "scientific" evidence that women are wired to do relationship, obviates alternative explanations, and colludes in maintaining current power relationships. In this regard, it is critical to take note of what research questions are asked and how answers are framed.

6. Relational-Cultural Theory emerged from dialogues about therapeutic relationships, considering the voices and experiences of women in therapy. In stark contrast with psychoanalytic models, it has grappled with the unequal power as it is present within this healing relationship. More recently, Relational-Cultural theorists have included in their thinking the notion that power-over arrangements form the bedrock of western socio-political and economic structures, and that these arrangements must be engaged not only on behalf of individual development, but on behalf of a social action imperative. Empowerment, seen in this context, extends beyond a strengthening of the individual self to collective strategies of resistance.

Theory does not develop in a sociopolitical vacuum. Twenty-five years ago the work of these theorists, Judith Jordan, Alexandra Kaplan, Jean Baker Miller, Irene Stiver, and Janet Surrey, all women working in hierarchical settings steeped in power-over models, was courageously radical. Today's world demands similarly courageous thinking and action.

## REFERENCES

Belenky, M.F., Clinchy, B.M., Goldberger, N.R., & Tarule, J.M. (1986). *Women's ways of knowing: The development of self, voice, and mind.* New York, NY: Basic Books.

Brabeck, M., Brown, L., Christian, L., Esoin, O., Hare-Mustin, R., Kaplan, A., Kaschak, E., Miller, D., Phillips, E., Ferns, T. & Van Ormer, A. (1997). Feminist theory and psychological practice. In J. Worell & Y. Johnson (Eds.), *Shaping the future of feminist psychology* (pp. 15-35). Washington, DC: American Psychological Association.

Coll, C.G., Cook-Nobles, R., & Surrey, J. (1997). Building connection through diversity. In J. Jordan (Ed.), *Women's growth in diversity: More writings from the Stone Center* (pp. 176-198). New York, NY: Guilford.

Fairbairn, W. R. D. (1954). *An object-relations theory of the personality.* New York, NY: Basic Books.

Fletcher, J. (1996). Relational theory in the workplace. *Work in Progress* 77. Wellesley, MA: Stone Center Working Paper Series.

Gilligan, C. (1982). *In a different voice: Psychological theory and women's development.* Cambridge, MA: Harvard University Press.

Goodman, E. & O'Brien, P. (2002). *I know just what you mean: The power of friendship in women's lives.* New York, NY: Fireside.

Hartling, L. & Sparks, E. (2002). Relational-Cultural practice: Working in a nonrelational world. *Work in progress,* 97, Wellesley, MA: Stone Center Working Paper Series.

Hill, M. & Ballou, M. (1998). Making therapy feminist: A practice survey. *Women and Therapy, 21,* 1-16.

Jordan, J. (1997a). Relational Development: Therapeutic implications of empathy and shame. In J. Jordan (Ed.), *Women's growth in diversity: More writings from the Stone Center* (pp. 138-161). New York, NY: Guilford.

Jordan, J. (1997b). A relational perspective for understanding women's development. In J. Jordan (Ed.), *Women's growth in diversity: More writings from the Stone Center* (pp. 9-24). New York, NY: Guilford.

Jordan, J., Kaplan, A., Miller, J.B., Stiver, I., & Surrey, J. (1992). *Women's growth in connection: Writings from the Stone Center.* New York, NY: Guilford.

Klein, M. (1975). *"Envy and gratitude" and other works,* 1946-1963. New York, NY: Delacorte Press.

Lerman, H. (1996). *Pigeonholing women's misery: A history and critical analysis of the psychodiagnosis of women in the twentieth century.* New York, NY: Basic Books.

Miller, J.B. (1986). *Toward a new psychology of women.* Boston, MA: Beacon Press.

Miller, J.B. & Stiver, I. (1997). *The healing connection: How women form relationships in therapy and in life.* Boston, MA: Beacon Press.

Riger, S. (1992). Epistemological debates, feminist voices: Science, social values, and the study of women. *American Psychologist.* 730-740.

Ruddick, S. (1995). *Maternal thinking: Toward a politics of peace.* Boston, MA: Beacon Press.

Tavris, C. (1992). *The mismeasure of woman.* New York, NY: Simon & Schuster.

Walker, M. (2002a). How therapy helps when the culture hurts. *Work in Progress* 9. Wellesley, MA: Stone Center Working Paper Series.

Walker, M. (2002b). Power and effectiveness: Envisioning an alternative paradigm. *Work in Progress* 94. Wellesley, MA: Stone Center Working Paper Series.

Winnicott, D.W. (1958). *The maturational processes and the facilitating environment.* New York, NY: International Universities Press.

Worell, J. & Remer, P. (1992). *Feminist perspectives in therapy: An empowerment model for women.* New York, NY: Wiley.

# Feminist Perspectives on Trauma

Denise C. Webster
Erin C. Dunn

**SUMMARY.** Feminist therapists, researchers, activists and scholars have long recognized that power differentials can have serious, sometimes fatal, consequences for women and children. Documenting the prevalence of problems such as rape, wife battering, and childhood sexual abuse, feminists began to dismantle social beliefs about gender, class and race that too often protect perpetrators of violence and blame victims for their own suffering. The authors cited (Burgess, Brownmiller, Herman, Koss, Harvey, NiCarthy, and Root) have combined scholarship with social activism to address the needs of the abused and develop social approaches to preventing violence. *[Article copies available for a fee from The Haworth Document Delivery Service: 1-800-HAWORTH. E-mail address:*

---

Denise C. Webster, RN, PhD, APRN, BC, is Professor in the School of Nursing, University of Colorado Health Sciences Center, Denver, Colorado. Her teaching, research, and practice for thirty years have been focused on women and mental health. Her experiences with women who have poorly understood conditions and chronic pain have reinforced the need to consider the long-term consequences of trauma and violence in women's lives. Erin C. Dunn, BS, MPH (candidate), is Research Coordinator at the Boston University Center for Psychiatric Rehabilitation and is also a graduate student at the Boston University School of Public Health. In addition to working with child and adolescent trauma survivors, she has participated in several research projects focusing on the long-term sequelae of trauma and violence against women.

Address correspondence to: Denise C. Webster, 2035 Kohler Drive, Boulder, CO 80305 (E-mail: Denny.Webster@uchsc.edu).

[Haworth co-indexing entry note]: "Feminist Perspectives on Trauma." Webster, Denise C., and Erin C. Dunn. Co-published simultaneously in *Women & Therapy* (The Haworth Press, Inc.) Vol. 28, No. 3/4, 2005, pp. 111-142; and: *The Foundation and Future of Feminist Therapy* (ed: Marcia Hill, and Mary Ballou) The Haworth Press, Inc., 2005, pp. 111-142. Single or multiple copies of this article are available for a fee from The Haworth Document Delivery Service [1-800-HAWORTH, 9:00 a.m. - 5:00 p.m. (EST). E-mail address: docdelivery@haworthpress.com].

http://www.haworthpress.com/web/WT
doi:10.1300/J015v28n03_06

**KEYWORDS.** Abuse, violence, trauma, rape, wife battering, domestic violence, incest, sexual abuse, memory

## INTRODUCTION

The theorists reviewed here are acknowledged for their contributions to feminist theory and therapy for trauma. Their work spans multiple forms of violence against women, including child sexual abuse, sexual assault and domestic violence. Although the authors are described separately for their contributions, we recognize that it is on the collective contributions that the progress of eliminating violence against women rests. Many other important contributors could not be included in this review due to space limitations. The women included represent many different disciplines (psychology, psychiatry, social work, sociology, nursing, journalism) and roles (researchers, therapists, theorists). Some have focused primarily on describing specific types of trauma and their sequelae, while others developed and refined theoretical explanations for these problems and still others emphasized the work of prevention of the problem and/or treatment of victims.

What all of the women reviewed here have in common is a commitment to shared feminist values that implicitly or explicitly frame the questions they ask and the implications they draw from the answers. As a group, they recognize the power differentials between men and women cross-culturally and internationally and the necessity of acknowledging the social and political contexts in which violence against women occurs. In doing so they depathologize the individual responses to violence and hold accountable those who perpetrate the violence or refuse to provide safety for all of a society's citizens. They value and validate the experiences of women by presenting their findings in the voices of those who would otherwise be silenced. They value cooperation and collaboration, as the work we review will demonstrate. They value and respect diversity, believing that answers will come from understanding differences and working together to create the changes that must occur at all levels.

In this review, we describe how these authors collectively brought public and professional attention to the existence of crimes against women and how they sought to challenge prevailing ideas about crimes against women. Anthropologist and psychiatrist Arthur Kleinman has described the importance of determining individual's understandings of a condition before conceptualizing and implementing any type of intervention (Kleinman, Eisenberg, & Good, 1978). Explanatory frameworks generally reflect social and socialized understandings of phenomena, i.e., how situations become recognized as problems, what they are called, how they came to be and what should be done about them. These frameworks also define how serious specific problems are, what maintains the problems, and who should be concerned about them. While recognizing the importance of honoring a culture's deeply held belief systems, these belief systems can also be oppressive to those who do not have the power to communicate their own definitions or modify socially accepted explanations that do not reflect their own experience. Widely believed explanatory frameworks often ignore or distort the perspectives of those without power while rationalizing the actions of those who do have power. Following Kleinman's depiction of explanatory frameworks, we seek to demonstrate how the feminist theorists in this chapter directly challenged the culture's dominant explanatory frameworks regarding violence against women. When feminists began to name women's experiences in this way, they were faced with exposing deeply rooted and widely accepted beliefs. They often addressed these widely accepted beliefs by labeling them "myths" and providing alternative explanatory frameworks. To do so, they had to provide convincing evidence to contradict powerful belief systems and seek nothing less than a major cultural shift. This review is divided into four sections as a way to capture the prevailing explanatory frameworks that were characteristic of each form of violence against women.

As we move from these collective contributions to each theorist's individual work, we discuss how each author's ideas, interests and opportunities evolve over time, alternately supporting, challenging and refining feminists' explanatory frameworks for violence against women. When possible we have addressed these shifts based on the themes identified in the author's work as well as the author's own perspectives on their work.

## RAPE

Rape was among the first forms of violence against women addressed by feminists. The 1971 version of *Our Bodies, Ourselves*

(Boston Women's Health Book Collective) outlined some of the "myths" of rape and how women might protect themselves. Among the myths they listed were that women (secretly) want to be raped, that the motive for rape is sexual, that it is an impulsive act, that it usually involves a stranger, and is frequently an interracial crime. Other myths at the time were that women invited rape by what they wore, that it occurred mostly among the lower classes, and was preventable if a woman really did not want to be raped. Most women believed it could never happen to them. Paradoxically, it was also believed (by some) that rape does not really injure women *and* that if a good woman was raped, she would go crazy. What was written about rape in the professional literature often described characteristics and psychodynamics of the victim as explanatory factors. The stigma associated with being raped meant families were shamed and victims were blamed. Few cases were reported to authorities and even fewer were prosecuted. Many of these ideas are still accepted by some people, but the treatment of rape victims has been immeasurably improved by the efforts of feminist theorists, therapists, writers and researchers. In our review of feminist contributions to the study of rape, we highlight the work of Ann Burgess, Susan Brownmiller and Mary Koss.

### Ann Burgess

In 1972, Ann Burgess, a professor of community mental health nursing, and sociologist Lynda Holmstrom started a rape crisis center at Boston City Hospital. They began to publish their findings in 1973, describing in nursing and medical journals what they called the "Rape Trauma Syndrome," a model that is cited as valid today (International Society for Traumatic Stress Studies, 2003). Based on a shared social perspective, they described rape as a social problem that needed to be addressed at a social level, both with services to individual victims and changes in institutional and social policies. As advocates in the broadest sense they provided direct services for physical and emotional trauma and also accompanied women to court if they chose to prosecute (Burgess & Holmstrom, 1973, 1974a, 1974b, 1979; Holmstrom & Burgess, 1975).

They described the symptoms they observed in rape victims (including nightmares, flashbacks, somatic symptoms and emotional responses) and linked these to crisis theory, Kubler-Ross's theories on dying and on traumatology (specifically Sandor Rado's theories of traumatophobia and to men's war experiences). Written near the end of the Vietnam War, there was no category of posttraumatic stress disorder (PTSD) in the *Diagnostic and Statistical Manual II* (1968). Burgess and Holmstrom described the range of normal responses seen in their study group that included representatives of all ages from many ethnic and racial groups. They addressed the myths of rape implicitly in their articles through the data they collected and reported. For example, they described the range of dress and attractiveness of the victims and emphasized that rape is not a sexual crime but a crime of violence. This position is made explicit in some instances, as in providing guidelines for talking with victims: "Use nonjudgmental language and speak about the issues of power, control, anger, and aggression, which are the salient features of the assault" (Burgess & Holmstrom, 1988, p. 38). They make it clear that the women they were seeing in emergency rooms felt they were in danger of their lives, and may barely have escaped murder.

Early in their descriptions of working with rape victims, Burgess and Holmstrom created profiles to provide some direction for providing assistance to victims. These profiles, however, were always based on what the women themselves were asking for. The authors described this approach as an overt shift from the view that the professional knows best to honoring the centrality of the woman's experience. Categories and descriptions of women's experiences were presented in the women's own words when possible. In articles and their book, *Rape: Victims of crisis* (1974c) and *Rape: Crisis and recovery* (1979a), Burgess and Holmstrom emphasized that rape victims may present a range of normal responses, from outwardly calm to visibly distressed. Three phases of recovery were described along with the physical, emotional and psychological needs at different phases. The first state or immediate phase involves acute fear, while the second stage is characterized by a phase of disorganization in which re-experiencing aspects of the assault may be particularly distressing. The third stage is a reorganization phase, the length of which can vary widely. Also described are "compounded" and "silent" rape reactions. The former is consistent with Herman's perspective on "complex PTSD" and the latter, described more by Koss, alerts health care professionals to the kinds of unexplained physical symptoms they may see in patients who have been assaulted in the past and/or more recently, but who have never spoken about it. Later publications have addressed institutional responses to rape (Holmstrom & Burgess, 1978) and sexual assault of children and adolescents (Burgess, Groth, Holmstrom, & Sgroi, 1978).

In the late 1970s Ann Burgess began to shift her work toward violence prevention by identifying risk factors associated with sexual perpetrators. She worked closely with John Douglas of the FBI to develop criminal profiling approaches for serial rapists and murderers and is now widely known for her work in forensics (Hazelwood & Burgess, 1987; Ressler, Burgess & Douglas, 1988; Ressler, Burgess, Burgess, & Douglas, 1993). Her current work involves looking at vulnerable populations and abuse of power, e.g., people who are cognitively impaired, and those who are in nursing homes or developmentally delayed, who may be without the language or memory (in some cases) or credibility (as witnesses to their own crime) to represent themselves. She was the chair of the 1996 National Research Council's Task Force on Violence Against Women.

### Susan Brownmiller

Susan Brownmiller is a journalist who began writing about rape in 1968. Self-described as "combative, wary, and verbally aggressive," she was skeptical in the early 1970s when her consciousness-raising group proposed that rape should be a concern of the women's movement. After she heard the testimony of women at the New York Radical Feminist's Speak Out that she had helped to organize in January of 1971, she became convinced that much of the history of women and of rape had never been adequately described and documented. Her ground-breaking book, *Against Our Will* (1975), marked an important shift in social, historical and cross-cultural explanatory frameworks when she presented evidence, in painstaking detail, of the use of rape as a formal and informal military weapon in the patriarchy's war against women. She came to believe that women's denial that they could be raped was what was keeping us from confronting the problem. She directly challenged the myths of rape by contrasting them with the realities, ranging from the Greek myths of rapists as heroes to the urban myths that women who are raped either do (or should) enjoy it.

Drawing from research, classic and contemporary literature, legal and military records, news reports, and women's personal testimonies, Brownmiller presented readers with disturbing evidence that rape too often has been romanticized, e.g., in both World Wars propaganda posters showed "the rape of Belgium" with Belgium portrayed as a beautiful woman. The reader who persevered learned that rape is far from rare, and is not an act of sex but of violence. Rape is a systemic way that men have kept women in "their place" for millennia. Traditional stories and fairy tales teach women that to be safe from all men a woman must be protected by one man, preferably a strong, overpowering one. Women have been discouraged from having strong minds and strong bodies; men find beautiful, passive and dependent women more attractive. Women are conditioned to be victims by cultural beliefs about women and men and the socialization of women to passivity. Passive, gentle young women are trophies; strong women are castrating. Even contemporary male writers, such as Updike, Solzhenitsyn, and Cleaver (and some females, such as Ayn Rand) apparently viewed rape either as not a crime or as justifiable (pp. 313-346).

Other myths and misconceptions of rape and rape victims were critically analyzed for accuracy and implications. She noted that women are given a double message about how dangerous rape is. For example, you must show evidence of extreme resistance to support the legitimacy of a rape charge, i.e., serious wounds . . . but if you resist you probably will be killed. Consent, she asserted, when one is threatened, is still forcible rape. Although there was a belief that a woman would only "cry rape" for revenge or because she "changed her mind" there was more evidence that men lie and that juries tended to believe the men. Movie images to the contrary, women do not fall in love with their rapists. In essence, the myths told us, there really is no such thing as rape; but if there is, it's the woman's fault. Not until Freud, and his follower Helene Deutsch, Brownmiller noted, could men take comfort in the belief that women wanted to be raped, as part of their inherent masochism (pp. 315-325).

Perhaps most chilling is Brownmiller's portrayal of rape as a "macho bonding exercise" carried out by groups of men in the wake of battle as the spoils of war, the right of the victor. Rape, torture and murder of women and children are not uncommon. Although charges were filed against American soldiers following the My Lai massacre and defendants were found guilty, the rape charges were later dropped. During the American Revolution and American Civil wars, there were reports of "lewd, lascivious and indecent acts," "much ravishment," and incidents involving "that most irreparable injury" (pp. 77, 119). And, of course, a man whose wife has been raped would never want to take her back once she had been "sullied" and was damaged property. Across cultures and history Brownmiller found reports of mass rapes of women and children as part and parcel of wars, pogroms, and riots. Forced sexual relations are somehow seen as justifiable when they involve oppressed groups, including slaves, minority religious groups, and defeated indigenous groups. Brownmiller's broad perspective puts the range of social and political traumas into a framework emphasized by Maria Root's work in more recent years. Complex interactions between race, sexuality, and power are outlined in discussions of the many unofficial undeclared wars, in domestic violence, southern lynchings, prison rape, and child sexual abuse. These were and are difficult truths to see and many would rather not.

Brownmiller has continued to speak difficult truths with clarity and passion in the intervening years since the publication of *Against Our Will*. An impressive array of her critical essays and interviews have illuminated readers about a wide range of topics (Brownmiller, 1984; 1992; 1994; 1999) but the topics of feminism and the aftermath of war have continued to engage her. In response to our questions about her current perspective on *Against Our Will* she wrote regarding her intent: "The last line of *Against Our Will* reads: 'My purpose in this book has been to give rape its history. Now we must deny it a future.'" The major point she was trying to make was that, "Rape is a crime of violence, not a crime of lustful sex." How successful was the attempt? The book has had "A lot of influence. The book became a classic text in feminism and therapy. Laws changed." One thing that has not changed is her views on the topic of rape. She wrote: "My views have not changed. The world has come to understand rape much more clearly, but we have not eliminated it." How does she think the work has held up over time? She responded that the "Assumptions and findings have held up brilliantly" (S. Brownmiller, personal communication, April 14, 2003).

## Mary P. Koss

In the early 1980s, research psychologist Mary P. Koss began studying rape by developing and revising a research instrument to measure sexual aggression by men and sexual victimization of women (Koss & Oros, 1982; Koss & Gidycz, 1985). Strongly influenced by Brownmiller's work. (M. Koss, personal communication, April 16, 2003), the development of this instrument was grounded in her observation that the incidence of rape was hidden by virtue of methodological flaws in viewing sexual victimization as a dichotomous variable. Rather than purporting that women were either victims or non-victims, Koss argued that a woman's understanding of her own sexual victimization could best be identified in a tool which considered a dimensional view of aggression and did not require a woman to label the experience as rape. What followed was the development of a systematic program of research to explore the prevalence, risk factors, consequences and impact of sexual assault.

Like other theorists described here and elsewhere, Koss argued that the prevalence of rape was dramatically underestimated and contrary to federally published rape statistics, rape was not a rare occurrence (Koss & Oros, 1982). Throughout her work she enumerated the myriad complexities involved in measuring the occurrence of rape and believed that these methodological issues were contributing to inaccurate rape estimates (Koss & Harvey, 1991; Koss, 1993; Koss, Goodman, Browne, Fitzgerald, Keita, & Russo, 1994). She argued that researchers' variations in the definitions of rape and in particular, the use of a conservative legal definitions (only penile-vaginal rape) to determine who qualifies as a victim may exclude women who were raped by other means (orally or anally). Furthermore, a woman's own definition of rape and her assessment of her victim status will vary based on a number of factors (i.e., conceptualization of the experience, acceptance of rape supportive beliefs, relationship to the perpetrator, perpetrator's use of force, whether rape was attempted or completed as well as the precise wording of questions about rape). Measuring the incidence of rape (occurrences in a given period of time) versus the prevalence of rape (occurrences throughout the lifetime) would also result in lower figures. In addition, the frequent exclusion of particular groups of women (e.g., mentally ill, homeless, mentally retarded, lesbian, imprisoned, ethnically and socioeconomically diverse, involved in the military) and flawed study designs (e.g., telephone surveys that are completed when a woman is in the presence of others, use of untrained, gender or ethnically unbalanced interviewers during face-to-face interviews) could all result in lower reports of rape.

In her classification of the forms of rape (Koss & Harvey, 1991), Koss identified a group of women who were hidden victims. In a series of articles based on her findings from a national sample of students in higher education, Koss observed that rates of victimization were 10-15 times higher and rates of perpetration were 2-3 times greater than originally reported by federal statistics. Almost half of the women who were raped did not disclose their rape to anyone, as Burgess earlier noted, while only one third of these women defined their victimization as rape, and only 5% reported their victimization to the police and/or sought victim services (Koss, Gidycz, & Wisniewski, 1987). Since rape reports are based solely on reported instances of rape from women who label their experiences as rape, she concluded that hidden rape victims were not represented in federal rape statistics.

Since the prevailing image of the rape perpetrator was a stranger who raped women in dark alleys late at night, Koss believed that the experiences of women who were being coerced into sex by intimate partners with little or no force were not identified as rape victims for several reasons. Despite meeting legal definitions of rape, Koss argued that women may not conceptualize their experience as rape based on their own acceptance of social and cultural beliefs about rape (Koss, 1993). Supporting this hypothesis she and her colleagues found that while forty-percent of women raped by family members described this experience as rape, over sixty-percent of these women either believed it was a crime, but not rape, or rather a miscommunication despite having been raped by their spouse or family member five or more times. As a result, only 44% compared to 73% of women raped by acquaintance told someone and sought help (Koss, Dinero, Seibel, & Cox, 1988). Furthermore, Koss observed that neither personality nor attitudes towards rape differentiated women who disclosed their rape from those who kept it hidden. Rather, the context in which they were raped determined their hesitancy or urgency to report; hidden rape victims were often raped in the context of a sexually intimate relationship, whereas women who disclosed their rape victimization to authorities had less of a prior relationship to their perpetrator (Koss, 1985). These studies were pivotal in conveying actual women's experiences to the world; not only was rape occurring more often than previously conceived, but a majority of these victimized women were living in secrecy after being victimized by spouses and acquaintances.

Based on the findings from her research, Koss focused on challenging societal perceptions of why men rape and why women are raped. Seeking to dismantle the myth of the deranged and psychopathic rapist, Koss found that 25% of men in one study used incrementally serious forms of coercion and aggression to achieve their sexual objectives leading up to attempted rape (3.3%) and rape (4.4%) (Koss & Dinero, 1988). Among a group of adolescents, women thought that non-consent was "extremely clear," whereas men for the most part thought it was "not at all clear" (White & Koss, 1993). She illustrated that while heterogeneous, men who rape commonly demonstrate developmentally progressive forms of aggression (Koss & Dinero, 1988; Koss & Harvey, 1991; Koss, Goodman, Browne, Fitzgerald, Keita, & Russo, 1994). Beyond individual psychological characteristics, family and peer socialization, Koss argued that institutional and societal forces support rape by failing to charge men for the crimes they commit and by giving women the message that not only will they not be believed, but they will be blamed for the crimes which were perpetrated against them. A woman would have to prove that rape had occurred (Koss & Cleveland, 1997). Like the early feminists, Koss believes the reason women are raped lies in men's need to exert intentional social control over women

(Koss, Heise, & Russo, 1994). Contrary to societal perceptions, she did not find overwhelming evidence for a particular group of risk factors that uniquely predicted women who were raped (Koss & Dinero, 1989). Rather, she concluded that rape happens to all women and the fear of rape is part of women's collective consciousness (Koss, Heise, & Russo, 1994).

Due to the high percentage of women who do not seek treatment immediately following rape (Koss, Gidycz, & Wisniewski, 1987), Koss urged both mental health and other professionals to become familiar with the needs of rape victims. In addition to her work with Mary Harvey, whose work will be described later, Koss believed that non-mental health treatment providers needed to be cognizant of the occurrence of violence against women and its aftereffects (Koss & Harvey, 1991; Koss, Goodman et al., 1994). She encouraged the medical community to routinely screen for rape victimization, provide referrals when needed (Koss, Woodruff, & Koss, 1990; Koss, Goodman et al., 1994; Koss, Ingram, & Pepper, 1997) and address the physical health concerns of rape victims including concern over pregnancy, sexually transmitted diseases and other physical health related problems (Koss & Woodruff, 1991; Koss, Heise, & Russo, 1994).

Koss's work demonstrates an awareness that male violence against women transcends racial, ethnic, socioeconomic, sexual orientation and age boundaries as well as state and national boundaries (Koss, Heise & Russo, 1994) and urges for improved research among ethnically diverse, lesbian and disabled women (Koss & Hoffman, 2000). What is most striking about Koss's work as a researcher is her reliance on accurate measures of the subjective experience. She takes the position that if the data do not support what we intuitively believe (e.g., that those with less education and income, who often use public transportation and live in central cities are more vulnerable to rape), then we need to see if the study methods used were flawed (Koss, 1993, p. 215). She notes that sensitivity to issues of diversity demands recognition that confidentiality may be a meaningless construct to participants who are historically skeptical and distrustful of institutions and people in positions of power (Koss, 1993), and that differences may exist in perception and expression of abuse (Lira, Koss, & Russo, 1999; Koss & Hoffman, 2000).

Through rigorous research and her ability to speak to multiple audiences, including psychology, law, medicine, and public health, Mary Koss brought the subjective experiences of women's lives into the objective realm of research. In doing so, her work helped to raise society's awareness of the magnitude of rape, of the secret pain of hidden victims and of the social forces that support its existence. In her current work, Koss is moving from theory to practice to explore social justice perspectives. She is currently involved in an innovative project based on concepts of restorative justice among Native American populations in Arizona in the belief that "Justice is healing" (M. Koss, personal communication, April 16, 2003).

## SEXUAL ABUSE

As with rape, there are numerous myths that deny the existence of the sexual abuse of children, or blame the child for the transgression when it is acknowledged to exist. Now, as in Freud's era, people prefer to believe that such things exist only in the fantasies of children who crave attention. Hence we are encouraged to believe the myths that child sexual abuse is rare, even rarer for prepubertal children, and that avoiding strangers will protect children from sexual abuse. We find comfort in the myth that only alcoholic or drug-crazed psychopaths would commit such acts, and that, if they do occur, it is a one-time occurrence that children will forget if it's not talked about. Most comforting, of course, is the belief it could never happen to us, to our children, or to anyone we know. Among the many fine feminist theorists, therapists and researchers who have addressed this topic we highlight the work of Judith Herman and Mary Harvey.

### Judith Lewis Herman

As a practicing psychiatrist and researcher, Judith Herman's work bridges the gap between grass roots social change efforts and interdisciplinary academic research. She describes the work as part of an ongoing "enlightenment" project to reveal truths based on empirical data and aimed at empowering victims of violence (Herman, 2002). Working with many different collaborators, Herman implements a clear program of research based in the reality of human experience rather than framed and constrained by predetermined theories. In studying incest, sexual abuse by therapists, and long-term consequences of repeated trauma, she first asks what the problem is and seeks answers from those who have experienced it. Risk factors for the problem are then identified as well as strategies that will prevent it or help people heal from the experience. Findings are reported to both lay and professional groups. In each case she makes clear the links between the social context in which apparently individual problems occur and the multilevel changes necessary to alleviate them.

Like most of the feminists described in this section, Herman was involved in anti-war and civil rights before coming to feminism. She credits her experience in a consciousness-raising group as giving her the ability to see and hear what the women she was seeing in practice were actually describing. While completing her psychiatric residency, she also volunteered in a storefront clinic and found similarities between the women she saw there and those who "sought shelter" in psychiatric hospitals. In 1975 she and her first collaborator, Lisa Hirschman, wondered why they were seeing so many incest survivors and battered women when the conventional wisdom was that these experiences were rare. When they published the findings from their first small study in *Signs* (Herman & Hirschman, 1977) they began to hear from victims and therapists all over the country that what they were seeing was far from rare and that the contemporary treatments based on psychoanalytic theory were not helpful in understanding the problem or helping victims.

The 1981 release of their book *Father-Daughter Incest* (Herman & Hirschman) brought to the public both the poignant words of victims and the disturbing statistics about the reality of sexual abuse in the family setting. In this book and related articles, Herman and Hirschman refuted the belief that sexual abuse is rare (citing that 1% of women have been victims of father-daughter incest and 10% of women report a childhood sexual experience with a relative) and that the consequences of sexual abuse are negligible (Herman, Russell & Trocki, 1986; Herman, Perry, & Van der Kolk, 1989). Also described were family risk factors for sexual abuse (Herman & Hirschman, 1981) and the family, social and institutional barriers (Schatzow & Herman, 1989) to disclosing the abuse. Much of Herman's subsequent work has been dedicated to documenting the pervasive and prolonged negative effects of early childhood sexual abuse from somatic symptoms, affective dysregulation and sleep disruption to disorders of personality and a range of self-destructive behaviors. In another study, Herman (1986) reviewed the records of 190 psychiatric outpatients and found nearly one-third of women had been physically or sexually abused and nearly as many (29%) of the male patients reported abusing others.

In the late 1980s Herman collaborated with Gartrell to study another abuse of trust and power: the prevalence of sexual abuse of vulnerable patients by psychiatrists. In a national survey of 1,423 randomly sampled psychiatrists, 98% of the respondents disapproved of sexual contact with patients and recognized it was harmful to patient (Gartrell,

Herman, Olarte, Feldstein, & Localio, 1987a). There was much less agreement, however, about the time that should elapse between the end of a therapeutic relationship and the possibility of engaging in a sexual relationship with a former patient (Herman, Gartrell, Olarte, Feldstein, & Localio, 1987). Most (86%) of the psychiatrists believed that there should be mandatory reporting of fellow therapists who have abused the therapeutic relationship; however they had only reported 8% of the situations about which they had knowledge (Gartrell, Herman, Olarte, Feldstein, & Localio, 1987b). A program to assess and rehabilitate sexually exploitive therapists was described in subsequent papers (Gartrell, Herman, Olarte, Feldstein, & Localio, 1988; Gartrell, Herman, Olarte, Feldstein, Localio, & Schoener, 1989).

With the 1992 publication of *Trauma and Recovery: The aftermath of violence from domestic abuse to political terror*, Herman wrote what many describe as a classic text on the topic. In an accessible academic writing style, reminiscent of Brownmiller's work, she leads the lay or professional reader through the compelling and disturbing cross-cultural history of the changing psychiatric beliefs about violence and its consequence in terms of human suffering. Herman takes the issue of trauma out of the gender battle by providing a scholarly description of the experience of trauma across many situations, from "shell shock" and combat-related traumas suffered by concentration-camp survivors, hostages, and prisoners (more frequently experienced by men) to the "combat neurosis of the sex war." The latter category includes survivors of domestic battering, childhood sexual and physical abuse, rape, and organized sexual exploitation (much more frequently experienced by women). Building on original observations of Freud, Janet, and Charcot, as well as contemporary trauma specialists, Herman uses multiple sources to develop her argument for a new Diagnostic and Statistical Manual of Mental Disorders (DSM) diagnosis of "Complex Post-Traumatic Stress Disorder." This diagnosis acknowledges that the effects of early and/or repeated acts of terror, captivity, and disconnection differ significantly from the trauma response associated with a single event that may have been experienced in the company of other victims (Herman, 1992b, 1995). The stages of recovery she describes (Safety, Remembrance and Mourning, Reconnection) link her own research with historical sources (van der Hart, Brown, & Van der Kolk, 1989), and contemporary work based on combat trauma (Scurfield, 1985), "complicated PTSD" (Brown & Fromm, 1986) and Multiple Personality Disorder (Putnam, 1989).

In *Trauma and Recovery*, now in its second edition (1997), as well as related research papers, Herman demonstrates her capacity to communicate in whatever language is most meaningful to different audiences. Because professional legitimization of any psychiatric condition currently requires verification of measurable, observable physiological evidence of neuropsychiatric damage, her collaboration with other scientists is crucial. At the same time, she grounds her presentations in the language of the men and women who have lived the experiences. Simultaneously poetic, passionate, well-documented and empirically-based, Herman's work maintains a feminist focus and identity without alienating everyone who is not a feminist. The social and political contexts of problems and their solutions are never lost. Nor do they drown out the voices of those who are suffering and need to be empowered as individuals.

Judith Herman's current efforts include teaching and research at Harvard, and ongoing practice in the Victims of Violence Program in Cambridge, Massachusetts that she co-founded with Mary Harvey. Her focus, like the feminist movement that has sustained her, has both broadened and deepened. She sees what is now an international women's movement as an opportunity to learn if the experiences of recovery from trauma can be understood more fully in a cross-cultural context. She is exploring, from a multidisciplinary perspective, what advocacy means to victims and what they would see as justice for the crimes they have endured. She asks how we can hold people accountable for their actions. And, because she has reminded us that there is no "magic bullet" or recipe for healing, the enlightenment project must continue (Herman, 2002).

## Mary R. Harvey

Like Judith Herman, Mary R. Harvey's contributions to feminist theory are well informed by her direct involvement in feminist grassroots organizations such as the Victims of Violence program. Based on her extensive experience as a treatment provider, Harvey has continued to bring the political forces that shape women's lives into the clinical domains of treatment and assessment. Her work has shaped the way treatment is provided both nationally and internationally and has promoted the recovery and resilience of victims of violence worldwide.

As the recognition of women's experiences took shape in prevalence studies, so too was the acknowledgement that violence against women was endemic to society. Feminists argued that violence against women was not an individual problem, but rather a community problem with a burden shared by all. To extend these ideas to clinical work, Harvey applied an ecological framework to describe the causes and clinical implications of trauma (Koss & Harvey, 1991; Harvey, 1996; Harvey & Harney, 1995). In doing so, she emphasized the salient role of the community in treating and preventing victimization by describing the multiple interrelationships between the individual and the community.

Harvey's work on her ecological framework of victimization placed the relationships among the person, event and environment at the focal point of discussion. Person characteristics (i.e., internal traits, abilities), event characteristics (i.e., components of the victimization, such as the nature, severity, frequency and duration of victimization) and environment characteristics (i.e., degree of safety and protection provided post-trauma, attitudes toward the victim and the resources available to her) form the individual's unique ecology and serve as the foundation from which recovery will occur. Harvey described how while the person and event characteristics are likely to be stable, the environment characteristics will range in the degree to which they promote or hinder recovery. Cultural norms or explanatory frameworks will inherently be transmitted to members of a given community. Consequently, women from communities that support a valued role for women and view violence against women as a form of patriarchy and oppression will likely fare better than women who are from communities which uphold patriarchal views. Moreover, since women belong to multiple communities simultaneously (i.e., cultural, racial, professional), victims of violence must negotiate their recovery amid potentially disparate messages heard from multiple communities. Harvey also described how the provision or absence of supports to heal within the community (e.g., availability of rape crisis centers) will shape the recovery process and play a vital role in buttressing women's well-being following trauma (Harvey, 1985; Koss & Harvey, 1991).

While Harvey demonstrates how the ecology of one's environment can empower or disempower recovery, she also stresses how the environment itself can serve as a mechanism to promote violence. Depending upon the nature of social, cultural, political and other environmental forces that are embedded in the ecology, ecological threats may prevail (racism, poverty, misogyny, patriarchy, and disinclination towards diversity and pluralism) to support violence against women, allowing men to use violence as a way to oppress women and exert their power over them. Given the pivotal role of the environment in preventing and intervening in victimization, Harvey underscores the need for social activism and community change to be at the heart of efforts to combat violence against women (Koss & Harvey, 1991).

Harvey also developed a model, based on the role of treatment, the ecological framework and stage models, to help clinicians provide the appropriate level of intervention to assist victims who are at different stages of recovery. Treatment assumptions within an ecological framework include the need to depathologize trauma by placing individual post-trauma reactions within the larger social context, recognition that recovery is multidimensional, and that effective treatment must be provided in the context of the person's unique ecology. Since victimization is the result of a loss of power and control, interventions must guide the victim in restoring these internal and external facilities (Koss & Harvey, 1991; Harvey, 1996).

The timing and level of intervention provided is based on awareness that not all victims of violence will develop post-traumatic stress disorder and as a result, many will benefit from a single session of crisis intervention (Koss & Harvey, 1991; Yassen & Harvey, 1998). At this stage it is important for clinicians to focus on the various reactions to violence and trauma (physical, psychological, relational, cognitive, behavioral and spiritual) and give power and control of the internal and external environment back to the victim by establishing physical and emotional safety, providing information, allowing for ventilation and validation of experience, mobilizing internal and external resources and preparing and planning for the future. Because clients often heal from trauma without intervention, having a history of trauma is not necessarily indicative of current treatment needs. In instances where the trauma is unresolved however, clinicians should begin to develop a relationship with the client and work towards assisting clients to process painful memories, manage disturbing symptoms, and integrate belief changes around the trauma, with the goal of restoring mastery, control and power. The egalitarian nature of group treatment approaches can provide multiple benefits for those who may feel isolated and stigmatized. Central to group treatment are opportunities for victims to validate feelings, foster safe attachments, share grief, confirm and assign meaning to the experiences (Koss & Harvey, 1991).

Beyond providing a structure for treatment, Harvey describes seven indicators of recovery that are applicable to all treatment types. Given the increased emphasis on the efficacy of treatment endemic to the current political climate, these recovery dimensions importantly provide a benchmark for therapeutic goals and clinical assessment. The indicators of recovery include (Harvey & Harney, 1995): (1) authority over the remembering process, (2) integration of memory and affect, (3) affect tolerance, (4) symptom mastery, (5) self-esteem and self-cohesion, (6) safe attachment, and (7) establishing new meaning. These components of recovery are fundamental to the several stage models of treatment developed by Harvey and her colleagues and account for the variation in goals of each stage, the amount of time clients typically spend during the stage and the oftentimes cyclical and non-linear nature of progression through the stages (Lebowitz, Harvey, & Herman, 1993; Yassen & Harvey, 1998). In her current work, she is focused on violence in general, including domestic, community, political violence (M. Harvey, personal communication, April 22, 2003) and is extending these ideas to examine recovery and resilience from the victim's perspective (Harvey, Mishler, Koenen, & Harney, 2000).

## DOMESTIC VIOLENCE/BATTERING

The myths about violence against women have often been incorporated into law and interpretations of the belief that women are men's property and that "family matters" should be private. Even with laws now changed in every state many of the myths about why women are battered and about those who batter continue to be widely believed. Among them are that few women experience battering, that it occurs primarily among low income groups, and that women often obtain satisfaction from being beaten, which is why they don't leave. Batterers are seen as either crazy or "just" under the influence of alcohol and their threats are empty. If women do leave, they will probably find someone else to batter them.

### Ginny NiCarthy

Directed at women who are in an abusive situation, Ginny NiCarthy's book *Getting Free* (1982) grew out of her experiences as a social worker with women in the early battered women's shelter movement. NiCarthy was the director of a battered woman's shelter in 1976 when she began to look for the experts who could provide guidance for helping women who were trying to escape violent relationships. She found, as she had earlier when working with rape victims, that the only real experts on the subject were the women who had lived the experience. Written as a self-help handbook that could help women decide how dangerous their own situation was, information also was provided about the signals that it might be getting more dangerous. Using the words of survivors and building on the successes and failures of these real experts, the book helped women evaluate the possibility of leaving their partners and identify the resources they would need. Practical information was provided about dealing with legal and social services, dealing with financial concerns, finding safe shelter and identifying options to overcome the pervasive and crippling sense of helplessness and terror. Checklists and values clarification exercises help a woman (who often is isolated) begin to frame her situation in terms that invite active problem-solving. It gave her hope that her life could be both different and much better. Now in its 2nd edition (1986, 1997) and 15th printing, *Getting Free* has been translated into many different languages and is still considered by many the "bible of domestic violence texts" (Amazon.com). Similarly, *The Ones Who Got Away: Women Who Left Abusive Partners* (NiCarthy, 1987), which presents the stories of 33 women and their escape from domestic abuse, is often cited as an invaluable resource for women who are trying to make sense of their own lives and identify the realistic costs and benefits of possible alternatives. Readers can confront their fears and take strength from the words of women who have risked leaving bad relationships, overcoming fear of poverty, retaliation, and loss of their children, for refusing to be treated badly.

NiCarthy originally had intended to write a succinct resource for women who were in abusive relationships, but as she added the exercises, examples, and information on all the relevant issues related to creating a new life, she found the book grew much larger than she anticipated. The publication *You Can Be Free: An Easy-to-Read Handbook for Abused Women* (NiCarthy & Davidson, 1989) is a shortened version of the step-by-step suggestions in *Getting Free*. Also translated into many languages, it is directed at women who will find the reading level more accessible, but the book also has the advantage of being brief enough to be used by women whose anxiety may limit their ability to concentrate or retain many details. It also is small enough to be concealed, if necessary.

At a time of these publications, services for battered women were just beginning to be developed and community responses were inconsistent. Although these realities still exist for many women in many places there is a much stronger public awareness that intimate partner violence exists and can no longer be dismissed as just an individual woman's problem, one considered "off-limits" within the private sphere of the family. When she first started running groups for battered women, NiCarthy found that what worked with other groups, did not work with battered women. These groups, involving women with very real fears and diminished self-esteem, provided major challenges to leaders in helping them make decisions. These observations resulted in a co-authored book, *Talking It Out* (NiCarthy, Coffman & Merriam, 1984) directed at group leaders who worked with abused women.

Ginny NiCarthy describes herself as driven by learning, challenge and change, noting that these were always present in the battered women's movement: women taught her. As they did, she realized she needed to constantly revise her evolving theories about patterns of abuse and the social and political contexts in which they occur. As evidence mounted that violence against women was not just physical, that it occurred among adolescents and could also be perpetrated by other women, she incorporated these observations into the revised version of *Getting Free* (1986). Chapters on emotional abuse, teen abuse, and lesbian abuse represented more complexity than the view that men beat women because they can.

Questions about the dynamics and abuse of power at all levels and the different ways they are managed in different cultural groups have continued to challenge her. Some of these questions are explored in *You Don't Have to Take It!* (NiCarthy, Gottlieb, & Coffman, 1993), a book about abuse in the workplace. Other questions relate to the tensions and paradoxes between assumptions feminists held the early battered women's movement and realities unfolding over time. For example, we want women to feel fine about who they are *and* we are hoping they will identify some ways to change their lives, through changing their own behavior and thinking (as well as through social change). And, as feminists, we recognize and honor cultural differences *and* at the same time we may support policies and laws that are incongruent with some cultural group's ways of managing conflict. In many cultural groups the idea of separating men from women for treatment (or the abuser from the abused) may be inconsistent with family and community-based values. Nor is it always clear how to proceed when a person may be an abuser in one instance and abused in another. Labels about abuse and privilege are seldom as distinct in reality as they appear to be in theory, once we consider class, race, life experience, disabilities, etc., as well as gender differences. Her ongoing concerns about the abuse of power between individuals and its relationship to abuse of power between nations have led her to some of the same larger questions raised by others reviewed in this section. Specifically, she wonders how people can be helped not to batter when, as humans, we all have the capacity to abuse others. She echoes the concerns of the other authors in this section in asking increasingly broad questions, such as "How do people of good will deal with people who are not of good will?" Simply excluding some nations from the human rights committee or telling women who are battered that they should leave are not solutions. Work against violence has to involve work toward community building. We are dealing with the same thing on global and individual levels and we should be able to take what we learn in one arena and transfer that to other arenas, or the violence will continue. How, she asks, are we going to deal with bullies in the world without being or becoming bullies? (G. NiCarthy, personal communication, May 1, 2003).

## GLOBAL PERSPECTIVES ON VIOLENCE AGAINST WOMEN

The work of one author in this review does not fit tidily into the aforementioned sections. Maria Primitiva Paz Root is discussed under this section because the scope of her work includes all forms of violence against women. Her theories are global perspectives in that they address all forms of violence against women. She asks critical questions concerning definitions of trauma and what groups of people have been included or excluded from these frameworks.

### Maria Primitiva Paz Root

Maria P.P. Root is a clinical psychologist whose contributions to feminist theory extend well beyond the study of trauma; her work spans two decades and includes numerous books and other publications on ethnic, gender and class identity development, cultural assessment and eating disorders (Root, Fallon, & Friedrich, 1986; Root, Ho, & Sue, 1986; Root, 1987; Root, 1990; Root, 2001). The work we review here is limited to her involvement in educating professionals about the long-term sequelae of victimization, reconceptualizing definitions of trauma and in guiding researchers studying violence against women of color.

As awareness of the prevalence of male violence against women was growing, so, too, was the recognition that these forms of violence may have long lasting effects on victims. During the mid 1980s, Root and her colleagues observed how women with bulimia had histories and symptoms that were reminiscent of women who were victims of interpersonal abuse, noting that the "bulimic often comes to therapy looking like a victim" (Root & Fallon, 1988, p. 161). Based on these clinical observations, Root conducted one of the earliest studies measuring the occurrence of interpersonal victimization in a sample of outpatient women with bulimia. In this study Root observed that 66% of the sample had been physically victimized, 25% raped, 29% were sexually molested, 29% were physically abused and 23% were battered (Root & Fallon, 1988). It was in these results that Root believed that disorders traditionally ascribed to women, such as bulimia and substance abuse, had overlapping expressions of post-trauma reactions and the disorders themselves were evidence of the various ways women tried to cope with interpersonal victimization (Root, 1989). These findings would prompt Root to assert that professionals could be more effective in treating women with these disorders if they began treatment by addressing the aftermath of victimization. To that end, she placed the onus of detecting interpersonal victimization on professionals from different treatment settings, calling on them to recognize warning signs potentially indicative of victimization by asking carefully worded questions to ascertain information about victimization history and by becoming comfortable discussing traumatic experiences with women clients (Root & Fallon, 1989; Root, 1989; Root, 1991).

Much of Root's work has been directed toward developing a broader definition of trauma; extending notions of what trauma is and who is seen as a victim. Many feminists, theoretical scholars and clinicians have criticized existing definitions of trauma and post-traumatic stress disorder (PTSD). These criticisms often have focused on how trauma responses tend to be viewed pathologically rather than in a normative perspective and how the system of diagnosis castigates victims, labeling them in ways that strip their experiences of meaning, history and context. Root extends these critiques by proposing a multidimensional definition of trauma and in doing so, she provides a framework that allows for understanding of the common and unique reactions observed across individuals and groups following victimization. It is also through this reconceptualization that Root extends the traditional definition of trauma, used by most of the foregoing authors, to include groups of people who may be "psychologically or spiritually wounded" as a result of being marginalized by race, ethnicity, religion or sexuality (Root, 1992).

Root's multidimensional definition of trauma is based on a number of limitations found in current thinking of trauma and its aftermath (Root, 1992; Root, 1997). First, consistent with Brownmiller and Herman's views, Root asserts that trauma should be defined as both an individual and collective set of reactions within a larger historical and socio-political context, since there are particular subgroups of people who have been excluded from trauma frameworks despite having experienced large scale atrocities (Japanese Americans, Holocaust survivors and Native Americans, for example). Second, the artificial separation of the mind and body in American culture neglects to incorporate the impact of trauma on one's spirit and spirituality, facets of the human experience particularly important to women of color. Third, concepts of what is traumatic need to become more elaborate and should include threat to life, chronic poverty, racism, homophobia and other forms of discrimination. Lastly, Root believes that by exploring the impact of trauma on dimensions of safety (physical, emotional/psychological, spiritual), professionals would be able to identify potential similarities and differences in trauma-responses based on the nature of the event.

In adopting a more comprehensive definition of trauma, Root sought to distinguish one form of trauma from another in two ways. First, she begins by categorizing trauma based on the proximity to the perpetrator (Root, 1992; Root, 1997): (1) Direct trauma includes traditional forms of trauma (war, accidents, natural disasters) as well as sexual and physical abuse, sudden or debilitating physical illnesses and culturally bound atrocities (internment of Japanese Americans, dislocation of native groups and genocide); (2) Indirect trauma is secondary trauma, whereby a person is traumatized by the trauma endured by another person. Friends, family members, direct witnesses to trauma, people who are habitually exposed to trauma (professionals who work with trauma victims or members of the media) could suffer indirect trauma. Women, as a result of being socialized to be relationship-dependent, may be more likely and vulnerable to indirect trauma; (3) Insidious trauma is form of psychological or symbolic threat based on individual characteristics that are directed towards a larger group of people who are marginalized by gender, race, ethnicity, age, religion, class, sexual orientation or physical ability. The effects of insidious trauma become part of a collective consciousness, leaving generations of people traumatized as a result of their ancestor's direct suffering.

Secondly, Root emphasized the perceived intent of trauma and interpersonal context in which trauma occurs (malicious vs. accidental; in isolation vs. with others) affects the attribution of blame, the support likely to be received as well as the process of healing (Root, 1992). In instances where the perceived intent of trauma is malicious, Root believes that society will tend to blame the victim because talking about this experience is uncomfortable and more often than not, people in society will be unable to identify with the person who has had this trauma inflicted upon her. As a result, victims of malicious trauma will likely suffer in isolation, receive little support and will be viewed as uniquely vulnerable. If the perceived intent of the trauma is accidental however, Root believes blame will be absorbed by society or an equally large force external to the victim and her characteristics. Additionally, her vulnerability will be considered universal. Moreover, Root introduces similar discrepancies based on the interpersonal context in which the traumatic event occurs. If the victim experiences the trauma in deliberate isolation, such as with sexual abuse, the coercion on behalf of the perpetrator will likely lead the victim to blame herself for the crime. The connection with at least one other person, on the other hand, will provide social support and diminish feelings of self-blame and vulnerability. However, when trauma occurs both in isolation and with others (i.e., racism) the affected individual and the community will be simultaneously marginalized and united and will experience feelings of universal and unique vulnerability.

Despite findings that abuse of power is witnessed cross-culturally, Root stresses how violence against women of color has not been explored extensively to date (Root, 1997). To address this gap, Root describes the multiple structural (language, economic disenfranchisement, conceptual, cultural and research) and other barriers that must be considered when conducting research among women of color. First, since women of color have been historically silenced and marginalized, it is imperative that researchers are cognizant of the effects of a traditionally devalued status in society; victims of trauma and particularly women of color may be disinclined to report their trauma out of fear of being mistreated, stereotyped or for fear that disclosing will have little or no effect. Second, researchers must provide ways for women to communicate in their native language. Third, economic status of both the perpetrator and victim and issues of privacy should be considered. Lastly, as Koss noted, researchers must consider how methods of data collection and analysis impact research outcomes; since these components are not independent of culture, Root promotes using ethnoculturally sensitive means of collecting and analyzing data to minimize researcher imbalance and bias and to allow the individual's cultural group to become visible, instead of upholding the viewpoints of the dominant group which have silenced women of color.

## *FEMINIST CONTRIBUTIONS TO THE MEMORY DEBATE*

As might be predicted from the history of any movement that challenges the status quo, a battle emerged during the mid-nineteen-nineties that created some strange bedfellows. Feminists found themselves in the same position Freud had been in when he challenged powerful belief systems nearly a century before (Herman, 1997). Proponents of the so-called "false memory syndrome" accused clinicians of pursuing and implanting nonexistent and distorted memories of abuse in their clients. Specific details and critiques of the scientific, legal, therapeutic and political implications of the backlash against feminist inroads are reviewed in Brown (2000) and Contratto and Gutfreund (1996). Along with other mental health advocates, Harvey, Herman and Koss disputed claims that members of the mental health community were using coercive techniques to conjure memories of nonexistent traumas. In a series of articles and book chapters, they illustrated the validity of clinical experience and shared their findings with respect to memories among victims of violence.

Through clinical vignettes and a study of adult childhood abuse survivors, Harvey and Herman (Harvey & Herman, 1994; Herman & Harvey, 1997) illustrated the three levels of trauma memories based on clients who enter therapy: (1) relatively continuous memories or complete recall with changing interpretations over time; (2) partial amnesia with a mixture of delayed recall and delayed understanding of meaning; (3) delayed recall following profound and pervasive amnesia. Rather than dichotomizing trauma memories as either present or absent, Herman and Harvey's classification underscores how memories are recalled in a continuous process with clients entering therapy at different stages in this process. Furthermore, they argue that distorted memory is part of the clinical presentation of trauma survivors who are diagnosed with PTSD and contrary to popular belief, most people do not enter therapy in search of memories, but rather seek treatment to acquire the strength and resources to cope with the symptoms related to the memories they already have.

Divergent thinking between researchers and clinicians was one of the many focal points of the false memory/recovered memory debate. Harvey questioned whether laboratory research findings (i.e., the finding that memories were malleable and subject to distortion) could be transferred to the therapeutic milieu since these two environments may be incompatible. Given this caveat, she encouraged the research community to consider the ecological validity of the therapeutic atmosphere and in doing so, become more respectful and accepting of clinical observations (Harvey, 1999). Koss also highlighted the differences between laboratory findings and actual or simulated memories in demonstrating that rape memories were distinguished from other unpleasant memories by being less clear, vivid, sequentially developed, well-remembered and talked about (Tromp, Koss, Figueredo & Tharan, 1995; Koss, Figueredo, Bell, Tharan & Tromp, 1996).

## CONCLUSION

We hope readers will be moved to read the author's original publications as the body of work described here is remarkable. The authors reviewed here have made significant inroads in shifting cultural beliefs about the invisibility and acceptability of violence against women. In the process of creating and writing about their research and clinical practices, they also exemplify feminist values of collaboration and cooperation. They acknowledge one another's efforts as important influences in the development of their own projects. They conceptualize gender and violence on a continuum rather than as a dichotomous variable of socialized characteristics and norms. They also recognize that the problems of rape and violence against women in all of its forms lie to a great extent in the social construction of femininity, masculinity and heterosexuality, as well as concepts of privilege associated with beliefs about class and race. They know that true social change means changes in traditional beliefs about the appropriate roles of men and women. And, perhaps most importantly, they know that the contributions they have made will be lost if others do not continue to build on their work and confront with each new generation what they will call the "myths" of the previous generation.

### Lessons for the Future

1.  Multilevel approaches are needed. Although individual treatment for women who have experienced trauma has an important role, the need for social interventions is crucial if trauma associated with violence toward women is to be prevented. Community resources can provide essential information to agencies, including schools and law enforcement. Changing the social structures that support or ignore domestic violence in its many forms requires working with social and cultural beliefs and definitions, and the influence of these beliefs on the development of policies and interpretation of laws.
2.  Remain grounded in the client's experience. Research and theories are useful to the extent that they are relevant in the client's

real world. Definitions of what constitutes violence and abuse and beliefs about how trauma is experienced and should be managed vary widely within and between cultures and sub-groups within cultures.

3.  Know the social and historical contexts of the problem. Beliefs about who has the right to name and control the experience of others is deeply embedded in every society's stories and laws. Confronting and contradicting those who benefit from the dominant perspectives in any situation will engender a vigorous response.

4.  Collaboration is essential to understanding, preventing and treating violence. Collaborations between clients and therapists, advocates and agencies, researchers and therapists, feminists and non-feminists, are all necessary to address complex problems. Disagreements can help refine our understandings. Supporting those who question taken-for-granted perspectives may diminish the effects of vicarious trauma and assaults from vested interests.

5.  Issues of trauma related to violence raise larger issues for several authors. For example "How do people of good will deal with people who are not of good will?" and "How do we deal with bullies without becoming bullies ourselves" (G. NiCarthy, personal communication, May 1, 2003) as well as "What would constitute justice from the perspective of victims?" (Judith Herman, 2002). Violence takes many forms and must be addressed at all levels.

## REFERENCES

American Psychiatric Association (1968). *Diagnostic and statistical manual of mental disorders, (2ⁿᵈ Ed.)* Washington DC: Author.

Boston Women's Health Book Collective (1971). *Our bodies, ourselves,* (pp. 92-97). New York, NY: Simon & Schuster.

Brown, D. & Fromm, E. (1986). *Hypnotherapy and hypnoanalysis.* Hillsdale, NJ: Lawrence Erlbaum.

Brown, L. S. (2000). The controversy concerning recovered memory of traumatic events. In A. Shalev, R. Yehuda & A. McFarlane (Eds.). *International handbook of human response to trauma,* (pp. 195-209). New York: Kluwer Academic.

Brownmiller, S. (1975). *Against our will: Men, women and rape.* New York, NY: Simon and Schuster.

Brownmiller, S. (1984). *Femininity.* New York, NY: Simon and Schuster.

Brownmiller, S. (1992). When men are the victims of rape. In M. S. Kimmel & M. A. Messner (Eds.), *Men's lives*. New York, NY: Macmillan Publishing Company.

Brownmiller, S. (1994). *Seeing Vietnam: Encounters of the road and heart*. New York: Harper/Collins.

Brownmiller, S. (1999). *In our time: Memoir of a revolution*. New York, NY: Dial Press.

Burgess, A., Groth, A. N., Holmstrom, L., & Sgroi, S. M. (1978). *Sexual assault of children and adolescents*. New York, NY: Lexington Books.

Burgess, A. & Holmstrom, L. (1973). The rape victim in the emergency ward. *American Journal of Nursing, 73*(10), 1741-1745.

Burgess, A. & Holmstrom, L. (1974a). Crisis and counseling requests of rape victims. *Nursing Research, 23*(3), 196-202.

Burgess, A. & Holmstrom, L. (1974b). Rape trauma syndrome. *American Journal of Psychiatry, 131,* (9), 981-986.

Burgess, A. & Holmstrom, L. (1974c). *Rape: Victims of crisis*. Bowie, MD: Robert J. Brady.

Burgess, A. & Holmstrom, L. (1979). Rape: Sexual disruption and recovery. *American Journal of Orthopsychiatry, 49*(4), 648-657.

Burgess, A. & Holmstrom, L. (1979a). *Rape: Crisis and recovery*. Englewood Cliffs, CA: Brady.

Burgess, A. & Holmstrom, L. (1988). Treating the adult rape victim. *Medical Aspects of Human Sexuality*, 36-43.

Contratto, S. & Gutfreund, M. J. (Eds.) (1996). *A feminist clinician's guide to the memory debate*. New York: Haworth Press.

Gartrell, N., Herman, J., Olarte, S., Feldstein, M. & Localio, R. (1987a). Psychiatrist-patient sexual contact: results of a national survey, I: prevalence. *American Journal of Psychiatry, 143*, 1126-1131.

Gartrell, N., Herman, J., Olarte, S., Feldstein, M. & Localio, J. (1987b). Reporting practice of psychiatrists who knew of sexual misconduct by colleagues. *American Journal of Orthopsychiatry, 57*(2), 287-295.

Gartrell, N., Herman, J., Olarte, S., Feldstein, M. & Localio, R. (1988). Management and rehabilitation of sexually exploitive therapists. *Hospital and Community Psychiatry, 39*(10), 1070-1074.

Gartrell, N., Herman, J. L., Olarte, S., Feldstein, M., Localio, R. & Schoener, G. (1989). Sexual abuse of patients by therapists: Strategies for offender management and rehabilitation. *New Directions for Mental Health Services, 41*, 55-66.

Gottlieb, N., Burden, D. S., McCormick, R. & NiCarthy, G. (1983). The distinctive attributes of feminists groups. *Social Work with Groups, 6*(3/4), 81-93.

Harvey, M. R. (1985). *Exemplary rape crisis programs: A cross-site analysis and case studies*. Rockville, MD: National Institute of Mental Health.

Harvey, M. R. (1996). An ecological view of psychological trauma and trauma recovery. *Journal of Traumatic Stress, 9*(1), 3-23.

Harvey, M. R. (1999). Memory research and clinical practice: A critique of three paradigms and a framework for psychotherapy with trauma survivors. In L. M. Williams

& V. L. Banyard (Eds.), *Trauma & Memory*, (pp. 19-29). Thousand Oaks, CA: Sage Publications.

Harvey, M. R. & Harney, P. (1995). Individual psychotherapy. In C. Classen & I. D. Yalom (Eds.), *Treating women molested in childhood,* (pp. 63-93). San Francisco, CA: Jossey-Bass/Pfeiffer.

Harvey, M. R. & Herman, J. L. (1994). Amnesia, partial amnesia and delayed recall among adult survivors of childhood trauma. *Consciousness and Cognition: An International Journal, 3*(3/4), 295-306.

Harvey, M.R., Mishler, E.G., Koenen, K. & Harney, P.A. (2000). In the aftermath of sexual abuse: Making and remaking meaning in narratives of trauma and recovery. *Narrative Inquiry, 10*(2), 291-311.

Hazelwood, R. & Burgess, A. (Eds.). (1987). *Practical rape aspects of investigation: A multidisciplinary approach.* New York, NY: Elsevier.

Herman, J. L. (1986). Histories of violence in an outpatient populations: An exploratory study. *American Journal of Orthopsychiatry, 56*(1), 137-141.

Herman, J. L. (1992, 1997). *Trauma and recovery.* New York, NY: Basic Books.

Herman, J. L. (2002, November). *Response to Feminist Therapy: Honoring our Legacy and Facing the Future.* Paper presented to the meeting of the Advanced Feminist Therapy Institute, Boston, MA.

Herman, J. L., Gartrell, N., Olarte, S., Feldstein, M. & Localio (1987a). Psychiatrist-patient sexual contact: Results of a national study: II: Psychiatrist's attitudes. *American Journal of Psychiatry, 144* (2), 164-169.

Herman, J. L. & Harvey, M. R. (1997). Adult memories of childhood trauma: A naturalistic clinical study. *Journal of Traumatic Stress, 10*(4), 557-571.

Herman, J. L. & Hirschman, L. (1977). Father-daughter incest. *Signs, 2*(4), 735-756.

Herman, J. L. & Hirschman, L. (1981, 2000). *Father-daughter incest.* Cambridge, MA: Harvard University Press.

Herman, J. L., Perry, J. C. & Van der Kolk, B. A. (1989). Childhood trauma in borderline personality disorder. *American Journal of Psychiatry, 146*(4), 490-495.

Herman, J. L. Russell, D., & Trocki, K. (1986). Long-term effects of incestuous abuse in childhood. *American Journal of Psychiatry, 143*(10), 1293-1296.

Holmstrom, L. & Burgess, A. (1975). Assessing trauma in the rape victim. *American Journal of Nursing, 75*(8), 1288-1291.

Holmstrom, L. & Burgess, A. (1978). *The victims of rape: Institutional reactions.* New York, NY: Wiley.

International Society for Traumatic Stress Studies. (2003). www.istss.org/What/history3. htm [website].

Kleinman, A., Eisenberg, L. & Good, B. (1978). Culture, illness, and care. *Annals of Internal Medicine, 88,* 251-258

Koss, M. P. (1985). The hidden rape victim: Personality, attitudinal, and situational characteristics. *Psychology of Women Quarterly, 9*(2), 193-212.

Koss, M. P. (1993). Detecting the scope of rape: A review of prevalence research methods. *Journal of Interpersonal Violence, 8*(2), 198-222.

Koss, M. P. & Cleveland, H. H. (1997). Stepping on toes: Social roots of date rape lead to intractability and politicization. In M. D. Schwartz (Ed.), *Researching sexual violence against women: Methodological and personal perspectives*, (pp. 4-21), Thousand Oaks, CA: Sage.

Koss, M. P. & Dinero, T. E. (1988). Predictors of sexual aggression among a national sample of male college students. *Annals of the New York Academy of Sciences. 528*, 133-147.

Koss, M. P., Dinero, T. E, Seibel, C. A. & Cox, S. L. (1988). Stranger and acquaintance rape: Are there differences in the victim's experience? *Psychology of Women Quarterly, 12*(1), 1-24.

Koss, M. P. & Dinero, T. E. (1989). Discriminant analysis of risk factors for sexual victimization among a national sample of college women. *Journal of Consulting and Clinical Psychology, 57*(2), 242-250.

Koss, M.P., Figueredo, A.J., Bell, I., Tharan, M. & Tromp, S. (1996). Traumatic memory characteristics: A cross-validated mediational model of response to rape among employed women. *Journal of Abnormal Psychology, 105*(3) 421-432.

Koss, M. P. & Gidycz, C. A. (1985). Sexual Experiences Survey: Reliability and validity. *Journal of Consulting and Clinical Psychology, 53*(3), 422-423.

Koss, M. P., Gidycz, C. A. & Wisniewski, N. (1987). The scope of rape: Incidence and prevalence of sexual aggression and victimization in a national sample of higher education students. *Journal of Consulting and Clinical Psychology, 55*(2), 162-170.

Koss, M. P., Goodman, L. A., Browne, A., Fitzgerald, L. F., Keita, G. P. & Russo, N. F. (1994). *No safe haven: Male violence against women at home, at work, and in the community.* Washington, DC: American Psychological Association.

Koss, M. P. & Harvey, M. R. (1991). *The rape victim: Clinical and community interventions.* Thousand Oaks, CA: Sage Publications.

Koss, M. P., Heise, L. & Russo, N. F. (1994). The global health burden of rape. *Psychology of Women Quarterly*, 18(4), 509-537.

Koss, M. P. & Hoffman, K. (2000). Survivors of violence by male partners: Gender and cultural considerations. In R. M. Eisler & M. Hersen (Eds.), *Handbook of gender, culture and health*, (pp. 471-489). Mahwah, NJ: Lawrence Erlbaum Associates.

Koss, M. P., Ingram, M. & Pepper, S. (1997). Psychotherapists' role in the medical response to male-partner violence. *Psychotherapy: Theory, Research, Practice and Training, 34*(4), 386-396.

Koss, M. P. & Oros, C. J. (1982). Sexual Experiences Survey: A research instrument investigating sexual aggression and victimization. *Journal of Consulting and Clinical Psychology, 50*(3), 455-457.

Koss, M. P., Woodruff, W. J. & Koss, P. G. (1990). Relation of criminal victimization to health perceptions among women medical patients. *Journal of Consulting and Clinical Psychology, 58*(2), 147-152.

Koss, M. P. & Woodruff, W. J. (1991). Emerging issues in women's health. In J. Sweet & R. Rozensky (Eds.), *Handbook of clinical psychology in medical settings*, (pp. 201-221). New York: Plenum.

Lebowitz, L., Harvey, M. R. & Herman, J. L. (1993). A stage-by-dimension model of recovery from sexual trauma. *Journal of Interpersonal Violence, 8*(3), 378-391.

Lira, L. R., Koss, M. P. & Russo, N. F. (1999). Mexican American women's definition of rape and sexual abuse. *Hispanic Journal of Behavioral Sciences, 21*(3), 236-265.

NiCarthy, G. (1982). *Getting Free: A handbook for women in abusive relationship.* Seattle, WA: Seal Press.

NiCarthy, G., Coffman, S. & Merriam, K. (1984). *Talking it out: A guide to groups for abused women.* Seattle, WA: Seal Press.

NiCarthy, G. (1986, 1997). *Getting Free: You can end abuse and take back your life.* Seattle, WA: Seal Press.

NiCarthy, G. (1987). *The ones who got away: Women who left abusive partners.* Seattle, WA: Seal Press.

NiCarthy, G. & Davidson, A. (1989). *You can be free: An easy-to-read handbook for abused women.* Seattle, WA: Seal Press.

NiCarthy, G., Gottlieb, N. & Coffman, S. (1993). *You don't have to take it!* Seattle, WA: Seal Press.

Putnam, F. (1989). *Diagnosis and treatment of multiple personality disorder.* New York, NY: Guilford Press.

Ressler, R. K., Burgess, A. W. & Douglas, J. E. (1988). *Sexual homicide: Patterns and motives.* New York, NY: Lexington Books.

Ressler, R. K., Burgess, A. W., Burgess, A. G., & Douglas, J. E. (1993). *Crime classification manual.* London, England: Simon & Schuster.

Root, M. P. (1987). An eight-week group treatment program for bulimia. *Journal of College Student Psychotherapy, 1*(4), 105-118.

Root, M. P. P. (1989). Treatment failures: The role of sexual victimization in women's addictive behavior. *American Journal of Orthopsychiatry, 59*(4), 542-549.

Root, M. P. (1990). Resolving "other" status: Identity development of biracial individuals. *Women & Therapy, 9*(1-2), 185-205.

Root, M. P. P. (1991). Persistent, disordered eating as a gender-specific, post-traumatic stress response to sexual assault. *Psychotherapy: Theory, Research, Practice, Training, 28*(1), 96-102.

Root, M. P. P. (1992). Reconstructing the impact of trauma on personality. In L. S. Brown & M. Ballou (Eds.), *Personality and psychopathology: Feminist reappraisals,* (pp. 229-265). New York, NY: Guilford Press.

Root, M. P. P. (1997). *Filipino Americans: Transformation and identity.* Thousand Oaks, CA: Sage Publications.

Root, M. P. P. (2001). *Love's revolution: Interracial marriage.* Philadelphia, PA: Temple University Press.

Root, M. P. P., Fallon, P. & Friedrich, W. N. (1986). *Bulimia: A systems approach to treatment.* New York, NY: Norton Publishers.

Root, M. P. P. & Fallon, P. (1988). The incidence of victimization experiences in a bulimic sample. *Journal of Interpersonal Violence, 3*(2), 161-173.

Root, M. P. P. & Fallon, P. (1989). Treating the victimized bulimic: The functions of binge-purge behavior. *Journal of Interpersonal Violence, 4*(1), 90-100.

Root, M., Ho, C. & Sue, S. (1986). Issues in the training of counselors for Asian Americans. In H. Lefley & P. Pedersen, (Eds). *Cross-cultural training for mental health professionals*, (pp. 199-209). Springfield, IL: Charles C. Thomas.

Schatzow, E. & Herman, J. (1989). Breaking secrecy: Adult survivors disclose to their families. *Psychiatric Clinics of North America, 12*(2), 337-349.

Scurfield, R. (1985). Post-trauma stress assessment and treatment: Overview and formulations. In C. R. Figley (Ed.), *Trauma and its wake*, (Vol. 1, pp. 219-256). New York, NY: Brunner/Mazel.

Tromp, S., Koss, M.P., Figueredo, A.J. & Tharan, M. (1995). Are rape memories different? A comparison of rape, other unpleasant and pleasant memories among employed women. *Journal of Traumatic Stress, 8*(4) 607-627.

van der Hart, O., Brown, P. & van der Kolk, B. A. (1989). Pierre Janet's treatment of post-traumatic stress. *Journal of Traumatic Stress, 2*, 379-395.

White, J. W. & Koss, M. P. (1993). Adolescent sexual aggression within heterosexual relationships: Prevalence, characteristics, and causes. In H. Barbaree & W. Marshall (Eds.), *The juvenile sex offender*, (pp. 182-202). New York: Guilford Press.

Yassen, J. & Harvey, M. R. (1998). Crisis assessment and interventions with victims of violence. In P. M. Kleespies (Ed.), *Emergencies in mental health practice: Evaluation and management*, (pp. 117-144). New York, NY: Guilford Press.

# Location, Location, Location: Contributions of Contemporary Feminist Theorists to Therapy Theory and Practice

Natalie Porter

**SUMMARY.** This chapter describes and analyzes the contributions of contemporary feminist therapy theorists Ellyn Kaschak, Laura Brown, Mary Ballou, Pam Remer and Judith Worell, and Bonnie Burstow. Themes common to all of the authors are presented, including: (1) the deconstruction of patriarchy in the service of understanding the lived experience of women, (2) the position that there is no single reality, no one "right" feminist theory or epistemological position about women, and (3) the understanding that the relationship of women's multiple realities, experiences, and roles is central to feminist theory building. The approaches of these theorists to the critical analysis of mainstream therapy, to feminist theory building, and therapy applications are described and compared. *[Article copies available for a fee from The Haworth Document Delivery Service: 1-800-HAWORTH. E-mail address: <docdelivery@haworthpress.com> Website: <http://www.HaworthPress.com> © 2005 by The Haworth Press, Inc. All rights reserved.]*

---

Natalie Porter is Vice-Provost at Alliant International University. She has contributed to feminist therapy theory primarily in the areas of supervision, ethics and multiculturally informed feminist therapy.

Address correspondence to: Natalie Porter, PhD, Alliant International University, 2728 Hyde Street, Suite 100, San Francisco, CA 94109.

[Haworth co-indexing entry note]: "Location, Location, Location: Contributions of Contemporary Feminist Theorists to Therapy Theory and Practice." Porter, Natalie. Co-published simultaneously in *Women & Therapy* (The Haworth Press, Inc.) Vol. 28, No. 3/4, 2005, pp. 143-160; and: *The Foundation and Future of Feminist Therapy* (ed: Marcia Hill, and Mary Ballou) The Haworth Press, Inc., 2005, pp. 143-160. Single or multiple copies of this article are available for a fee from The Haworth Document Delivery Service [1-800-HAWORTH, 9:00 a.m. - 5:00 p.m. (EST). E-mail address: docdelivery@haworthpress.com].

**KEYWORDS.** Feminist therapy, feminist therapy theory, feminist social constructivism.

This article addresses the theoretical and therapy contributions of feminist therapists over the last decade, specifically the works of Ellyn Kaschak, Laura Brown, Mary Ballou, Pam Remer and Judith Worrell, and Bonnie Burstow. Common themes run through the works of these theorists, particularly the deconstruction of patriarchy in the service of understanding the lived experience of women, the assertion that the multiple contexts of women's lives must be addressed in theory and in therapy, and the recognition that feminist therapy theory must involve the reconstruction of therapeutic goals, values, frameworks, and theory. Although none of these theorists would be characterized as post-modern theorists, and in fact, would take issue with the value-neutral connotations of that epistemological standpoint, they all share the position that there is no single reality, no one "right" feminist theory or epistemological position about women. Rather they would claim that understanding of the relationship of women's multiple realities, experiences, and roles is central to feminist theory building. "Location, location, location," are central features of contemporary feminist theory development. The location of the feminist theorist, the location of the feminist therapist, and the location of the client must all be brought to the endeavor of feminist theorists and therapists understanding the contexts of women's lives and working toward the well being and healing of women.

The commonalities and differences of the theorists listed above, their approaches to feminist epistemology and therapy theory, and the ways they have extended feminist theory and practice will be covered in this piece. Each author's feminist analysis/critique, or deconstruction, of gender and psychotherapy, her re-construction or reformulation pertaining to feminist epistemology and therapy theories, and her specific extensions of feminist therapy will be presented. The impact of these works on contemporary feminist therapy practice and implications for the future will be offered.

## *FEMINIST DECONSTRUCTION: GENDER, SOCIETY, AND PSYCHOPATHOLOGY*

Contemporary feminist theorists continue to provide rich critical analyses of contemporary society and the necessity of understanding women in the context of race, ethnicity, gender, class, sexual orientation, disability and age. The deconstruction of gender by Ellyn Kaschak, of psychopathology by Judith Worell and Pam Remer and by Laura Brown and Mary Ballou, and of violence by Bonnie Burstow will be addressed in this section. These authors have taken on the "usual suspects" in their critiques of traditional psychology theory, empiricism and scientism and the myth of value free science. They have also addressed the problems of some of the early feminist epistemologies that espoused essentialist, dichotomous gender-based categories, albeit with positive, even heroic feminine characteristics replacing the negative stereotypes of traditional psychology.

Among Ellyn Kaschak's many contributions to feminist psychology, her writings in the areas of feminist epistemology and the deconstruction of patriarchal social structures are at the core of the field. Her early work is rooted in the family therapy and systems theory movements, where epistemological questions, that is, making known the rules or meaning of "meaning," undergird the theoretical enterprise. She began by deconstructing family therapy itself, demonstrating how the "rules" of the family as well as those underpinning family therapy and therapists remained based on patriarchal structures and assumptions (Kaschak, 1990). The following quote by Kaschak embodies how both authors view the role of gender in society: ". . . the masculine always defines the feminine by naming it, containing it, engulfing, invading, and evaluating it. The feminine is never permitted to stand alone or to subsume the masculine" (1992, p. 5).

In *Engendered Lives: A New Psychology of Women's Experience,* Kaschak (1992) takes on what it means to truly understand the nature of the gendered world. By taking the noun, "gender," and transforming it into a verb form, she is already providing insight into the epistemology of gender. In a gendered, or engendered world, gender is not static. Gendering is an active, interactive, and continuous process that is embedded in all aspects of our existence, our relationships, and our meanings. To truly understand the embeddedness of gender throughout our social structures means to recognize that changes in these relationships and structures cannot occur within the context of the same "rules." Kaschak (1992) argues that women are always the targets of these rules. Women are penalized for being too feminine as well as too masculine. They are presented with the paradox that, on the one hand, as a female, to follow gender-based rules is to be confronted with negative consequences for being female, and on the other hand, to not follow the rules is to be confronted with negative consequences for not being female enough. As women walk this tightrope between expressing too little or too much femininity, there are few payoffs for doing what is expected.

Kaschak (1992) offers the Antigone myth as the extension of the Oedipal myth/complex of psychoanalytic theory. The Oedipal myth explains the patriarchal domination of the family and the culture. The Antigone myth elaborates women's roles in the patriarchal family. It is emblematic of the realization that men exist always with the expectation that they are entitled to the love and caretaking of women. In a patriarchal, gendered society, women's development is tantamount to preparation to serve men. Women's identity is synonymous with patriarchal definitions of women's roles, bodies, and expectations. Attachment to one's mother or other women or even conscious attempts to raise children in nonsexist ways cannot change these relationships or alter the course of gender in the broader context. In fact, in an Oedipal/Antigone world, women are separated from each other, because the role of mothers is to prepare their daughters for the same male servitude.

Kaschak (1992) provides examples of the pervasiveness of the embeddedness of gender. Self-concept is "embodied" for women, meaning that it exists only within the context of the female body. For women, esteem is the result of the internalization of a social rather than an individual construct that revolves around the attributions given to women by men about women's bodies. Relational, according to Kaschak, is defined as being responsible for the success of relationships with others or for being sensitive to the needs of others, even when these needs go unexpressed or even unrecognized by men who assert their independence and separateness while expecting nurturance and support.

Mary Ballou and Laura Brown have been central in providing a feminist critique of psychological constructs pertaining to personality and psychopathology. In *Personality and Psychopathology: Feminist Reappraisals* (1992) and *Rethinking Mental Health and Disorder* (2002), Ballou and Brown challenge both the traditional notions of personality and personality theories as well as the diagnostic "enterprise" that has shaped the field's views of psychopathology, mental health and illness. Ballou and her colleagues (Ballou, Matsumoto and Wagner, 2002) question the scientism of the past two centuries that embraced logical positivist and empirical forms of scientific inquiry as the only ways of knowing. In their work, Brown and Ballou (1992, 2002) have exposed the inadequacy of these approaches for understanding women's distress, their psychological development, or the static construct called "personality" as it pertains to women. Not only have the authors called for a more contextual view of women's development, health, and distress, but they have also pointed out that no psychological theories or constructs that fail to account for oppression in the lives of women can ever effectively be used to understand or treat women. Brown (1992) has demonstrated how the "personality disorders" found in the Diagnostic and Statistical Manuals are severely flawed; they possess problems of methodology, reliability, and validity and are contaminated by cultural biases, including sexism and other forms of oppression. Brown points out how current diagnostic nomenclature fails to account for physical and psychological trauma as the etiology and shaping forces behind women's distress. Women are not only oppressed by their being on the receiving end of physical, sexual, and psychological violence in society but are further oppressed by the mental health establishment that confers stigmatizing labels for the resulting distress or trauma.

Worell and Remer (1992, 2002) have elaborated on the ways in which sexist dimensions have biased the psychological assessment and diagnosis of women. They listed:

> (a) disregarding or minimizing the effect of the environmental context on individual's behaviors; (b) different diagnoses being given to women and men displaying similar symptoms; (c) therapist's misjudgments in selection of diagnostic labels due to sex-role stereotyped beliefs; and (d) using a sex-biased theoretical orientation. (p. 151)

Worell and Remer (1992, 2002) have developed a schema depicting how racial/ethnic and gender bias can impact mental health diagnosis and treatment at multiple levels. How mental health and pathology are defined; how symptoms are described, interpreted, and identified; which diagnostic labels are applied and which interventions are seen as appropriate all constitute stages of diagnosis that are vulnerable to bias. The broader cultural context (e.g., legal, social, cultural, economic, and educational structures), the attributes, perspectives, history, behavior, education of the clinician and of the client comprise the potential sources of bias that interact with the various stages listed above. The permutations generated by these interactions substantially raise the odds that a client will be labeled with a stigmatizing and sexist or racist diagnosis or receive an inappropriate intervention.

In *Radical Feminist Therapy: Working in the Context of Violence*, Bonnie Burstow (1992) elaborates a critique parallel to those of Kaschak, Brown, and Ballou. Like Kaschak (1992), Burstow argues that woman is reduced to "Body" (p. 4) by men and patriarchy. Not only is "woman" synonymous with "body" in male dominated societies, but this body is then fetishized by men, and the body exists not "as for-itself or for-herself but as for-him" (p. 4). Just as Kaschak proposes the paradox of women's lives as being punished for either behaviors that are too femininely gendered or not gendered enough, Burstow points out that women are objectified as a series of body parts with the sole purpose of serving the male. Female pleasure is irrelevant; and when pleasure is associated with females, it is viewed as "uncomely . . . [and women as] insatiable and are 'bestialized'" (p. 4).

Continuing the work of other radical feminists such as Dworkin (1974) and Daly (1978), Burstow categorizes the various ways in which violence is committed against women, ranging from (1) sexualization of the female body; (2) physically harmful and painful "beautification" practices embedded in different cultures; (3) compulsory and male-dominated heterosexism; (4) physical and sexual violence; (5) exploitation of women as domestic laborers. The woman-as-body phenomenon serves to separate women from each other and maintain this separation in service to men, through a complex interaction of the eroticization of the younger woman (daughter), which Burstow labels as a form of incest, and the exploitation for labor of the older woman (mother). Burstow relates the story of Persephone, daughter of Ceres, abducted and used sexually by her uncle, king of the underworld. This myth serves as the symbol of father-daughter exploitation and eroticization and mother-daughter separation that occurs because of the mother's inability to protect her daughter or provide the same power and privilege seemingly provided by the father.

## FEMINIST RECONSTRUCTION: ADDRESSING CONTEMPORARY ISSUES PERTAINING TO WOMEN IN ALL OF THEIR COMPLEXITY

Although the themes of these contemporary feminist theorists are wide-ranging, there are common themes in the topics they have pursued. Attention to context, the diversity of women's lives, and the impact of multiple oppressions, such as race, ethnicity, class, or sexual orientation on women are central to the work of these theorists. These authors have struggled to move beyond gender as a dichotomous category to expose the impact of all forms of oppression on women, and to describe women's development, growth, and dilemmas in all of their complexity and depth.

Kaschak's resolution of the Antigone complex symbolizes the feminist re-construction of theory and practice as that which is life affirming and central to women, based on women making meaning from their own experiences, perceptions, and knowing. The Antigone complex is resolved when women leave the world of their fathers, do not ". . . settle for a place in a man's world [and] . . . take courage in behalf of themselves and other women, the courage to make their own meanings" (1992, p. 88). "Resolution of the Antigone complex requires a reconnection with other women and a reaffirmation of the positive quality of this connection, of women and of oneself as a woman" (1992, p. 226). In this phase, a woman:

> Faces own vulnerability.
> Develops interdependence and flexible boundaries.
> Develops own identity as a woman and a human being, and only then can deal with men. Experiences self in context.
> Redefines meaning of physicality. Moves beyond fragmentation of body parts and psychological aspects of the self to integration. Uses eyes to see for herself. Develops her own sense of nonexploitive entitlement. Doesn't demand that others also see her way.
> Mothers stop making males central and helping to domesticate other females. (Kaschak, 1992, p. 84)

The radical feminist therapy theory of Burstow is based on the intersection of feminist therapy theory with the radical therapy/antipsychiatry movement. Burstow (1992) characterizes radical feminist therapy as primarily a political activity "grounded in woman-woman solidarity" (p. 40). Female empowerment and the rekindling of woman-woman connections signal the re-construction of the woman in service to herself. Resistance is the hallmark of woman's "being for-itself" (p. 16). Burstow describes resistance in much the same way Kaschak wrote of the resolution of the Antigone complex:

> Women's vision may be seen as an act of resistance in its own right. Seeing out of our own eyes is in itself disobeying the patriarchy. Women also resist more concretely. As women we are beings who act and whose actions can be our resistance. (p. 18)

She continues to characterize resistance as occurring in varying degrees or efficacy from those that draw psychiatric diagnoses to more deliberate and systematic action in the service of social change. Brown (1994) describes this resistance as the refusal to "merge with the dominant culture" (p. 23).

Ballou, Matsumoto, and Wagner (2002) have expanded contextual and social constructivist theoretical perspectives into a feminist, multicultural, ecological framework. In part, this model was derived from Ballou's synthesis of 11 aspects of contextual feminist multicultural psychology, which addressed recognizing the intersection of class, race/ethnicity, and gender and the status hierarchy implicit in these intersections, the understanding of the "personal" as both structural and symbolic, the understanding of how power and resources are allocated, the study of the psyche in context, the belief that activism and social justice must accompany therapy and the development of a critical consciousness, the awareness of the privilege given to the dominant patriarchal paradigm, and the need for a multi-leveled and interdisciplinary feminist analysis and practice (2002).

The Feminist Ecological model, which incorporates this synthesis of feminist therapy theory with multicultural psychology, liberation psychology, and ecological theory, was intended to represent . . . " multiple dimensions of human existence, of real-world complexity, of multiple models of living and ways of knowing, of multidirectional interactions between the person and her or his contexts, and of direct, contiguous, and distal influences" (Ballou, Matsumoto, & Wagner, 2002, p. 118).

Figure 1 depicts the ecological model, which contains four levels (individual, microsystem, exosystem, and macrosystem levels), two "meta" levels (planetary/climatic conditions and time/history), and four demographic characteristics (sex/gender, race/ethnicity, age, and class) that are considered coordinates because they cut across all levels. The individual level incorporates the intellectual, emotional, physical and spiritual dimensions of the individual. These dimensions interact with the coordinates (sex/gender, race/ethnicity, age, and class) to signify that each aspect or experience of the individual results from the mutually interactive processes between dimensions and coordinates and the interaction between the individual level with the other levels of the model.

The second level, the microsystem, includes all aspects of the individual's environment that directly and routinely interact with the individual. Included at this level are family members, close relationships, the workplace or school, the neighborhood, community, and local government. The impact of these factors is mediated by the demographic variables; for example, cultural practices and values may shape the immediacy or intimacy of family relationships for the individual.

FIGURE 1. The Ecological Model

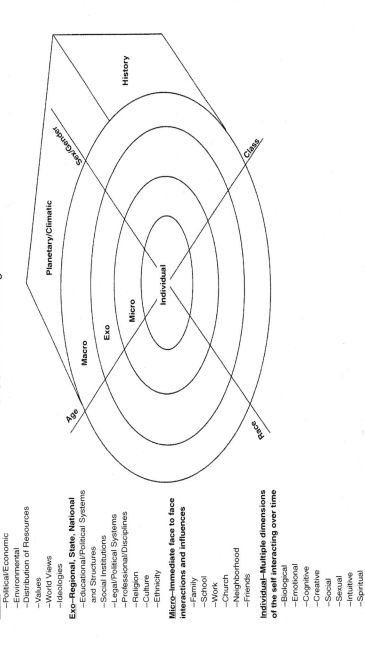

**Macro—Global**
 –Political/Economic
 –Environmental
 –Distribution of Resources
 –Values
 –World Views
 –Ideologies

**Exo—Regional, State, National**
 –Educational/Political Systems
  and Structures
 –Social Institutions
 –Legal/Political Systems
 –Professional/Disciplines
 –Religion
 –Culture
 –Ethnicity

**Micro—Immediate face to face
interactions and influences**
 –Family
 –School
 –Work
 –Church
 –Neighborhood
 –Friends

**Individual—Multiple dimensions
of the self interacting over time**
 –Biological
 –Emotional
 –Cognitive
 –Creative
 –Social
 –Sexual
 –Intuitive
 –Spiritual

Source: Ballou, M., Matsumoto, A., and Wagner, M. (2002), Toward a feminist ecological theory of human nature: Theory building in response to real-world dynamics. In M. Ballou & L. S. Brown (Eds.), *Rethinking mental health and disorder: Feminist perspectives* (pp. 99-144). New York: The Guilford Press. Reprinted with permission.

The third level, the exosystem, includes social institutions and other institutions at the regional, state, or national level that impact the individual more indirectly. The macrosystem includes the structural and environmental forces more distally related to the daily functioning of the person. Economic principles, structural and environmental forces, values, worldviews, and distribution of resources at a global level all constitute aspects of the macrosystem.

## NEW MODELS OF FEMINIST PSYCHOTHERAPY

Kaschak articulates the relationship between theory and practice that characterizes much of the work this group of feminist theorists:

> Feminist psychotherapies and epistemologies share a focus on making visible the hidden effects of gender in ordinary life. They are both oriented toward exposing masculinist meanings and their damaging effects in general and in particular, and toward developing alternative meanings and choices based upon the actual lived experience of girls and women. (1992, p. 210)

Worell and Remer (1992) have based their therapy model on three well-established feminist principles, "the personal is political, egalitarian relationships, and valuing the female perspective" (p. 91). Ballou (2002) proposes five overarching themes that are found throughout the feminist therapy theory literature that overlap with the preceding themes: (1) the valuing of women's experience; (2) the belief that socio-cultural factors underline women's psychological distress; (3) the belief that power issues must be addressed at both "local" and societal levels; (4) the placement of gender within a hierarchy of oppressions and; (5) the need for feminist therapy to incorporate social as well as individual change.

Burstow (1992) has articulated similar premises: that power imbalances both create and exacerbate women's personal problems and that the role of therapy is to aid women in understanding this connection in the service of resistance to societal demands; that individuals who are similarly "located" socioculturally are better able to understand each other, with female therapists better able to work with women clients, disabled women with disabled women therapists, women of color with each other, etc.; and that feminist therapy should be a collaborative, empowering process where therapists eschew the "expert" role and its trappings.

Brown (1994) has emphasized the role that social change, multiculturalism, and anti-domination must always play in feminist therapy:

> The purpose of psychotherapy is not to soothe, but to disrupt, not to adjust, but to empower. . . . Feminist therapy requires a theory that defines therapy as not simply a healing art, although healing is likely to take place. Therapy must also be a conscious and intentional act of radical social change. . . . It involves questioning fundamental values and assumptions. (pp. 29-30)

These principles are characteristic of the work of the theorists described throughout this article. In this section, aspects of the models of feminist therapy of Worell and Remer, Brown, Burstow, and Kaschak will be described as emblematic not only of these principles but of the theoretical advances that have occurred over the past decade in approaches to feminist therapy. I will primarily address the areas in which each author has made distinctive contributions because of the overlap and synergy between much of their work.

Brown's contributions to feminist therapy theory and practice have been wide ranging. She has assisted many, many practitioners from all disciplines in understanding the lives and experiences of the clients with whom they engage everyday–clients who, because of the traumatic lives they have lived, are often difficult to get to know or understand and are frequently avoided or stigmatized even by mental health professionals. She has been an articulate and effective voice in analyzing and critiquing oppression such as white privilege, class privilege, heterosexism, and homophobia. She has explored models for changing oppression in her articles about antiracism, anti-domination, multiculturalism, diversity, and lesbian/gay psychology. She has addressed ethical and boundary issues, fee and contractual issues, and has added immensely to the understanding of feminist treatment of distress brought on by trauma.

One salient question for all feminist therapists is whether "feminist therapy" is an oxymoron. That is, does the act of therapy itself, which typically is making the political personal, undermine the political to such an extent that it is contrary to feminist values and goals? Although each of the authors has struggled with this issue, Brown (1994) has articulated the role the therapist must play to maintain the political edge within the therapy act. She asserts that to be truly political, the therapy must "continually trace the path back from the personal to the political, its interpretations and understandings on feminist political analysis and feminist strategies for action" (p. 37). In her work, Brown demonstrates the commitment to maintaining this political focus in all associations and interactions with her clients. This interweaving of the personal and the political and the implicit and explicit analysis of gender, power, social justice issues, and oppression serves as a model for feminist and radical therapists who are committed to fostering higher order change such as social change and justice rather than their clients making peace with their oppression. In this context, Brown also takes on another key issue in feminist theory, the "tension" (p. 67) between essentialist and constructivist positions. Rather than viewing this issue from one standpoint, Brown addresses the dialectic. She argues that the tension between essentialism and constructivist standpoints serves to illuminate the individual lives and experiences of women in all of their diversity, and in important ways, so long as they don't become essentialist about gender.

Brown has also pushed feminist therapy theory to truly address diversity, particularly to attend to multiculturalism and white privilege and anti-domination. She has challenged the field to move beyond the superficial attention paid to multiculturalism to integrated and complex understandings of how feminist therapy approaches that have ignored diversity, and particularly race and class, have undermined the values and practice of feminist therapy for all women. Brown describes a multicultural feminist analysis as that which:

> moves understanding of oppression and domination beyond dichotomies toward a more accurate and nuanced representation of how these dynamics are experienced in life by people who rarely, belong entirely to groups that occupy the role of most powerful or oppressor. (p. 74)

She questions and rejects the monocultural approaches that are typically associated with white women therapists and used with white clients (and far too often with clients of color) and the ways in which white feminist therapists do not challenge themselves or their clients to address white privilege and domination in all aspects of our lives. Through Brown's work, a white feminist therapist is able to move along a path of addressing diversity (Brown 1990), to embracing multiculturalism and antiracism (Brown, 1991), to adopting an anti-domination stance, which requires an active understanding of how to become an ally to those whom we oppress as white women and to undermining these structures worldwide (Brown, 1993). Brown's vision of a therapist-client relationship in feminist therapy is one where the therapist must question their own values, view, and standpoints about gender, race, class, culture, sexual orientation, age, and disability and bring this self-awareness into the therapeutic realm. The therapist must understand how these factors have been "constructed in each of their lives and how they will gain meaning to them" (Brown, 1994, p. 100). Brown's work lays out the complexity and radical nature of these actions, which are too often superficially understood and casually addressed.

Worell and Remer (1992, 2002) have provided a comprehensive feminist therapy practice and training model that encompasses not only their work but also the theories and practice of other contemporary feminist therapists, including several featured in this chapter. They have prepared a framework that pairs the feminist therapy principles of initiating social change, developing egalitarian relationships, and valuing women's perspectives with specific counseling goals. The author's empowerment model then provides therapy techniques that can be implemented in the service of each of these principles and goals.

The authors have also gone beyond the gender-bias critique of mainstream theoretical perspectives to offer an analysis of whether and how to transform these theories into nonsexist theories and therapy orientations. Although this approach is less radical than that of many of the other authors included in this chapter, it is more accessible to feminist-oriented therapists who themselves are embedded in these mainstream theoretical perspectives. They are modeling the feminist process of starting with the reader's theoretical and epistemological perspectives and then moving to expand their understanding and practice of feminist principles. This approach provides therapists with not only the content and information needed for a comprehensive overview of the etiological factors and interventions from a feminist perspective, but a blueprint for thinking about women, their psychological well-being and their distress.

Kaschak advocates for an integrated model of feminist therapy that breaks with established models of psychotherapy. Her model is based on the contextual model of personality development described previously. The aim of therapy is to make explicit and then change the meanings, both social and private, that have been embedded in the experiences of every women. Additionally, the therapist must simultaneously attempt to view the words of the client through three sets of lens, the client's eyes, her (therapist) own eyes, and the eyes of patriarchy. The therapist should be "questioning her own meanings as well as those of the client and ferreting out the indeterminate observer who will be hiding in them as well as in those of her client" (1992, p. 212).

The therapist uses a "mattering map" (Kaschak, 1992, p. 215) to understand the client's experiences. It includes:

1. Quality and centrality of relationships with other women, men, and children. How much and in what ways do these relationships determine the sense of self and of self-esteem? What particular aspects are enhancing and debilitating to others and to the woman herself?
2. History and current personal experience of limitations imposed by parents, peers, teacher, the media, and other significant sources and of more apparent violations including, but not limited to the more obvious ones involving violence, incest, and rape.
3. Own evaluation of appearance and its centrality on her mattering map.
4. Physical presentation of self, including habitual aspects of posture, carriage, gait, expression, musculature, movement, as well as situational variations when dealing with specific issues and experiences in therapy.
5. Degree of fragmentation experienced physically and psychologically.
6. Sense of invisibility and hypervisibility or exposure in general and in particular circumstances.
7. Eating/diet strategy.
8. Losses and disappointments, especially loss of the possible and of the sense of self.
9. Anger at and loss of the mother and enmeshment with an individual father or cultural fathers.
10. Degree of identification with the indeterminate [male] observer.
11. Extent of sense of responsibility for events and behaviors of people whom she cannot control.
12. Experiences of shame.
13. Sense of self and of self-esteem. (Kaschak, 1992, p. 215-216)

In assessing the individual client and developing meaning, the therapist must maintain sight of both the individual woman and the categorical woman. Kaschak asserts that both the personal and the sociopolitical must be understood and addressed. She concludes:

Feminism and therapy both involve understanding the meanings of ordinary, everyday life and focusing not just on the figure but on the ground upon which it stands–ground shifting if not ground breaking.... the ground can never be taken for granted and can become figure at any unpredictable moment. Similarly, one can never study gender relations as a category or a monolithic construct involving woman in isolation. One is always a self-in-context. The self is as much a part of the context as the context is of the self. (1992, p. 225)

Burstow's assessment includes a series of questions that the therapist asks herself based on observation and interviewing of the client. They are aimed at understanding the potential levels of multiple oppressions of the client, her identification with male or female-oriented culture, her level of comfort with herself and potential capacity for resistance, the extent to which she is being physically, emotionally, or sexually exploited, and the sources of power and satisfaction in her life. Solidarity is a key ingredient in the empowerment work used by Burstow with women. She describes we-statements as potent empowerment tools for they "(a) identify our commonality as women, (b) proclaim our bond as women, (c) empathize with our sister client, (d) identify oppressor and oppressed groups, (e) analyze sexist situations, and (f) invite ongoing solidarity and analysis" (p. 51-52).

Methods geared toward client empowerment in radical feminist therapy include identifying, naming, understanding, and rejecting social scripts that have served to oppress and restrict women; developing and strengthening the bonds between women; doing body work as well as psychological work, and encouraging social action and links back to other members of the client's oppressed communities (Burstow, 1992).

## CONTEXTUALISM, YES. MORAL RELATIVISM, NO.

Contextualism and social constructionism are key aspects of the work of each of the feminist theorists described above. However, none subscribe to the moral relativity associated with a post-modern philosophical stance. For each, feminist theory and practice represent moral enterprises. Kaschak (in Kaschak and Hill, 1999) labels feminist therapy as moral therapy, because it stands against oppression and takes judgmental positions. She argues that therapy must promote responsibility and accountability not only on the part of therapists to their clients but on the part of clients to those with whom they are in relation–their families, victims, broader society. Each of the other authors delineates clear moral values and paths that they associate with feminist stand-points.

## FUTURE VISIONS–MAINLY QUESTIONS

As young women have turned away from feminism, one explanation that permeates popular culture is that feminism is passé, because women have made significant gains in society. For example, women now are the majority of the student body in higher educational institutions. Walls, if not glass ceilings, have tumbled (supposedly) in industry, in the professions, and the academy. It is said that women are reaping economic benefits as never before; they are free to marry (or not), they are freer to be out as lesbians, they are freer to define their own goals and lifestyles.

The question remains, are these assertions true? Is this freedom purely an illusion? The paradox described by Kaschak (1992) seems truer than ever. More women are experiencing eating disorders than ever before. Popular culture is overflowing with pornographic, sexualized, and sexist images of women. Women have not escaped the forced domestic labor of their homes, in spite of their working outside of the home, and men still do not share this work to any great extent. Violence against women has not abated. The sexual freedom of women in the West continues to be defined by patriarchy and in the service of men. This "freedom" has drawn the ire of more conservative cultures both in the West and in other parts of the world, which also wish to define women on their terms. The conflict between Western, Eastern, and Middle Eastern definitions of female agency, activity, and image are all male dominated views of women. However, women are experiencing the backlash of these culture wars.

So where are women and feminist therapy in this context? Does women's freedom merely mean freedom to choose the same scripts for which women have been socialized? Are women more unified in their quest for self-definition, identity, and actualization or are they more splintered and isolated than ever before? As more middle class women work, are they realizing their own goals and values or are they now exploited in two labor arenas, just as has been true for poor women for centuries?

How will feminist therapy theory address these issues? Does the illusion of freedom and economic and social freedom make women less interested in understanding their plight? Are women recognizing the oppression they face? Does this oppression produce radicalizing insights; or are women too tired from their multiple roles and too intimidated by the need to be perfect to recognize the treadmills they are on? Are women accepting medical solutions, such as daily doses of medications to solve their everyday problems, ranging from depression and alienation to sexual "problems," rather than choosing pro-women therapies? Has feminist therapy become so mainstream that it no longer addresses the issues central to its founding, central to the theories delineated above? How are we continuing to construct theories and practice therapy that is truly radical, multicultural, and constructivist? How are we integrating anti-domination perspectives into our lives, theories, and practices? How do we truly integrate ecological and anti-domination into feminist therapy theories in ways that provide the blueprint for action sought by both therapists and their clients?

## REFERENCES

Ballou, Mary. (2002). Personal communication.

Ballou, Mary & Brown, Laura S. (2002). *Rethinking mental health and disorder: Feminist perspectives*. New York: Guilford.

Ballou, Mary, Matsumoto, Atsushi, & Wagner, Michael. (2002). Toward a feminist ecological theory of human nature: Theory building in response to real-world dynamics. In M. Ballou & L.S. Brown (Eds.), *Rethinking mental health and disorder: Feminist perspectives* (pp. 99-144), New York: Guilford.

Brown, Laura S. (1990). The meaning of a multicultural perspective for theory-building in feminist therapy. In L.S. Brown and M.P.P. Root (Eds). *Diversity and complexity in feminist therapy* (pp. 1-22), New York: Haworth.

Brown, Laura S. (1991). Antiracism as an ethical imperative: An example from feminist therapy, *Ethics and Behavior, 1*, 113-127.

Brown, Laura S. (1992). A feminist critique of the personality disorders. In L.S. Brown and M. Ballou (Eds.). *Personality and psychopathology: Feminist re-appraisals*, New York: Guilford, 206-228.

Brown, Laura S. & Ballou, Mary. (Eds.). (1992). *Personality and psychopathology: Feminist reappraisals*. New York: Guilford

Brown, Laura S. (1993). Anti-domination training as a central component of diversity in clinical psychology education. *The Clinical Psychologist, 44*, 83-87.

Brown, Laura S. (1994). *Subversive Dialogues*. New York, Basic Books.

Burstow, Bonnie. (1992). *Radical feminist therapy: Working in the context of violence.* New York, Sage.

Daly, Mary. (1978). *Gynecology: The meta ethics of radical feminism.* Boston: Beacon.

Dworkin, A. (1974). *Woman hating.* New York: E. P. Dutton.

Kaschak, Ellyn. (1990). How to be a failure as a family therapist. In H. Lerman and N. Porter (Eds.). *Handbook of feminist ethics in psychotherapy,* New York: Springer.

Kaschak, Ellyn. (1992). *Engendered lives: A new psychology of women's experience.* New York: Basic Books.

Kaschak, Ellyn & Hill, Marcia (Eds.). (1999). *Beyond the rule book: Moral issues and dilemmas in the practice of psychotherapy.* New York: Haworth.

Worell, Judith & Remer, Pam. (1992). *Feminist perspectives in therapy: An empowerment model for women.* New York: John Wiley & Sons.

Worell, Judith & Remer, Pamela, P. (2002). *Feminist perspectives in therapy: Empowering diverse women.* New York: John Wiley & Sons.

# From the Past Toward the Future

Marcia Hill
Mary Ballou

How do we know where we are going?
How do we know where we are headed
till we in fact or hope or hunch
arrive? You can only criticize,
the comfortable say, you don't know
what you want. Ah, but we do.

–Marge Piercy, *The perpetual migration,* 1982

Marcia Hill, EdD, is a psychologist in private practice in Montpelier, VT. She is a former editor of *Women & Therapy* and has edited ten books about psychotherapy. She is also the author of *Diary of a Country Therapist* (2004).

Mary Ballou is Professor of Counseling Psychology at Northeastern University, a practicing psychologist who holds a Diplomate from the The American Board of Professional Psychology, Co-Chair of the Graduate Consortium of Women's Studies Programs in the Boston area, and Chair of The Feminist Therapy Institute.

Address correspondence to: Marcia Hill, EdD, 25 Court St., Montpelier, VT 05602 (E-mail: marcia.hill@worldnet.att.net).

[Haworth co-indexing entry note]: "From the Past Toward the Future." Hill, Marcia, and Mary Ballou. Co-published simultaneously in *Women & Therapy* (The Haworth Press, Inc.) Vol. 28, No. 3/4, 2005, pp. 161-163; and: *The Foundation and Future of Feminist Therapy* (ed: Marcia Hill, and Mary Ballou) The Haworth Press, Inc., 2005, pp. 161-163. Single or multiple copies of this article are available for a fee from The Haworth Document Delivery Service [1-800-HAWORTH, 9:00 a.m. - 5:00 p.m. (EST). E-mail address: docdelivery@haworthpress.com].

http://www.haworthpress.com/web/WT
doi:10.1300/J015v28n03_08

The principles of feminist therapy form the basis for the work described by the previous authors; they also form the foundation for the possibilities imagined by the authors in this second section. These are: valuing women's experience ("the personal is political"), recognizing the sociocultural contributions to psychological distress, attending to power in the therapy relationship, integrating an analysis of gender with that of other oppressions, and prioritizing the creation of social change (Hill & Ballou, 1998). In the section that follows, the authors apply these principles to an imagined future for the practice of therapy, the education of therapists, and community.

Consider what you might imagine as a future informed by these feminist principles. If you are thinking in terms of practice, do you imagine differences in what clients bring to therapy? In how your practice is structured? In how you are reimbursed? In your function in the community? Or think perhaps of how therapists are educated: what would change there? Do you see changes in the role of the teacher or the relationship between teacher and student? Changes in the relationship between the academy and the community? And all of us live in community. How might our lives be altered in a community that is feminist? As you read about the thoughts of these feminist therapists, consider that the ideals described here are based on assumptions not only about feminist principles, but also about the root causes of our current difficulties and limitations. If you believe that economic disparities and the power of corporate-driven capitalism is the most critical factor, you will imagine a different solution than if you focus more on racial, gender and other oppressions, although all are important and relevant.

As you consider your vision, remember also that human nature is varied and often difficult. People do in fact injure one another, and those injuries beget others in a ripple effect. Some people, if only genetically or biochemically, need more stimulation and risk than others, are vulnerable to depression or anxiety, are likely to self-medicate. The challenge to imagining a transformed society, as well as transformations in its microcosms of education or therapy practice, is to include attention to the barriers to change and to incorporate methods to address those barriers.

In our final chapter, Mary Ballou looks at some of the challenges to a feminist future. Hegemony and the increasing reliance on "best practices" bring real threats to any discussion of the sociopolitical causes of distress and to the possibility of deconstructing cultural meanings, a central element of feminist therapy and the education of feminist therapists. The conservative political forces identified in this final essay may be intimidating, but they also show us how critical it is to envision a feminist direction at this point in history. With funding shifting away from justice and human needs and toward national ideological control and international domination, taking community action is very different from what it was in the liberation movements of the 1960s and 1970s.

Ballou's essay ends with a discussion of a new paradigm, which includes collaboration with other progressive forces. We do not need to all have the same vision, but we must all have a vision. Perhaps these authors will suggest a starting point for yours. In the melding of these feminist visions with those of other allied movements lies our hope for the future.

## REFERENCES

Hill, M. & Ballou, M. (1998). Making therapy feminist: A practice survey. In M. Hill & M. Ballou (Eds.), *Feminist therapy as a political act,* (pp. 1-16). New York: The Haworth Press.

Piercy, M. (1980). The perpetual migration. *Circles on the water: selected poems of Marge Piercy* (p. 273). New York: Alfred A. Knopf.

# Feminist Therapy Practice: Visioning the Future

## Marcia Hill
## Gail Anderson

**SUMMARY.** The authors describe a small group process of visioning what the practice of therapy would be like if feminist principles were valued and instituted. This visioning process was held at the annual conference of the Feminist Therapy Institute in Boston, MA, on November 3, 2002. Differences in the practice of psychology are imagined in a world where oppression and misuse of power are addressed or eradicated; those changes are imagined on local as well as global scales. Participants also looked at how the practice of psychotherapy might be different for the therapist. The vision stretches to include some of the ways to move toward this ideal from the present. *[Article copies available for a fee from The Haworth Document Delivery Service: 1-800-HAWORTH. E-mail address:*

Marcia Hill, EdD, is a psychologist in private practice in Montpelier, VT. She is a former editor of *Women & Therapy* and has edited ten books about psychotherapy. She is also the author of *Diary of a Country Therapist* (Haworth Press, 2004). She can be reached at 25 Court St., Montpelier, VT 05602 (E-mail: marcia.hill@worldnet.att.net). Gail Anderson, MA, has been a psychotherapist for eighteen years in Minnesota. She is currently employed by a non-profit agency working with children in play therapy, adolescents, couples and adults. She can be reached at Lutheran Social Service of MN, P.O. Box 6069, St. Cloud, MN 56302 (E-mail: gailoa125@tds.net).

Author note: While we have tried to represent the group discussions accurately and to attribute ideas and quotations correctly, we have doubtless made some mistakes. We apologize to the discussion participants for any errors.

[Haworth co-indexing entry note]: "Feminist Therapy Practice: Visioning the Future." Hill, Marcia, and Gail Anderson. Co-published simultaneously in *Women & Therapy* (The Haworth Press, Inc.) Vol. 28, No. 3/4, 2005, pp. 165-176; and: *The Foundation and Future of Feminist Therapy* (ed: Marcia Hill, and Mary Ballou) The Haworth Press, Inc., 2005, pp. 165-176. Single or multiple copies of this article are available for a fee from The Haworth Document Delivery Service [1-800-HAWORTH, 9:00 a.m. - 5:00 p.m. (EST). E-mail address: docdelivery@haworthpress.com].

**KEYWORDS.** Feminist therapy, feminist vision, ideal feminist world, feminist principles

Can you imagine the best possible context in which to practice therapy? Two of the groups of therapists attending the Feminist Therapy Institute (November 3, 2002) in Boston did just that. They elicited dreams of what the practice of therapy would be like if feminist principles were woven into the entire fabric of shared life. Participants imagined that sociocultural problems related to power and oppression were addressed or eliminated. They pictured society valuing emotional well-being. Visions significantly transformed feminist therapy practice in scope, purpose and attributes. Finally, behavioral steps leading toward realizing these feminist visions were identified.

## THE VISION

*Sociocultural problems related to power and oppression would be addressed or eliminated.* Not surprisingly for a group of feminist therapists, the initial focus of people's imaginings was on the larger picture of sociocultural change. The Feminist Therapy Institute's code of ethics (Feminist Therapy Institute, 2000) says that "feminists recognize the impact of society in creating and maintaining the problems and issues brought into therapy." These experienced therapists clearly agreed that it was not possible to imagine the ideal practice of therapy without also imagining a world changed in ways that supported justice. That is, therapy was envisioned as beginning not with a client's initial visit to a therapist, but rather with the kind of environment in which the client lived.

After a guided imagery asking the participants to imagine that such changes had already happened, Natalie Eldridge commented, "I wasn't afraid to go out at night. That startled me." This comment speaks to fundamental concerns of physical safety; others took that further to imagine the implications of living in a context of emotional safety. Dorsey Green: ". . . people were respected. All relationships where power imbalances now exist were different; they had more respect." Gail Walker talked about people being "a lot more curious about each other and more open about their answers to each other." People could state, "This is who I am" and there would be no shame. Here is the basic feminist principle of respect for others, including appreciation of differences. But these comments, particularly Walker's mention of shame, also point to how much discomfort about one's differences is currently woven into the fabric of everyday life. It would be transformative to live openly as one's self and to expect acceptance. As Brown, Riepe, and Coffey state in this volume, ". . . the concept [of] 'woman' is a multifaceted phenomenon. One important lesson emanating from the writings of these authors is that the complexity of women's identities, social locations, and biopsychosocial contexts must be affirmatively embraced." This group clearly agreed, making it clear that feminist therapy in the future must be firmly built on a foundation that recognizes, appreciates, and takes into account differences among people.

Claudia Pitts raised a point of clarification. She noted that what might make her feel secure might cause conflict for others. She referred to issues arising from conflict about transgendered person's presence at the Michigan Womyn's Music Festival. Eldridge concluded, "There would always be power imbalances. What we want to change is how we treat differences." Dorsey Green agreed, "It is how we mediate difference that is the most important variable." Clare Holzman paraphrased feminist writer and teacher Jeanne Adleman who said, "We should listen with intent to learn. We need to hold the trust that we are both right in order to transcend the polarity." This bit of conversation is a good example of the difficulties inherent in imagining the unimaginable, a future that we have not lived. The conflict about transgendered persons in what has traditionally been "women only" space is predicated on the need for women-only space, which in turn is a result of powerful and pervasive sexism that has made any geography inhabited by men potentially, if not actually, dangerous for women. It also, of course, assumes only two genders. In a transformed world, gender would be irrelevant as a predictor of danger. Women-only space would be unnecessary; further, gender would be unlikely to be binary.

Feeling welcome for who one is means the elimination of the negative consequences currently associated with various differences such as sexual orientation or age. Thus, changing or eliminating cultural trauma resulting from issues of race, class, gender or other differences would be a priority according to Marcia Hill. In addition, vulnerable populations such as children would be protected (Carolyn West). Tal Astrancha surmised that activists and therapists would be allied, again reinforcing the notion that the practice of feminist therapy cannot be separated from working toward a better world.

Lauree Moss stated that her practice would be very different. "None of my clients who now have a borderline diagnosis would have been abused." This statement in itself implies vast cultural change, as the frequency of sexual abuse is a symptom of misogyny, difficulties with power, family stressors, and so forth. There would be less trauma-based therapy and a focus on growth versus repair.

In a feminist world there would be no place for war, according to Gail Anderson. She imagined that political processes would be based on feminist principles. The Feminist Therapy Institute Code of Ethics (FTI, 2000) states: "A feminist therapist acknowledges the inherent power differences between client and therapist and models effective use of personal, structural or institutional power." If those principles were to extend to governments, they would recognize that power differentials exist among nations and would (in the words of the FTI Code of Ethics) "pledge to not take control or power which rightfully belongs . . ." to another nation. Instead, governments would seek to understand and respect cultural differences, and our world order would be radicalized. In another extension from the FTI Code of Ethics from therapist/client to nation/nation, Anderson surmises that a government would take responsibility "to confront and change any interfering, oppressing, or devaluing biases" (FTI, 2000) each country has. Feminist therapists would be valued consultants on the ethics of governmental processes and choices.

Note that, in imaging the ideal practice of therapy, these therapists implicitly eliminated many factors that currently bring people to therapist's offices: struggles with sexual harassment, the prevalence of rape and battering, the stressors of living with racism or with barriers and negative attitudes about disability, anxieties about war or terrorism, the grinding difficulties associated with being poor. Feminist therapists know that much of what brings clients to their offices is culturally caused; we would choose to solve societal problems politically rather than case-by-case in our offices.

*Society would value emotional well-being.* At this point, the conversation moved from attitudes in general to the particulars of social support for the business of therapy, which is the emotional well-being of individuals. The group looked at the way mental health might be defined and conceptualized. Hill noted that antiracist and economically just standards would be considered crucial to a psychologically healthy culture; that is, that the valuing of differences discussed previously would be sought at least partly because they were necessary components of emotional health. Susan Barrett noted that vulnerability and connection would be treasured and so emotional and relational development would be encouraged. This points to a prioritizing of connectedness, reminiscent of West who, earlier in this volume, suggests a sense of "a therapeutic presence that not only includes cognition, but asks for a quality of 'being-with,' fully and in the present moment."

Again, the participant's perspective was both broad (global) and deep (addressing cultural assumptions). Gail Walker said, "If we had a web of connectedness it would help us think more about others and our impact on them. It takes living much more simply, less acquisitively, with less hunger." She suggested that people would think ahead for seven generations from now, a Native American concept. Gail Anderson agreed that living simply would allow resources to be shared globally. "People would think of themselves as citizens in a global community." There would be no homelessness or poverty. Access to psychological care, suggested Hannah Lerman, would be available globally as well as nationally.

Thus, the conversation circled from a just society to the valuing of connection and back around to the notion of justice. In the vision of these therapists, there can be no individual emotional well-being without respect for others and the cultural changes that this implies. In this volume Barrett also recognizes how feminist therapists have challenged the European American dominant way of thinking:

> Western psychology is poised on the edge of a major paradigm shift away from believing . . . one understanding of human beings, away from a central dominant view against which all are measured . . . The interplay of gender, race, culture, class, sexual orientation, etc. is more than the sum of all parts and the nuances and shadings of meaning will influence how we understand ourselves.

*Therapists and therapy would be valued.* What, then, would be the effect of these changes on therapy itself? The group first addressed attitudes toward therapy and those who practice it. Barrett imagined that there would be appreciation for psychological expertise. Feminist therapists would not need to explain their work; it would be respected and understood, others concluded. Mary Margaret Hart identified that therapy would be normalized, not seen as shameful. In both of these comments, we see the implication that emotional health would not only be considered important, but would be addressed as comfortably and naturally as physical health. Both Susie Kisber and Hannah Lerman noted that therapists would be well-paid, with payment no longer being a barrier to access. Today's struggles with adequate payment are accurately seen as a reflection of cultural discomfort with matters psychological as well as an inadequate valuing of human happiness. In addition, the emotional care giving of therapy is a traditionally female task, another factor that may result in its being both undervalued economically and associated with "weakness" in today's climate.

*Therapy would be integrated into the community.* If the nature of therapy cannot change without changing the nature of society, similarly, change in the practice of therapy would involve changes in the community. Webster and Dunn, in this volume, note that "Collaborations between clients and therapists, advocates and agencies, researchers and therapists, feminists and non-feminists, are all necessary to address complex problems." These therapists followed that directive and envisioned therapy integrated seamlessly with other forms of community support. The community as a whole would take responsibility for the well-being of its members so there would be fewer people who needed treatment, according to Hart. For those who did need treatment, the access point for therapy would be integrated into other services such as education, suggested Juli Burnell. Prevention would be a priority (Lerman) and would take many forms. For example, conflict resolution skills and other psychological knowledge would be integrated into school curricula (Barrett). Parvin and others identified that there would be easy availability of peer support groups for various concerns. In this vision of the future with emotional well-being prioritized, therapists would be seen as protective forces in the community and used as consultants. Because prevention mattered, there would be increased general knowledge about psychology, similar to the way most people now know about good nutrition or exercise, usually because of frequent media coverage, according to Hill. She also anticipated a general awareness of the common traumatic life difficulties (e.g., divorce, major loss) likely to need intervention. This again would imply a knowledge and acceptance of psychological needs not unlike that which currently enables most people to judge when to seek out a physician and to be able to do so comfortably. The picture here is one of a community caring for its members psychologically as well as in other ways. This community would be informed about the effects of life challenges, responsive to the needs of its members for support, and eager to make help readily available to its members.

*Therapist's work environments would be nurturing.* Next, the discussion turned more specifically to the immediate work world of the therapist. Therapists work very much in isolation and with limited support for themselves. The Feminist Therapy Institute code of ethics (FTI, 2000) identifies therapist self care as an ethical imperative, and these participants imagined settings and methods of practice that would support the practitioner as well as the client. In addition, the Relational-Cultural model described earlier (West, this volume) addresses the centrality of connection to well-being. Recognizing this, the group envisioned a work environment rich in connection. Therapists would have collaborative, not isolated, work environments in Denny Webster's feminist world. Parvin fantasized, "Every afternoon, I could sit with sherry or coffee with friends and talk about cases. I wouldn't feel like my practice was all on my own shoulders."

Some participants saw less isolation and greater connectedness between student and non-student with mutual learning as the preferred model. Kathryn Bruning and Lynn Jones envisioned a mentoring program between and among established feminist therapists and graduate students who also felt isolated. Parvin also envisioned that the barrier between the student and the non-student would come down; learning would go back and forth among experienced therapists and students with fresh ideas.

Self-care would be built into therapist's schedules. Therapists would write collectively in retreat settings with options for hiking and shared meals, Parvin decided. Hill anticipated campuses as "think tanks" where therapists gathered to exchange ideas and to write. Kisber saw those settings as interdisciplinary. Lerman described paid sabbaticals allowing time and money to think and write together or singly. Liz Margolies got excited thinking, "We would be free to think about the next cutting edge thing, even beyond feminist therapy. Some of us like to be at the front, as "outlaws." Now that our work is mainstream, we can move forward. Like, here we are advocating for women and the transgender movement is calling it all into question. What is a girl?"

It is noteworthy that many of these ideas are elaborations on the notion of available, paid time for activities other than direct service delivery. That means time for therapists to do other kinds of work, such as writing; time for consultation and support from colleagues; and time simply for "recharging one's batteries." The emphasis on collaboration and on activities other than direct service highlights two of the primary difficulties in practicing therapy as it is currently structured: isolation and the heavy emotional demand of direct service. These therapists emphasized balance in the therapist's work life by focusing especially on changes in these areas.

All of these ideas come down to adequate resources. Pitts concluded there would be standardized rules and forms by third party payers, thus simplifying and limiting time spent on paperwork. Others predicted that the value of therapy would be so integral to culture that the government would use shared resources to pay for therapy services for all who need it. The identities of therapists and clients would reflect greater sociocultural variety as therapy became truly accessible. A general wish was that therapy would be accessible to all without such barriers as cost, managed care restrictions or cultural insensitivity. Therapist's energies would be spent more productively toward learning and focusing on client's specific needs and/or community interventions. Liz Margolies called into question how feminist therapists see themselves. "We as feminist therapists need to stop fighting as underdogs and see ourselves as privileged. We then need to act from that place."

## *HOW TO GET TO THE VISION*

A vision for the future can be enormously energizing. It can also feel overwhelming. How are we to got from here to there? The groups brainstormed possibilities, some general ideas and some small actions that anyone can take.

*Reducing sociocultural problems related to oppression.* Contratto and Rossier identify key concepts in feminist therapy earlier in this volume including "a commitment to listening to women as experts in their own lives and to political action . . ." These therapists saw a political perspective and political action as inextricably entwined with therapy. The heart of radical feminism is to find ways to address the root causes of oppression, and people discussed how to do so at some length. Changing oppression at its roots means working for justice (Hill & Ballou, 1998) in both the larger political arena and in the politics of how we work. Political action is the first and most obvious of these, and includes all the familiar tools of grass roots collective action: demonstrations, writing to elected representatives, lobbying, leafleting, civil disobedience, boycotts, and so forth. Direct political action is much of what has won us the gains we have achieved so far. Forming coalitions with other like-minded groups is a way to make an even greater impact. In addition, we can speak up and write about our feminist values and perspectives on a variety of issues (Green), both in our local communities (e.g., newspapers), as suggested by Kisber, and in our professional communities, as proposed by Barrett. Several participants talked about taking a moral stance when that is indicated, i.e., identifying some behaviors as not just politically opposed to a feminist stance, but morally wrong in some cases. It is a powerful statement, for example, to overtly declare racism as morally wrong.

Working toward justice happens in our offices as well as in congress; we live the vision immediately and personally. Earlier in this volume Porter asks "How are we integrating antidomination into our lives, theories, and practices? How do we truly integrate ecological and antidomination into feminist therapy theories in ways that provide the blueprint for action sought by both therapists and their clients?" Juli Burnell described the possibility of giving clients direct information about the specifics of their power in the therapy relationship. Clients can be informed that they have the right to terminate therapy or to ask for a referral, to set the agenda, to ask for a different approach, to disagree with the therapist's interpretation, and so forth. Hart recommended that therapists explicitly state their philosophy of practice in the materials they offer clients when starting therapy. "The concerns you bring to therapy are not located solely in you," said Hart, as an example of such a statement.

Feminist therapists already politicize their work, of course, in a variety of ways, from what materials they choose for their waiting rooms, to educating clients about sociocultural aspects of their concerns, to modeling feminist values, to restructuring various therapy techniques in ways that are more inclusive and respectful (for a good description of some of these specifics, see Hill & Ballou, 1998, and Weiner, 1998). Each of these small acts is a step toward a more just world.

*Valuing emotional well-being.* How can we help to create a society that lives the values of interdependence, diversity and connection? Denny Webster reminded the group that we can learn from existing models, echoing Barrett's observation (this volume) that "Gender roles are different in different cultures." Some cultures are more collaborative than others, and the group agreed that finding a balance between a collaborative stance and the mainstream U.S. emphasis on individualism would be important. Hill pointed out that self-disclosure in the community, e.g., talking about one's own struggles with depression, is one way to help change the discourse. After all, some things like rape or sexual abuse were rarely discussed until feminists began to talk about them.

The current "voluntary simplicity" movement also implies a shift toward valuing emotional well-being. With less emphasis on material things, there potentially would be a greater focus on relationships and personal emotional and spiritual development. (For example, a hand- lettered sign in downtown Tucson, Arizona, says "Buy Less; Be More.")

Valuing therapy and therapists. Perhaps the best way to encourage greater valuing of what we do is to make that more visible. As long as therapy is mysterious, as long as therapists are sequestered in their offices, it will be difficult for people to appreciate what we know and do. Therapists can offer consults to local human service and other nonprofit groups. Many organizations, from libraries to senior centers, can do with the occasional bit of expertise about how to handle problems with patrons. Developing relationships with physicians and other health care providers not only brings referrals, but also educates these providers about what therapy has to offer. A column in the local paper applying psychological expertise to everyday life would be another venue.

*Integrating therapy into the community.* Here again, the way to achieve our goals is to move our work into the community. Therapists can offer skills and information to the community through classes at the local "Y" and other non-therapy venues, as Hill suggested. Barrett's idea of teaching conflict resolution in schools is appropriate here. Parvin had talked previously about the importance of peer support groups, and therapists can be instrumental in setting those up and teaching participants the fundamentals of effective group structure and process. Finally, as described previously, the media provide an excellent opportunity to educate the community and make psychological knowledge a more normative part of everyday life.

*Developing a nurturing work environment.* Self care is both personal and interpersonal. Personally, we can attend to our physical health (exercise, nutrition, rest) as well as our emotional and spiritual health (family and friendships, spiritual practice, life balance). We need to ask ourselves: "What brings me joy?" and see to it that the answers to that question are priorities in our lives. The groups discussed how critical a supportive home base is, somewhere to find the understanding, encouragement and challenges of respectful colleagues. For many, of course, this was the Feminist Therapy Institute. Susan Barrett described the support she experiences as a member of a group practice in which differing perspectives in a context of mutual appreciation provide a rich resource. Those of us in individual practice or in unfriendly organizational settings may want to create consultation groups outside of the work context. E-mail contact with colleagues is another possibility. Whatever the means, the ability to count on frequent consultation was seen as central to self-care.

Hart reminded the group how important it is not to get overwhelmed with the task before us. If we remember that every step counts, we will more easily stay energized. And Walker reminded the group that whatever invigorates each of us personally, spiritually and otherwise, will help to propel us toward political action. Thus, our vision of change comes full circle.

## CONCLUSION

Our visioning groups saw a society largely rid of oppression and the misuse of power over those social groups now punished or excluded for their differences. Instead, diversity was valued because that diversity enriched all communities through a web of connectedness. While there were still differences which came into conflict, the process of resolving those differences was respectful with parties choosing to be vulnerable and to listen with intent to hear. After conflicted parties have a shared understanding of the other's view, the goal would be to build a connection despite differences; this process was seen as a more complex definition of political action. Participants thought in bigger terms (as global citizens) and for longer periods of time (for seven generations). There was less isolation and more connectedness.

Communities valued psychological and multidisciplinary knowledge and those who shared it in a variety of settings. Therapy was radically different because it was focused more on growth than repair. It was integrated into all facets of the culture via multiple avenues such as media. There was common knowledge about basic psychological skills such as conflict resolution as well as understanding of the kind of transitions and injuries likely to require intervention. Therapists were supported emotionally and financially in self-care, study and writing, collaborative efforts, sabbaticals and cutting-edge theory-building. Graduate students were supported intellectually in learning liaisons where knowledge among experienced feminist therapists and students was freely exchanged.

Many of the steps toward making these visions possible were identified. Avenues toward political action were envisioned widely, from a variety of grassroots and more mainstream political efforts to specific changes in the way therapists practice. Groups looked at methods to integrate psychological knowledge into the community, likely resulting in greater valuing of therapists and their expertise. A nurturing work environment was seen as critical to our ability to practice well, live well, and bring energy and focus to the task of creating a better world.

# REFERENCES

Feminist Therapy Institute (2000). *Feminist therapy institute code of ethics.* (Available from Marcia Chappell, Administrator, Feminist Therapy Institute, 93 Five Islands Rd., Georgetown, ME 04548.

Hill, M. & Ballou, M. (1998). Making therapy feminist: A practice survey. In M. Hill (Ed.), *Feminist therapy as a political act.* New York, NY: Haworth.

Weiner, K. (1998). Tools for change: Methods of incorporating political/social action into the therapy session. In M. Hill (Ed.), *Feminist therapy as a political act.* New York, NY: Haworth.

# Visions and Aspirations:
# Feminist Therapy and the Academy

Meredith M. Cohen
Mary Ballou

**SUMMARY.** This chapter explores key characteristics of an ideal feminist educational environment, one that specifically focuses on the intellectual development and training of feminist therapists. Such an environment is dependent on an ongoing relationship among three entities–students, instructors, and the institution–and characteristics of each of these three entities are discussed. The chapter evaluates the present climate within universities, and whether that climate offers the potential to promote or stifle a feminist environment. *[Article copies available for a fee from The Haworth Document Delivery Service: 1-800-HAWORTH. E-mail address:*

Meredith M. Cohen is a graduate student enrolled in the doctoral program in Counseling and School Psychology at Northeastern University. Her research and applied interests include prevention within schools and feminist therapy. Mary Ballou is Professor of Counseling Psychology at Northeastern University, a practicing psychologist who holds a Diplomate from the American Board of Professional Psychology, Co-Chair of the Graduate Consortium of Women's Studies Programs in the Boston area, and Chair of the Feminist Therapy Institute.

The ideas within this chapter were initially generated through a focus group that took place during the 20th Annual Feminist Therapy Institute, Honoring Our Legacy Facing Our Future, and have been elaborated and extended through the experience and resulting viewpoints of the authors. The authors would like to thank the members of the initial focus group for their candor and willingness to share and build on various perspectives on this issue within the short time period we were together.

[Haworth co-indexing entry note]: "Visions and Aspirations: Feminist Therapy and the Academy." Cohen, Meredith M., and Mary Ballou. Co-published simultaneously in *Women & Therapy* (The Haworth Press, Inc.) Vol. 28, No. 3/4, 2005, pp. 177-188; and: *The Foundation and Future of Feminist Therapy* (ed: Marcia Hill, and Mary Ballou) The Haworth Press, Inc., 2005, pp. 177-188. Single or multiple copies of this article are available for a fee from The Haworth Document Delivery Service [1-800-HAWORTH, 9:00 a.m. - 5:00 p.m. (EST). E-mail address: docdelivery@haworthpress.com].

http://www.haworthpress.com/web/WT
doi:10.1300/J015v28n03_10

*177*

**KEYWORDS.** Feminism, feminist pedagogy, learning environments, feminist therapy

Any feminist discussion of education is of necessity multileveled and complex. This one on feminist education as related to feminist therapy was no exception! It is our belief that the function and overall operation of an ideal feminist academic environment, which emphasizes training of feminist therapists, depends on the synergy of three independent, yet coexisting, standpoints: (1) students; (2) instructors; and (3) the institution. Each standpoint, consisting of its own non-exclusive group of individuals, must encourage dialogue that ensures comfort in expression accompanied by accountability through the conscious transfer of ideas to action. This is a somewhat different conceptualization of academic environments because we are interested in the relationship within and among standpoints, rather than formal power and the making and implementation of policy. Here, we will review the characteristics of each standpoint in this ideal environment as we interrelate the roles and responsibilities between and within each of the three levels. Once we have illustrated the ideal characteristics of this environment, we will question its application, and overall existence within the contemporary climate of the university, and whether present conditions could, or ever would, enable its development.

## STUDENTS IN THE FEMINIST ACADEMY

The student of feminist therapy offers a natural place with which to begin our discussion of the ideal feminist academic environment, in part because, as Contratto and Rossier point out in their discussion of key feminist concepts, feminist principles direct us toward consideration of egalitarian relations. We start with discussion of those whom the enterprise is meant to serve. Since most students who pursue training in therapy have completed undergraduate study, when we refer to "students" here, we are assuming graduate student status. While the student of feminist therapy is beginning what will become an ongoing learning process, it is believed that the student should enter both practical and academic training with certain attributes or skills. Cognitive and affective, and perhaps intuitive, abilities to learn competence in course work that provides the corpus of knowledge, and course work that provides clinical practice and professional role and ethics socialization are all essential. The student in feminist therapy training, however, would be selected for existing abilities to prize basic intra and interpersonal skills and values that would allow her/him to relate to others (West, this volume). In addition, feminist training programs would emphasize general helping qualities and values, along with appropriate technical skills of communication and intervention, as highly as research abilities, comprehensive exams and assisting faculty with their teaching and publication. The student of feminist therapy would also have a sense of personal awareness and political consciousness along with active knowledge of various feminist principles. This would be actively applied and further developed through conceptualizations and direct interactions with clients, other students and faculty and community.

Students studying and practicing feminist therapy should also be ready and willing to further develop an understanding of, and dedication to, feminist standpoints. These would be advanced through feminist literature in and outside of psychology, and would be used to consider existing mainstream theory, methods of assessment, diagnosis and psychopathology. In accordance with what Barrett discusses (this volume), feminist, multicultural and other critical theory analyses would also be applied to the entire curriculum including research and professional socialization customs, practices and organizations. Students would recognize the key similarities among feminisms–a collective acknowledgment and analysis of women's oppression, along with the oppression of other non dominant groups, and a commitment to changing oppressive conditions and structures. In addition to the similarities among feminisms, the students will develop the ability to comprehend the politics of knowledge as a new aspect of oppression. The contemporary expansion of feminist epistemology extends political analysis to the process of knowledge generation. The feminist academy will explicate and transcend the repression of information, which structures thought, thus escaping the control of knowledge.

Furthermore, students should be prepared to develop a further sense of personal social responsibility that will lead to challenge, rather than maintenance, of the status quo, currently advanced in the United States by capitalism combined with the myth of meritocracy. Students in feminist practice training programs must be able to identify and challenge oppression in everyday life, which is generated and maintained by those groups and structures in power. Feminist therapy students must also be able to delineate the manner(s) in which such oppression trickles down and harmfully affects nondominant groups and individuals. This understanding, an important form of social action, would translate to an understanding and readiness for the manner(s) in which various disparities caused by social forces would surface within the therapeutic arena. In short, the student of feminist therapy would be prepared to further develop the skills necessary to deconstruct social messages and effects of multiple oppressions, leading to the recognition of, and dedication to, social change.

Through the ability to engage in conceptual deconstruction, the student would further develop the ability to understand that the oppressed have capacities to survive and cope that are often obscured from, and devalued by, the dominant culture of which mainstream psychology and its organization are part. The link between this perspective and the dynamics of feminist therapy is invaluable. Much of the current work of progressive research and theory building in feminist, multicultural and critical psychology is centering precisely on the strength and coping and resistance of those who live within nondominant identities. Without obscuring the oppressive conditions that cultural, gender and class identifiers may bring, the student of feminist therapy would explore sources of strength and coping that also surface.

Given these demands of feminist therapy, multiple views must be held at one and the same time. Perhaps the strongest example of this double and triple simultaneous and sequential vision might come with the expectation that the student be able to view therapy as mutual connection in the service of the client, as well as a relationship that also calls for working for social change and may involve advocacy. At the same time, the student would understand professional ethical expectations, and also see that those come from prescription that belongs to power and privilege.

The student within this environment would deeply question mainstream psychology and its supportive organizations, particularly with respect to research and theory. In response to such questioning, the student would involve her/himself in consciousness raising activities that focus on gender, class, race, ethnicity and sexualities, especially as they relate to normative standards and social control. As a consequence, the student would develop an appreciation for interdisciplinary approaches, and would begin to insist on interdisciplinary views and multiple methods to address and conceptualize therapy, as well as academic issues.

Therefore, while working with clients, the student would be able to explore a variety of methods of change, including social change.

Evaluation of students in traditional programs is a difficult, stressful and opaque concept. In a feminist training program, clear expectations for achievement and increased awareness would be a priority; this is imperative due to the multiple goals and the importance of the work of feminist therapy. However, the attitude would be very different. The goals would be to facilitate the development of multiple views, a broad range of action and clinical skills and a consciousness and value base so clear as to serve as a solid foundation for analysis and action, especially since this will sometimes be outside of the rewarded mainstream. The goal in a feminist training program would not be to sit in judgment of the students who achieve this by virtue of their innate ability and individual hard work to assure that some ill defined, but conformist, standards are met. Rather, the emphasis in a feminist training program would be on the mutual responsibilities of institution, faculty and students. A student's failure to achieve would also rest on the inability of the faculty to guide and teach, and the institution's inability to mentor and meet the needs of the student.

Typically there is substantial competition among students in graduate programs. Perhaps our general competitive culture, most likely the admissions criteria and process, and certainly the faculty and institution's fostering of comparisons and relative status all contribute to competition among students. Honorary societies, graduate assistantships/fellowships, favored positions, competitions for training sites and a general attitude of who is weak and who is strong are influencers of this hierarchical notion of achievement. In a feminist training program, considerable efforts would be taken to make conscious and reduce competition in the service of collaboration. This is in accord with feminist principles and an important structural learning opportunity for later feminist work in institutions. Efforts to obviate the notion of scarce resources that the clever and strong get, to hold faculty and the institution responsible for functional pluralistic actions and attitudes, and to create mutually supportive relationships within the training community would indeed go a long way to repair the competitive patterns set by the mainstream culture and its institutions.

## THE ROLE OF THE EDUCATOR

Teaching, from a feminist perspective, involves a mutual engagement in process and content (Fisher, 2002; among others). In the feminist educational relationship, power asymmetries are reduced between the instructor and the student, and emphasis is instead on mutual respect and trust between the instructor and student(s). Education becomes a process of multiple discussions between faculty and students, in which students are valued as the endpoint of learning, and in the end, their own best experts. Through appropriate self-disclosure, instructors model open communication, which helps students connect abstract concepts with real life issues; this approach facilitates both cognitive and emotional (body, intuitive) knowledge.

It is assumed and necessary that the feminist educator would keep her/himself up to date of latest trends within the field of psychology, as well as other disciplines, so that she/he is able to address issues within discussions in a way that is clear, current and interdisciplinary. In addition, it is important to remain in touch with occurrences within local, state, national and international news in anticipation of how these events might shape the lives of individual clients and communities. Michele Fine (1985), a social psychologist, writing on this topic for feminist psychology stated,

> Integrating and synthesizing a carefully considered approach to feminist philosophy with a theoretical and intervention framework informed by psychology principles requires a willingness to read and study widely, attend to interdisciplinary perspectives and examine congruencies and inconsistencies between one's practice and assumptions. (p. 173)

Michele sets very high aspirations here. They have been approached in some women's psychology and feminist therapy courses, and are often discovered in women's studies graduate courses but 18 years later they are still far too invisible and missing. The instructor's role in our vision for teaching of feminist therapy includes Michele's hopes for feminist standpoints, interdisciplinary perspectives and integrated practice. Using postmodern views with narrative language, we thought that feminist therapy instruction might also include some additional attributes. Through the formulation and telling of disciplinary, and multidisciplinary, stories in the context of dominant group histories, a social activist stance would permeate teaching in this ideal feminist academic environment, as feminist educators who specialize in feminist therapy question and reshape the discipline of psychology. Paths for critical thinking and analyses would always explore the existing bodies of knowledge and articulate embedded assumptions within the mainstream academy. Through these critical analyses, there would be allowance for the creation and re-creation of a feminist perspective, embedded within input and student discussions, which also aligns with an interdisciplinary approach to various issues and modes of instruction.

The personal and the political would continue to live on as teaching emphasizes consciousness-raising within students as individuals and within practice as feminist therapists. Students would be encouraged to examine how external environmental forces, reward structures and related messages influence individual lives and choices. Feminist educators would encourage students to help both their clients and themselves to adopt active methods for responding to inequity and conscripted learning expectations as they come to consciousness and readiness. In addition, students would be encouraged to question the politics of research, professional organizations and state licensing boards through a feminist lens, both within classroom walls and outside. Also opened for question and narration would be the aspects of ethics that are controlling and that reinforce oppressive tendencies of the mainstream, as well as the important ethical aspects of feminist therapy.

The actual practice of classroom teaching from a feminist perspective has been addressed by many (i.e., Fisher, 2002; Tomlinson & Fassinger, 2002; Worrell & Oakely, 2000) and it has been noted that the topic of feminist pedagogy, much less programs specifically devoted to feminist therapy, has little representation within psychology (Tomlinson & Fassinger, 2002). An actual cookbook of techniques or ideal syllabi may not exist, however overall principles must be present and adhered to. For example, feminist educators would be aware of their own biases, and would be ready to address issues pertaining to bias with students, and ready to endure the conversations that would inevitably surface, particularly when they do not feel especially positive but do result in growth for students. Such discussions should be present within every course and module, and not limited to a single course on gender or multicultural issues.

Feminist educators must already posses a feminist consciousness. That is, their own process of becoming aware and conscious of their gender, race/ethnicity, class and other identities is critically important. Important also is their reflection on these experiences, their effects on self, and analyses of the socio-economic, ideological and spiritual underpinnings. One's developing feminism with all its strengths and weaknesses is a central component of necessary qualities for a feminist therapy educator. Similarly necessary is competent familiarity with the range of feminist standpoints as well as multicultural and other critical theories. Educators must be able to bring a variety of analyses to a discussion. They must also bring their own conscious awareness of gender, class and culture and identity politics to the classroom. They must be experienced in and have reflected upon a range of feminist practice in order to draw from lived experience in the didactic engagement with students.

Instructors must also be well informed about their own discipline and interdisciplinary perspective as well as a range of knowledge generation methods. They must also be committed to teaching and the education process, rather than viewing it as a one requirement among many some of which–administration, research, and clinical practice–may have higher priority. A faculty that teaches because it is required, but lives for research or professional status as a source of steady income, is certainly understandable in college and university environments but not good enough to qualify for feminist therapy educator.

Another aspect of the practice of teaching in feminist therapy is the emphasis on lived experience. Mainstream education values theory and research, which affirms theory more highly than raw experience. However, feminism inverts this hierarchy by insisting that abstract ideas must be tied to concrete experiences. Further, feminist teaching perspectives would insist that intellectual conversations also include other important levels of understanding beyond the mere rational. This makes for an alive and vital mutual engagement rather than an expert passing on of known truths that the student must consume, remember and reason from in practice.

It would of course be important that instruction lead to the competencies already discussed. Much discussion, critical analysis, knowledge creation (theory and research), and development of practice and ethics have already gone on in feminist therapy. The polis need not be rediscovered for each student and in each generation. We do sit with our older sisters. So too may theoretical insights and clinical practices contained within mainstream psychology and other critical theories are necessary and useful. A broad base of well-defined areas of competence must be the goal of and standard for instruction within feminist therapy. And the instructor's role should be to facilitate this development. No student fails alone, but teachers fail to reach and educate students and institutional structures often stand in the way of successful education.

## THE INSTITUTION

A feminist academic institution would maintain a non-hierarchical governing structure accompanied by clear expectations that would maximize strengths of administrators, faculty/educators and students. This would be evident through standards of evaluation and promotion, an organized curriculum, and dedication to promote the development of socially responsible citizens who are prepared to enter the profession of feminist therapy. The overall goal would be to work toward consensus among administrative committees and within the classroom and practical instruction, thereby creating an atmosphere that would allow all participants to be treated fairly. Administrators, faculty and educators would be held accountable to uphold the governing principles and to serve as model educators in the classroom and beyond. Within the institution, tenure promotion would be based on ability to fulfill standards that are made salient to all academics, rather than on number, or volume, of publications.

As mentioned above, a central goal of any feminist therapy training program should be the promotion and creation of socially competent graduates, trainees and citizens. Since the university, or academic institution, would be held accountable to create such individuals, a system should be present through which to monitor faculty as well as student progress. In contrast to practices within traditional academic departments, a feminist training program would restructure many of the institutional activities that surround teaching. For example, faculty would be routinely evaluated on their ability to acknowledge bias and incorporate critical analysis of mainstream thought into each and every core course.

Faculty/educators who are unable to respond to this level of accountability would face the option of obtaining additional training or education on matters relating to personal as well as collective social bias, and if unable to incorporate these understandings into their personal lives and curriculum, would be asked to pursue other employment options. Also, student's ability to respond appropriately would be continuously assessed, and administrators would regularly revisit the question regarding student's intellectual development in this arena, and whether it is commensurate with performance in practical/training sites. If neither were satisfactory, students would be encouraged to consider obtaining additional supervision that focuses on the relation between the personal and the political, and ultimately, if unable to make the connection, should be advised to seek alternative career paths.

## CONCLUSION:
## IS IT POSSIBLE? WHAT IS AND WHAT COULD BE

The ideal feminist academic environment, which emphasizes the intellectual development and training of feminist therapists, would encourage dialogue that enables both comfort in expression and accountability through the conscious transfer of ideas to action. The relation between thoughts and active social change would be evident within non-hierarchical, clear standards and expectations that comprise a universal governing system to which administrators, instructors and students would be held accountable. In addition, this environment would promote and respect acknowledgment of bias, and the multiple social and structural lenses through which various biases are created.

An institution that teaches feminist therapy would require a reinvention of structure that flattens hierarchy, and would optimally result in a respectful environment that tolerates challenge among and between colleagues. Overall, the ideal feminist environment would encourage collaborative skills and maintain a certain accountability of students, faculty, deans and administration. The university itself would also be judged by its involvement in social change and education. However, given the increasing demand within the academy to make money through funding research and tuition dollars, increasing economic threat to those institutions who resist, and given the regulatory functions of professional organization approval of training programs and the complicity of state licensing boards and ethics boards resting on the same curricular and professional culture, and the quest for status within educational institutions by submitting to these narrow definitions, it may be necessary to state that education of feminist therapists ought occur in institutes outside the universities.

Gender and culture have been included in most curricula but they have not been allowed to transform the curriculum. Hopes in the 1970s and '80s of the academy embracing feminist and other progressive thought has turn to disillusionment in the 1990s and 2000s and has squeezed out, trivialized and co-opted feminist and other progressive thinking, actions and programs.

It is also imperative to recognize the relationship between Universities and the dominant group they serve, a relationship often negotiated through research funding and program approval. The agenda in the social sciences is to please the funders and controllers, not to explore values and social forces or to educate aware multi-perspective change agents. The link between the government and the university is also necessary to acknowledge. Government and the advanced capitalism it serves are rewarding and overtly controlling the university. The notions that the academy is protected from government and that learned societies protect free inquiry, as may have been true for the sons of upper class European white men in the 18th century University, is not the pattern today.

In this chapter, we have considered at least in broad terms the kind of institution that would accommodate the characteristics necessary to teach feminist therapy. As a result we conclude that there is enormous need for an institute to teach feminist therapy outside of academy. Rich traditions already exist in approaches being developed outside of the academy. Gestalt, psychoanalytical, family, hypnotherapy, biofeedback and trauma institutes all have developed their approaches in detail, trained practitioners and academics, and generated inquiry and theory outside of the universities of their times. One might wonder if the university is perhaps a bit cautious and conservative. Alternatively, one might hold that the careful scholar only acknowledges that which fit her or his world view of separations between knowledge and experience, confirmations through repeated research findings and inquiry supported by the status figures of the era. In the end both imply a hegemonic link among social/political/economic forces of the state, the corporation and the academy are in the early 21st century in North America.

If the training of feminist therapist is to proceed on these broad outlines, an institute independent of a university structure is likely the best model. Such an institute would probably be best created to offer additional training and certification to counselors, psychologists, social workers, psychiatric nurses and psychiatrists already graduated at the practice level with clinical and disciplinary competency. They would also already meet, or be meeting, those post-degree clinical supervision, state and supervision professional regulations required for practice. The feminist therapy practice institute would seek to meet needed interdisciplinary feminist analysis, including transformative multicultural perspectives such as systemic, structural and historical competencies. It would also engage in education that increased individual awareness and would lead to a critical consciousness and an ethic of social change. Feminist therapy theory and practice would be central to the education and practice. Social change and individual advocacy as well as other related feminist practices would be a focus of the institute. Finally, feminist therapy and feminist practice theory would be further developed.

# REFERENCES

Brabeck, M. M. (Ed.). (2000). *Practicing feminist ethics in psychology.* Washington DC: American Psychological Association.

Collins, L. H., Dunlap, M. R., & Chrisler, J. C. (Eds.). (2002). *Charting a new course for feminist psychology.* Westport, CT: Praeger.

Fine, M. (1985). Reflection on a feminist psychology of women: Paradoxes and prospects. *Psychology of Women Quarterly, 9*(2), 167-183.

Fisher, B. M. (2001). *No angel in the classroom: Teaching through feminist discourse.* Oxford: Rowman & Littlefield Publishers.

Tomlinson, M. J., & Fassinger, R. E. (2002). The faces of feminist pedagogy: A survey of psychologists and their students. In L. H. Collins & M. R. Dunlap & J. C. Chrisler (Eds.), *Charting a new course for feminist psychology* (pp. 37-64). Westport, CT: Praeger.

Worrell, J., & Oakley, D. R. (2000). Teaching as transformation: Resolving ethical dilemmas in feminist pedagogy. In M. M. Brabeck (Ed.), *Practicing feminist ethics in psychology* (pp. 167-188). Washington DC: American Psychological Association.

# Fostering Feminist Principles in Our Community: How Do We Get There?

## Dorcas Liriano

**SUMMARY.** In a recent focus group discussion at the Feminist Therapy Institute conference participants outlined a vision for a future community based on feminist principles. It is built on five critical ideals, including more equitable distribution of resources, genuine respect for human diversity and varying world views, caring and compassionate members, increased connections and collaborations, and political/personal empowerment. While the challenges inherent to such vision must be acknowledged, greater attention will be placed on ways in which we can begin to foster environments and micro communities that are conducive to feminist practice and ideology. *[Article copies available for a fee from The Haworth Document Delivery Service: 1-800-HAWORTH. E-mail address: <docdelivery@haworthpress.com> Website: <http://www.HaworthPress.com> © 2005 by The Haworth Press, Inc. All rights reserved.]*

Dorcas Liriano obtained her doctorate degree in counseling psychology from Northeastern University. She is currently affiliated with Cambridge Hospital and Boston Medical Center where she conducts assessments and provides psychotherapy to women and children affected by violence.

Address correspondence to: Dorcas Liriano, P.O. Box 398050, Cambridge, MA 02239.

[Haworth co-indexing entry note]: "Fostering Feminist Principles in Our Community: How Do We Get There?" Liriano, Dorcas. Co-published simultaneously in *Women & Therapy* (The Haworth Press, Inc.) Vol. 28, No. 3/4, 2005, pp. 189-200; and: *The Foundation and Future of Feminist Therapy* (ed: Marcia Hill, and Mary Ballou) The Haworth Press, Inc., 2005, pp. 189-200. Single or multiple copies of this article are available for a fee from The Haworth Document Delivery Service [1-800-HAWORTH, 9:00 a.m. - 5:00 p.m. (EST). E-mail address: docdelivery@haworthpress.com].

**KEYWORDS.** Feminist therapy, feminist practice, community, social justice

Recently, a group of women came together at the Feminist Therapy Institute conference in order to acknowledge many pioneers who had made significant contributions to the development of feminist therapy. In addition to honoring the past, we also hoped to explore some of the current day challenges facing feminist therapy and generate a vision for its future. To complete the latter part of this task, participants were asked to break up into small focus groups with each group taking responsibility to think critically about the future of feminism as it related to a particular domain of interest. Our group chose to address the question of how feminist principles could be applied to a community setting. Our task was not only to dream of the possibilities, but also to identify some concrete steps that would help move feminist therapy (as well as each one of us individually) towards this goal.

I would like to begin by highlighting that the ideas expressed below are not mine alone, but are the product of a discussion among the six women named below. As such, it is with great gratitude that I would like to acknowledge Erin Dunn, Kathy Peres, Linda Edelstein, Kim Wands, and Jamie Suvack for their participation in the group, their wonderful insight, and their contributions to this chapter.

## THE VISION

Integrating feminist principles into a community setting has not been at the forefront of feminist therapy; however, it is not a completely novel idea. Mulvey (1988) provides us with at least one article that sets the groundwork for identifying theoretical links between feminist and community psychology. Nevertheless, for most of us participating in the discussion group, this was the first time we had been asked to consider how we could practically implement feminist ideals into our vision of a future community. We were both energized and challenged by the prospect ahead.

A community consists of women, men, and children of varying ages, ethnicities, cultures, religions, and social and economic privileges. Therefore, if we were going to adopt a literal understanding of community, our vision would have to extend to all human beings, not just women, and not just privileged and educated women. In reviewing principles of feminist therapy, one can see that feminist therapy does make allowances for focusing and considering these differences mention above. Ballou and West (2000) write that feminist therapy is rooted in the search for and valuing of all women's experiences (pp. 274-275). They further add that modern feminists have extended beyond the boundaries of womanhood and seek to bring about social change by speaking out against oppression and imbalance of power as it relates to all human beings. In doing so feminist therapy seeks to build egalitarian relationships and respect the inherent worth and dignity of all individuals while seeking to "expose subtle and overt manifestations of oppression directed at gender, race, class, religion, age, ethnicity, sexual orientation, disability, and the identities that flow out of belongings anchored in multiple cultural contexts" (Ballou & West, 2000, p. 275).

Keeping in mind the words of the feminist writers mentioned above, our group's discussion was centered around five main principles that we believed to be guiding forces in the implementation of feminist thinking to a community agenda. Inherent in our vision of a community based on feminist ideology were the following: (1) greater availability and access of resources, (2) genuine value and respect for human diversity and self-determination, (3) caring and compassionate members, (4) increased value placed on personal connections and collaborations, and (5) political empowerment. These values are interconnected and interactive and therefore, it is important to focus on all of them as we pursue our ideal feminist community setting.

## *Availability of Adequate Resources and Access to Resources*

We imagined a community that would strive to meet, if not ensure, each individual's basic human needs and rights. In order for any community to begin to undertake this philanthropic endeavor, there must be a greater availability of resources and relatively easy access to these resources, as well as a heartfelt obligation on the part of the community as a whole to help its members attain basic necessities. Given the frequent existing and/or manipulated states of scarcity, community members would feel a social responsibility to allocate existing resources as fairly as possible. Responsible, more equitable distribution of resources would be implemented at both the micro and macro level.

At the micro/individual level, each community member would have access to core basic needs such as food, quality housing, safety, and healthy and nurturing relationships with others. At the macro, the community would actively pursue measures to distribute wealth and material privileges in a manner that would be conducive to abolishing poverty and substandard living conditions. Along these lines, illiteracy would need to be aggressively addressed and all community members (regardless of their status in the community) would be provided with an equal opportunity to access education and information. Health care needs would be met by a comprehensive universal health care system that includes mental health parity. Viable alternatives and care options would be available for families with young, ill, or elderly dependents. Social policies would be enacted that would allow and/or require human service agencies and other similar programs to be proactive about identifying areas of need and closing any gaps in services. In conjunction with these agencies, community members would be willing to help each other and pursue less traditional methods of obtaining resources (such as bartering of services and considerate, communal sharing of goods and services).

In cases in which resources are being offered through a governmental or other type of organized institution, it is not sufficient for services to be available; they also need to be easily accessible and be user friendly. Ideally, a centralized system of service access could be established to provide all community members with information and access to these services. The goal would be to minimize the degree to which unnecessary bureaucratic policies, along with language and transportation barriers, hinder anyone from seeking out desperately needed assistance. Centralization of the existing social service agencies would also facilitate greater communication and cooperation between the many services providers.

### Genuine Value and Respect for Human Diversity and Self-Determination

Feminist therapists, multicultural counselors, and community psychologists have all highlighted the importance of honoring individual physical and cultural differences. Earlier in this volume, Carolyn West in particular speaks eloquently regarding the contributions of relational-cultural theory to the development of feminist principles that critically opposed racism, sexism, classism, and other bases for prejudice. Yet, these ideals have not been fully embraced. A healthy and productive society cannot realistically occur unless equity and respect of all of its members is adopted as an integral part of the social value system. Following these principles, this future community would validate, honor, and celebrate differences rather than using them towards divisive purposes. Social norms would call for all individuals to be treated with respect and dignity regardless of their gender, race, social-economic status, physical capacities, religion, or any other distinguishing characteristic. Multiple voices, opinions, and ideas would not only be heard, but also encouraged and valued. Maintaining respect for the numerous valid realities within the community would also promote mindfulness towards each individual's right to self-determination and choice. More importantly, this would be an ideal valued by all, not just activists or professionals in human services.

## A Caring and Compassionate Community

A caring and compassionate community is characterized by both interpersonal connections and personal safety. This would occur in various ways and at different levels. This community would nurture fluid community boundaries that would facilitate supportive community networks and a genuine mutual concern among members. Individual community members would frequently collaborate with and support one another when needed. As mentioned above, neighbors would then be redefined as viable resources for each other in the face of parenting issues, home improvement projects, and financial or emotional crises. Earlier in this volume, Susan Barrett urges us to redefining our notion of what constitutes a family to better match our current day families that extend beyond the two-parent nuclear, heterosexual family. In our vision, the family unit is not as much defined through blood lineage, but rather as a unit of close-knit relationships and support systems. When a community allows for a more tribal definition of family, then its members often begin to see themselves as interconnected and become more invested in helping and supporting one another.

Ensuring physical and emotional safety within the community would also be important. The state of security would not be promoted by organized law enforcement but rather by community initiatives. On the whole, kindness and respect would replace aggression and penetrate into all levels of society. This would facilitate the abolishment of random physical assaults, domestic violence, abuse and neglect of vulnerable citizens (young, ill, elderly). If and when violence occurred, the entire community would come together to support the individual(s) whose right to safety was violated and to confront the aggressor. Aggression in any form and to any degree would be looked down upon and would not be tolerated by this community. Major felonies, as well as misdemeanors such as malicious destruction of property, verbal assaults, and public ridicule/humiliation directed towards any person would be viewed as a violation of the community as a whole.

### Connections and Collaboration Between Individuals

The idea of connection and collaboration was highlighted several times throughout our discussion. While it is addressed above as it pertains to the individuals within the community, it is also important to extend the idea of collaboration to the professional service arena. Webster and Dunn (earlier in this volume) speak to the importance of professional, lay people, and community collaboration to facilitate addressing complex social problems. For example, therapists, social worker, parents, community leaders, and law enforcement officials would work in conjunction to address issues of violence, drugs, and other social concerns from both a prevention and intervention standpoint. Working together could produce a greater flow of ideas, a sense of comradery, and make even the greatest challenge appear more manageable.

### Political Empowerment

Finally, our vision for a future community called not only equitable distribution of resources, but also for political power to be distributed more evenly among the community. This could mean a number of things. First, there would be an institution of a truer democracy in which all of the community members could have fair and equal representation. In order for this occur, it would mean that each able-minded citizen's individual right to vote would be honored regardless of any mitigating factors (i.e., legal resident status). At minimum, in the case of undocumented citizens, social policy or legislation could be brought forth to allow undocumented citizens to voice their opinion on important political issues. In turn, each community member would need to take personal responsibility to exercise the right to vote and maintain an awareness of social and political issues facing the community.

Much of the political endeavors and movements in the community would be carried out via community meetings and grassroots efforts in order to allow greater activism and participation of the ordinary individuals in the decision making process. These collaborative efforts would be a more common occurrence and would be valued by community members and politicians alike. In time, such venues for community activism could lead not only to political empowerment of the community and its individual members, but also build in safety and checks against oppression and abuse of power. Having a strong, resilient and politically active constituency would in turn also serve to sustain the motivation of elected officials to continue to work diligently to represent their constituents and remain informed of pertinent issues facing the community.

While the five main principles identified above were generated solely from our group discussion, there is existing literature from the field of community psychology that supports our thinking. More specifically, Prilleltensky and Nelson (2000) identified key values that they believed to be essential in promoting a more just society and standing against oppression. These are as listed, "health, caring and compassion, self-determination and participation, human diversity, and social justice" (p.167). Despite the distinctions in language, there are many similarities between the author's core community values and our five main principles identified in the focus group. In addition to offering guiding ideology to support the actualization of these community values, Prilleltensky and Nelson further expand on their understanding and conceptualization of social justice and discuss implications for theory, research, and training in the field of community psychology.

## *HOW DO WE GET THERE?*

Despite some misgivings, the group's vision of a community influenced by feminist principles took shape quickly. We were transported to a world so different than our own, so far removed from current US mainstream values and therefore seeming so difficult to reach. In short, our vision appeared somewhat unrealistic and Pollyannaish. A humane and well functioning society, such as the one we envisioned, does not seem plausible on a large scale unless humanity can genuinely embrace social protocols based on justice, fairness, respect for human dignity, and acknowledgment of the interdependent nature of our existence. How could we achieve our community ideal under the prevailing climate of war, hunger, poverty, political persecution, and the entrenched racist, sexist and classist ideologies of our society? How could we, humankind, shift towards building compassionate, just, equitable and collaborative environments? We reminded ourselves that if our vision were to remain faithful to feminist practices, it would not only need to be authentic, but also completely voluntary on the part of those involved. We were faced with a great dilemma. In order to truly address issues related to racism, sexism, oppression, poverty, and other societal ailments, it would be essential to move toward adopting a collective mentality rather than one that is mainly focused on individual goals and achievements. This would require a willingness to share resources and power, as well as genuine and respectful mindedness towards all. To achieve this, individuals would have to be willing to give up the primacy of self-interest and self-serving aims that render some of us privileged and others not. While the vision and its underlying principles may be desirable to many, it may be too threatening for some individuals who find great comfort and benefits in their privileged and powerful standing. How does one envision and/or create a society based on feminist ideology and not allow room for these voices of dissention?

While history has taught us that changing core societal values is possible, such radical transformation of ideals is slow, arduous and sometimes comes at a high personal and professional cost to those who spearhead the initiative. Though challenging, the picture is not entirely bleak. While the current global climate may not be ready to foster our community vision, there are ways that we as individuals can begin to implement these ideals into smaller community settings and in our daily interactions with others. For example, we could begin to implement the above feminist community principles (outlined above) in our homes, a place in which we have greater control. We may also want to seek out other agencies and institutions whose ideology is congruent with these beliefs (i.e., community agencies, health care settings, places of worship).

In keeping with the second part of our agenda; that is, identifying concrete steps that would move us towards realizing the vision, we attempted to identify some concrete steps that each of us can take to begin to set the stage for change.

### Begin to Create the Environment

It is possible for each one of us to begin to plant seeds that may ultimately foster a more humane, democratic and feminist society. One simple place to start would be to begin to talk about feminist concerns with other individuals who are willing to engage in this dialogue. This continuous flow and interchange of feminist ideas could be instrumental in raising our collective social conscience and shifting towards greater mindfulness of social justice within our society. Sharing and modeling of feminist principles can be done at a more intimate level with our families and friends or at a larger scale with other professionals and/or colleagues.

Those of us who parent, teach, and mentor children are in unique positions to influence our young and guide them in such ways that they are more mindful of social injustices and have greater respect for the dignity and rights of all. We can model kindness and compassion in our interactions with others and by doing so, we may be indirectly teaching children the values that will foster love, solidarity, and respect. If we acknowledge that today's children are the future of tomorrow, then teaching our children more altruistic and feminist values is a wonderful method of bringing about social change.

Outside our homes, we could also try to implement principles of feminist therapy to whatever degree possible. This would mean honoring each person's right to self-expression, acknowledging/allowing for multiple realties and multiple truths, creating spaces and safe places for silenced voices and ideas to be heard, and seeking out collaborations and connections with others. Once this safe base has been established, we could begin to take greater risks and engage in critical thinking about the many ways in which we hold or lack power and privilege. Being cognizant of the ways in which we are or are not privileged, we can choose not to stand in the way of other's efforts to empower themselves.

Joining and working with disciplines and movements that share ideologies that are similar to those of feminist therapy, is not only positive step in the desired direction but also provides an opportunity for mutual learning and support. For example, we can look to other disciplines (such as multicultural psychology, community psychology) to highlight converging thinking and identify common goals. On a more practical level, we can also begin to reach out and seek to establish better communication and working relationships with similar valued professionals in the faith community and other social activists to address issues related to social injustices and other pertinent concerns.

However, before we begin to take some of the steps outlined above, we need to first engage in an earnest personal self-inventory. That is, we must take a good look at our value system and pay attention to what drives and motivates us. We must come to determine the nature of our goals and intrinsic motivators. Are these spiritual and non-material, or are we mainly driven by status and material aims? In short, we need to have decided if our personal value system is indeed compatible with feminist ideology. If we fail to take this important step, then we risk creating a process that lacks integrity, as our participation may not be genuine.

## Get Involved in Social Activism and Politics

Becoming involved in social activism and political causes is another way that we can begin to effect meaningful change. We should not be afraid to become involved in the complex political system, but rather learn to use the existing structures to affect change from the inside out. At first glance, this can appear as a daunting task for those of us who do not feel comfortable or confident in political venues. However, there are many ports of entry into the social political system. Some of us may be able to foster philosophical and systemic changes by seeking an elected office and creating just and fair legislation. Others can do this by using their power and their voices to communicate to politicians the values and ideals based on social justice. Bottom-up approaches such as grass roots and community-based efforts are also very powerful means of addressing political and social concerns. We can also contribute to change and social consciousness raising by smaller scale organized efforts such as school boards, neighborhood initiatives, and community collaboratives. We can participate in these venues as an extension of our roles as parents, educators, professionals, and community members and as such we need not redefine ourselves as activists or politicians. Lastly, we can also think about how to use the popular media to voice political and social concerns. For example, writing (articles, prose or poetry) for newspapers or magazines, seeking television and radio talk show opportunities, and theatrical works are all powerful and creative methods in which we can communicate important sociopolitical ideas.

## Work Towards Continued Personal and Professional Growth

Finally, we must continue pursue personal and professional growth that will help sustain our commitment to the vision and its underlying principles. An important part of maintaining this commitment requires that we identify ways to care for ourselves and remain resilient. Coming together and seeking out the supportive guidance of our peers is instrumental in reenergizing and motivating us towards continued action. We can do this by smaller scale support efforts consisting of two or more individuals or by joining already existing professional organizations. Either venue is a very useful way in which we can protect ourselves and each other from burning out and becoming inactive in our pursuit of our ideals.

It is also important to recognize our limitations. We must remember that one's stage of life and other familial responsibilities may have a significant effect on what one is able to do. Some of us may be have greater opportunities to act and participate in this vision, while others may be hindered by familial, professional, or financial commitments and responsibilities. However, we must all respect and value each person's contribution.

Mentoring of younger women is a key way to foster resiliency in the movement as a whole. Through the mentoring process we can not only create cross-generational collaboration, but also bring in new energy and new ideas. Mentoring relationships can also serve to educate and inspire younger women to take on new challenges and new struggles. Mentors also benefit from this collaboration as they receive opportunities for mutual learning and experience other benefits and intrinsic rewards.

Lastly, in order for us to continue to grow in personal and professional realms we need to think "outside the box" and come up with creative alternative ways of viewing and solving the existing problems/challenges. We need to continuously work toward "making it better" and not become complacent with the status quo. We need to believe that the vision is possible within a broad range of community settings and celebrate every small step or success that we (individually or collaboratively) can take towards our vision of a future community.

## CONCLUSION

There have been many women before us who served as pioneers in the field of feminist therapy. Many of these women were also challenged as they moved against the grain to change gender based inequities for women. However, as a result of their labor, persistence, and voice, the field of feminist therapy has made many advances. Yet, we cannot become complacent; there still remains a lot of work to do. We are now embarking on a new vision, one that involves building communities based on feminist principles. This vision is one that requires us to engage in efforts at collaboration and to incorporate a social justice agenda into our conceptualization of community. While society may not be ready to embrace our vision, we can begin to implement and practice these ideals in smaller settings. At the same time, we need to find opportunities to extend beyond our communities and our comfort zone and reach out to others. We need to express ourselves and communicate our vision within our circle, but also to those in nearby parameters and those who for one reason or another remain in the margins. As a field, we need to continue to work to find ways to resolve the inherent tensions present in feminist therapy. We need to balance our individual drive for self-determination with our collective need for connection. As women, we also need to continue to pay close attention to the importance of other factors (race, class, religion, age, sexual preference, physical ability, etc.) in creating our identity. All of these things are key as the field of feminist therapy strive to continue to move forward.

## REFERENCES

Ballou, M. & West, C. (2000). Feminist therapy approaches. In M. Biaggio & M. Hersen (Eds.), *The psychology of women* (pp. 274-275). New York, NY: Kluwer Academic/Plenum Publishers.

Mulvey, A. (1988). Community psychology and feminism: Tensions and commonalties. *Journal of Community Psychology, 16,* 70-83.

Prilletensky, I. & Nelson, G. (1999). Community Psychology. In D. Fox & I. Prilleltensky (Eds.), *Critical Psychology: An Introduction* (pp. 166-184). London: Sage Publications.

# Threats and Challenges
# to Feminist Therapy

Mary Ballou

**SUMMARY.** A discussion of three current forces that deeply affect feminist therapy and other progressive positions in mental health is the content of the chapter. Hegemonic relationships among best practices, conservative politics and a new paradigm are the three themes for the discussion. *[Article copies available for a fee from The Haworth Document Delivery Service: 1-800-HAWORTH. E-mail address: <docdelivery@haworthpress.com> Website: <http://www.HaworthPress.com> © 2005 by The Haworth Press, Inc. All rights reserved.]*

**KEYWORDS.** Feminist therapy, challenges, hegemony, best practices, advanced capitalism, empirical, conservative politics, paradigm, progressive approaches

There are several threats to the future of feminist therapy and other progressive approaches to mental health. The purpose of this chapter is to enumerate many of these threats in the hope that we shall be better

Mary Ballou, PhD, is Professor of Counseling Psychology at Northeastern University, a practicing psychologist who holds a Diplomate from the American Board of Professional Psychology, Co-Chair of the Graduate Consortium of Women's Studies Programs in the Boston area, and Chair of the Feminist Therapy Institute.

[Haworth co-indexing entry note]: "Threats and Challenges to Feminist Therapy." Ballou, Mary. Co-published simultaneously in *Women & Therapy* (The Haworth Press, Inc.) Vol. 28, No. 3/4, 2005, pp. 201-210; and: *The Foundation and Future of Feminist Therapy* (ed: Marcia Hill, and Mary Ballou) The Haworth Press, Inc., 2005, pp. 201-210. Single or multiple copies of this article are available for a fee from The Haworth Document Delivery Service [1-800-HAWORTH, 9:00 a.m. - 5:00 p.m. (EST). E-mail address: docdelivery@haworthpress.com].

able to see and resist them. Feminist therapy in both its original definition and its ethical principles advocates working toward social change. If we see the threats we are more able to meet the challenges. Some of the threats named in this chapter are unique to the current historical period, while some are long standing and are re-energized by the current interlocking, conservative, nationalistic, fear-based, advanced capitalistic forces. Feminists are not alone in being threatened at this juncture as many progressive and indeed even liberal positions and policies are being centrally challenged.

The challenges are at several levels and in many directions. A variety of analyses and standpoints are brought together here as we try to bring to sight some of the threats and challenges facing feminist practice and other progressive movements. Other progressive movements might include multiculturalism, human rights, post-modern analyses, interdisciplinary perspectives, social justice activism, LGBT rights, prisoners' rights, environmentalism, etc.

## HEGEMONY AND BEST PRACTICES

One threat especially significant to mental health work is the hegemony that has come to exist among the medical model, traditional science, funding for research and training, corporate managed insurance, both APAs and state licensing and ethics boards. The interlocking interests and controlling influence is seen quite clearly in the current notion of best practices. At first glance the idea of best practices is actually quite compelling. Selecting the treatment that has been demonstrated to work most effectively with a certain kind of illness or problem, especially with the vast array of existing interventions and theoretical orientations, seems to be a very good idea for a variety of reasons. It would offer a guide for practitioners and for patients in selection of interventions. It would also offer a set of criteria for judging competency of the practitioner for training programs and licensing boards, and for ethics committees considering complaints against individual practitioners. On a closer look however, the idea of best practices assumes that there is uniform agreement among disciplines and professionals, and that thorough and comprehensive empirical research validation exists indicating which treatment is the best practice for which disorder.

If one assumes that the medical model of mental illnesses is correct nosologically and ontologically; and one assumes that empirical research based on inferential and linear propositions can discriminate effectiveness among all interventions; and one assumes that the only dimensions of import are measured or observed cognitions and behaviors; and one assumes that acceptable outcomes are those defined by dominant social norms; then thorough agreement with best practices makes a great deal of sense and is a genuine improvement in competent training and practice of mental health services. Yet each of these four assumptions should be and is debated.

The medical model has been useful and heuristic in western physical medicine. Indeed an empirical understanding of the functioning and abnormalities of the human body is one of the great advances of the modern era. That said, debate exist even in the realm of physical, e.g., "alternative or complimentary medicine" such as the Chinese, mind-body medicines, etc. Further, the illness-based model is not so convincing when applied to other dimensions. There is, for example, no "science of the soul" or empirically validated decision-making in ethical realms such as: when or whether to remove life support, abortion, assisted death. The valued based and ethical dimensions call for other modes of knowing and choice-making. Questions of mental health and rightness of behavior, adequate coping, normal perceptual processing, and developed and functional affect are quite different phenomena from the amount of hydroid being released into the blood stream or the existence of malignant cells growing in the body. Three related issues exist here.

## MEDICAL MODEL MENTAL ILLNESS?

The first issue is the question of whether mental illness is correctly characterized within the medical model. Certainly major mental illness is real and the experience of it, disabling. But other disorders and some related features of major mental illness are not well fit to the medical model. By now this discussion is common, since thinkers from a variety of standpoints within and outside of mental health have engaged in the discussion. The discussion of ill fit of the medical model to psychological disorders perhaps started with the anti-psychiatry movement of the '60s, continued on in the '70s with theories as diverse as behaviorism and humanism, and certainly feminism from the '70s consistently forward. To this mix we could add critical psychology; postmodern perspectives; and, within psychology, social construction; and in the '90s some multicultural discussions and patient's rights community organizations. The discussions do vary but are quite consistent in raising important questions about the problems with the medical model for conceptualizing mental functioning and pathology. One's sense of self, relationships, possibilities available in a given culture, the damage caused to one from external forces–both interpersonal (trauma) and structural (economic system and dominant group construction of merit)–and others have been delineated as crucial aspects of human functioning not well fitting with the medical model. Feminist therapy theory has been among the clearest to articulate strong analyses and arguments against the medical model. Yet the medical model is even more dominant now in mental health, despite forty years of objection. Strong hopes for assisting individuals with psychiatric dysfunction, and strong forces of and links between pharmaceutical, insurance, and professional corporations have nearly muted the discussion.

## HEALTH OR ILLNESS

The difference between illness and health is a second issue. While we all want the absence of illness and hope for effective and efficient intervention to facilitate client's return to a non-ill status, the concept of health is very different. Indeed there are so many ideas about what constitutes health that it remains largely undefined and yet it is known! In mental health practice, the normative social standards of the dominant society become the equivalent of the normal range of functioning in the physical medical practice. So while having fasting blood sugar of a 100 or within the range of 80 to 120 is normal, we are hard pressed to find similar quantification for mental health. We can, of course, also give psychometric tests but they rest on unseen constructs and must compare self reported responses to group norms. These group norms are established through test development which essentially compares an individual's response or set of responses to an averaged response of a group taken as normal by the researchers. Norm groups are researcher constructed which is importantly different from the old science claim of representative of the universal or in psychometrics, normal. In the end, those dominant in the social structure have developed the tests based on their views of normality, and their trained representatives continue to interpret these tests on the bases of dominant socio-cultural normative standards. Mental health does not have the empirically verified normal ranges that physical medicine does and so relies on conventional behavior and functioning of the dominant group, sometimes directly as in clinical evaluation and sometimes through psychometric measurement.

So assessment and who decides what is effective/right/optimally functioning (normal) is one issue in applying the medical model to mental health.

## OLD SCIENCE

The third issue is the artifact of empirical measurement. Material things or their stand-ins, operationally defined variables, constitute what can be measured and hence what can be researched. Basing best practices on those interventions that have resulted in empirically verified significant change for a certain diagnostic category is very limited. Basically cognitive-behavioral interventions and psychotropic medications are the interventions being demonstrated to bring about significant measured change–i.e., operationalized thoughts and behavior and psychologies stand in for physical change! Other meaningful human dimensions: awareness; functioning through one's own choices according to principles; authentic communication; empathic connection with partners, children and friends; living in the present and planning for the future; fellow feeling; living in care and peace with one's body; etc., are not easily measurable empirically and hence not included in best practices. Yet they constitute healthy functioning and are very appropriate subject matter for intervention. Dimensions of importance to health are left out of the medical model and instead measurable variables which are brought into line with single dominant norms become the focus.

While this state of affairs may seem very limiting to clients and some practitioners, the hegemonic influence of those who are the major controllers in this era are well served. Insurance corporations; research grantors; academic faculty seeking recognition and status, as well as approval for their training programs; professional associations acting for inclusion in the corporate and government benefits; state boards changed with assuring competent licensees; and ethics boards adjudicating complaints, all benefit by a clear set of best practices to use a normative criterion in deciding funding, granting status and assuring competence. The best practices as limited above are easy to research, less expensive to fund, provide rather clear rules for judgments of competence and ethics. Yet do they serve the needs of people and understanding of mental health well?

At the practice level, mental illness and managed benefits have thrust the medical model and empirically based treatment upon therapists as the requirement for payment and as the standard of care. If therapists ignore them, they cannot participate in third party payment and are at risk for sanctions from licensing boards and ethics committees for incompetent and unethical treatment. Both APAs have run to embrace the financial aspects of the corporately defined mental illness. Psychiatry's training is increasingly exclusively biological, and their practice is prescribing and managing psychotropic medication. Many psychiatrists struggle to continue to do therapy. Psychology's APA is seeking prescription privileges and is selling new ethics codes and malpractice insurance. It seems to be a "me too" pact for decreasing treatment dollars and for regressive, biological research funds. It is also very much in keeping with the next threat to Feminist Therapy: conservative politics.

## CONSERVATIVE POLITICS

Focus on the economy has long been a central feature of United States politics. As a nation we have been content to elect leaders who tend the national wealth and power, and our own money. The phrase "we vote through our pocketbooks" captures much in U.S. elections. The invisible hand of the rich and the very visible presence of the upper middle and professional classes guide our nation toward materialism and consumerism, both requirements for advanced capitalism. Government involvement in social issues, here health care and poverty, has been much talked about but little done. Under Clinton the economy soared but social supports eroded and restraint of money making by corporations in health care was lifted, once efforts at universal insurance failed. But under George W. Bush, even the appearance of government involvement in social supports has evaporated.

President Bush's people have abridged individual rights, given priority to moneyed interests, reduced complex international and national situations to good guys versus bad guys, in order to dominate and control. Whether it be terrorism with its incantation of the dangers of others (e.g., dark skinned foreign Islam men), women's bodies, restorative justice to oppressed groups, access to affordable health care, earning a living wage through employment, or an appreciation for and sustainable relationship with the environment, the current republicans are ethnocentric, patriarchal and nationalistic.

While it seems that the resurgence of the religious right and patriotism has found a supporter, some worry about the collapse of separation between church and state, as excessively conservative Christian views fuel changes in federal policy. Examples can be seen in faith based initiatives and restrictions of funding if certain procedures are done, for instance, pregnancy counseling that must exclude mention of abortion and birth control, and prohibitions on stem cell research. Some also wonder if this is a vehicle for corporate interests. Certainly the new imperialism is in line with advanced capitalism's need for cheap labor, environmental disregard, additional resource and new markets. Globalization is, in large measure, an economic control maneuver for the G7. Despite the too occasional rhetoric for human rights, liberation and social justice are apparently not a motivating factor, though perhaps they offer possibilities for action taking.

The conservative political turn, which found an advocate in the current president's administration, is a huge threat to Feminist Therapy and other progressive standpoints. The discomfort, fear and mind numbing disregard for justice and caring effects us all. Principles become slogans without any real action. At the same time government policies undermine even these slogans. Hard won struggles–affirmative action, abortion rights, federal funding for education and social needs, real participation in world organizations looking toward principle actions and decisions, global agreements to stop abusing the planet–are being taken apart, unfunded and opposed. These conservative politics are disabling, angering and frightening, our hope is that the severity of the threat turns people to action. Until then, the principles and actions of Feminist Therapists and other progressive peoples are threatened.

## A NEW PARADIGM

Even in the face of the materialism, empiricism and increasingly hegemonic relationship between government, corporate profit, and the professions and their academic departments, exciting thinking, important analysis and the coupling of action taking with them continues in the corners and shadows. There is a paradigm shift well under way. It might be described as systems thinking with relational consciousness and a social and environmental justice ethic. Said another way, interconnections among matter and processes, raised in theoretical physics and Buddhism, are increasingly understood and are taking hold in other disciplines, value systems and analyses.

This new paradigm also holds promise to consider deeply people and other life as well as non-living phenomena. New science, postmodern positions, social construction, transformative multiculturalism, ecological, interdisciplinary, ethical living, environmentalism, voluntary simplicity, mysticism, spirituality, liberation psychology, and feminism are clearly among the points of view influenced by and influencing the paradigm change. In feminist therapy, we see these influences working in concert with and extending feminist principles. In women's studies, we see interdisciplinarity at the forefront of scholarship. In counseling and therapy, we see the need for expanding contacts throughout human services and legal services as well as to policy and activism. In intellectual matters and in human action matters the old rules and structures are no longer fitting the contemporary complexity and values.

While there are many sightings and descriptions of the new paradigm, ranging perhaps from postmodern analyses, on the one hand, to liberation theology praxis on the other, Feminist Therapy is well positioned at the intersection of analysis and action and is supported by clear principles. This wedding of thought and action is vital to a paradigm shift. So too is the conception of consciousness with both its meaning of reflectivity and apprehension of other dimensions. The ideas and principles within feminist therapy theory are key to the truth of this new paradigm. These include multiplicity, i.e., considering human diversity and complexity; awareness of and action against multiple oppressions; valuing personal experience as politically and epistemologically informative. These are principles that we know within feminist therapy and we use them in doing therapy, supporting social causes and analysis. Yet even as we do, more distance is created from the dominant positivist paradigm.

The new paradigm eschews universal, known truth. Instead it considers knowledge-claims and power together and does not confuse them with true statements about reality. Indeed the linking of science with power and politics rather than an enlightened road to truth is one of the more challenging aspects of the newly developing paradigm. The new paradigm also points to the limits of materialism and enlightenment science in the mainstream European and American thinking. Some of the participants call for deeper and multiple consciousness–some for power and structural awareness and some for participation in other realms of perception/experience such as meditation, expanded awareness and spirituality. It speaks to the multiplicity of experiences and social organizations and to metaphysical stories as different from empirical reductionism.

Some sightings of the new paradigm feature ethics as central, not so much as a code for setting rules for behavior, but as a grounding for actions. It, for example, is not so much about avoiding dual relationships as it is about doing social justice and challenging oppression when it is happening. With the new paradigm, the door to ethical action and social justice is opened wide, and both feminist and liberation psychologists are walking through. Feminist positions and actions in feminist therapy is risky business and difficult to sustain. Maracek and Kravetz (1998) discuss finding feminist therapists hiding their feminism in public announcements and others who distort feminism to mere gender socialization. Some therapists also cover feminist therapy with phrases more appealing to their clients in order to decrease their own risk in their communities. We also see refocusing from women's issues to women's pathology oriented specialties such as eating disorders or depression. Too often women's studies have become gender studies with the resulting loss of the political and action dimensions within the paradigm shift.

Excitement, new possibilities and new voices are certainly features of these new sightings and descriptions. Discord is also present. Discord exists between the developing postmodern views and the modern period scholarly, disciplinary and professional authorities. But discord exists too among those describing these newer views. Relative importance of analyses and action is one area of difference. Another is the relationship between the kinds of consciousness such as spiritual and political. Yet another is how to handle relationships. Will equality be sought and egalitarian practices be honored or will new experts and authorities be crowned? Will the impulse to construct relative hierarchies be followed or will feminist commitment to coalition become the model? Some within feminist therapy are involved in the new paradigm in thinking and in actions. Indeed feminism has been a major contributor, yet as we do so in theory, in research, in practice and in structural challenge through social action within our professions and communities, we risk much.

The risks are quite real. The influence of feminist thinking has been used but rarely acknowledged by multiculturalism, by social construction, by postmodern writers, by narrative therapy. Laura Brown and Maria Root (1990) wrote of the importance of culture and taking antiracist stances in feminist therapy theory well before the current multicultural upsurge. Listening to and basing understanding in women's experiences has been a prime principle of feminist therapy since its beginning and certainly predated narrative therapy but no mention is made in most narrative therapy literature and training. Both Ellyn Kaschak's 1992 book *Engendered Lives* and Ballou and Gabalac's 1985 text *A Feminist Position on Mental Health*, clearly identified the embedded patriarchy in society and the bias and values within theoretical inquiry and practices of the professions and disciplines, arguments that postmodern American writers would later make but without acknowledgement that feminists had seen and said this.

Another risk can be seen in feminist work in trauma having been taken over by the bioscience specialists. Feminists listening to their client's stories and experiences have heard, over and over again, about sexual abuse. In bringing the unrare occurrence of sexual abuse to social awareness feminist therapists have faced the attempts by others to discount, demonize and denigrate them. Feminist therapists who carefully self-disclose for the benefit of the client or who encourage the client to join them in working toward social change in their communities, stand outside what the state may consider accepted practice. Feminists have challenged the authority of mainstream theory and conceptualizations of psychopathology. We have moved some good distance toward developing alternative understandings consistent with feminist principles. Critique is not enough; action is necessary. Feminists have gone beyond political and epistemological analysis to the development and use of new ways to help (Hill and Ballou, 1998).

In this volume we have looked at the theoretical and practical foundations of Feminist Therapy. We have offered speculation about possible visions and directions for Feminist Therapy's future. The analysis offered in this essay is drawn in part from the foundations and is embedded in the visions of the future. History, vision and analyses must now lead to action.

## REFERENCES

Ballou, M. & Gabalac, N. (1985). *A Feminist position on mental heath.* Springfield, IL: Charles C Thomas.

Brown, L. & Root, M. (1990). *Diversity and complexity in feminist therapy.* Binghamton, NY: Haworth.

Hill, M. & Ballou, M. (1998). Making therapy feminist: A practice survey. *Women & Therapy, 21,* 1-16.

Kaschak, E. (1992). *Engendered lives: A new psychology of women's experience.* New York: Basic Books.

Maracek, J. and Kravetz, D. (1998). Putting politics into practice: Feminist therapy as feminist praxis. *Women & Therapy, 21,* 17-36.

# Index

*Abnormal Psychology in a Changing World,* 47
Abortion, 69
Academic environment, for feminist
    therapists' training, 177-188
  educators in, 181-184
  the institution in, 184,186-187
  students in, 177-181
Acculturation, 32,33,76
Activism, 167-168,198
Activists, social class of, 80-81
ADDRESSING model, 85
Adleman, Jeanne, 167
Adolescents, sexual assaults on, 115
Advanced Feminist Therapy Institute,
    22-23
Advocacy, 77,180
African Americans,
        homophobia/heterosexism
        among, 48
African-American women
  class status of, 83
  gender roles of, 57
  lesbian, 48,66-67
*Against Our Will* (Brownmiller),
    116,118
Aggression, in rapists, 120
Aging and ageism, 70-74
  culturally-influenced attitudes
    towards, 57
Alliant International University, 31
Allodynia, ethnocultural, 38-39
Alternative or complementary
    medicine, 203
American Civil War, 117
American Psychiatric Association
    (APA), 202,206

American Psychological Association
    (APA), 202,206
  Award for Distinguished
    Professional Contribution to
    Public Service, 42
  Psychotherapy with Women
    Research Award, 47
*American Psychologist,* 72,75
American Revolutionary War, 117
Anderson, Gail, 168,169
Anger, women's inability to express,
    21
Anti-domination, 153,154-155,173
Antigone complex, 146,149
Anti-mutuality, 103
Anti-psychiatry movement, 203
Appalachian women, 71
Aron, Adrienne, 76-77
Asch, Adrienne, 67-69,85
Asian Americans, in therapy, 33
Assertiveness training, 21-22
Association of Women in Psychology
    (AWP)
  Distinguished Publications Award, 47
  Women of Color Psychologies
    Publication Award, 47
Astrancha, Tal, 167-168
Authority, 65
Autonomy, 28


Baker, Nancy Lynn, 82-83
Ballou, Mary, 29,65,144,145,150-152,
    162-163
  *Rethinking Mental Health and
    Disorder,* 146-147

# BOOK ORDER FORM!

Order a copy of this book with this form or online at:
http://www.HaworthPress.com/store/product.asp?sku=5384

## The Foundation and Future of Feminist Therapy

____ in softbound at $24.95 ISBN-13: 978-0-7890-0217-4 / ISBN-10: 0-7890-0217-5.
____ in hardbound at $39.95 ISBN-13: 978-0-7890-0201-3 / ISBN-10: 0-7890-0201-9.

**COST OF BOOKS** _____

**POSTAGE & HANDLING** _____
US: $4.00 for first book & $1.50
for each additional book.
Outside US: $5.00 for first book
& $2.00 for each additional book.

**SUBTOTAL** _____

In Canada: add 7% GST. _____

**STATE TAX** _____
CA, IL, IN, MN, NJ, NY, OH, PA & SD residents
please add appropriate local sales tax.

**FINAL TOTAL** _____
If paying in Canadian funds, convert
using the current exchange rate,
UNESCO coupons welcome.

❑**BILL ME LATER:**
Bill-me option is good on US/Canada/
Mexico orders only; not good to jobbers,
wholesalers, or subscription agencies.

❑**Signature** _____

❑ **Payment Enclosed: $** _____

❑ **PLEASE CHARGE TO MY CREDIT CARD:**
❑ Visa ❑ MasterCard ❑ AmEx ❑ Discover
❑ Diner's Club ❑ Eurocard ❑ JCB

**Account #** _____

**Exp Date** _____

**Signature** _____
*(Prices in US dollars and subject to change without notice.)*

**PLEASE PRINT ALL INFORMATION OR ATTACH YOUR BUSINESS CARD**

| | |
|---|---|
| Name | |
| Address | |
| City | State/Province | Zip/Postal Code |
| Country | |
| Tel | Fax |
| E-Mail | |

May we use your e-mail address for confirmations and other types of information? ❑ Yes ❑ No We appreciate receiving
your e-mail address. Haworth would like to e-mail special discount offers to you, as a preferred customer.
**We will never share, rent, or exchange your e-mail address. We regard such actions as an invasion of your privacy.**

Order from your **local bookstore** or directly from
**The Haworth Press, Inc.** 10 Alice Street, Binghamton, New York 13904-1580 • USA
Call our toll-free number (1-800-429-6784) / Outside US/Canada: (607) 722-5857
Fax: 1-800-895-0582 / Outside US/Canada: (607) 771-0012
E-mail your order to us: orders@HaworthPress.com

**For orders outside US and Canada,** you may wish to order through your local
sales representative, distributor, or bookseller.
For information, see http://HaworthPress.com/distributors

*(Discounts are available for individual orders in US and Canada only, not booksellers/distributors.)*

**Please photocopy this form for your personal use.**
www.HaworthPress.com

BOF05